AF540242

MARINE CONSERVATION BIOLOGY

MARINE CONSERVATION BIOLOGY

By

Dr. Veena Maurya

M.Sc., Ph.D.

Sri Guru Ram Roy Degree College

Pathribagh, Dehradun (Uttarakhand)

(India)

DISCOVERY PUBLISHING HOUSE PVT. LTD.

NEW DELHI-110 002

Published by:
Tilak Wasan

DISCOVERY PUBLISHING HOUSE PVT. LTD.
4383/4B, Ansari Road, Darya Ganj
New Delhi-110 002 (India)
Phone : +91-11-23279245, 43596064-65
Fax : +91-11-23253475
E-mail : discoverypublishinghouse@gmail.com
namitwasan9@gmail.com
sales@discoverypublishinggroup.com
web : www.discoverypublishinggroup.com

***First Edition:* 2013**

***Reprinted:* 2018**

ISBN: 978-93-5056-278-9

Marine Conservation Biology

© Author

All rights reserved. No part of this publication should be reproduced, stored in a retrieval system, or transmitted in any form or by any means: electronic, mechanical, photocopying, recording or otherwise, without the prior written permission of the author and the publisher.

This book has been published in good faith that the material provided by authors is original. Every effort is made to ensure accuracy of material, but the editor, publisher and printer will not be held responsible for any inadvertent error(s). In case of any dispute, all legal matters are to be settled under Delhi jurisdiction only.

Printed at:
Infinity Imaging Systems
Delhi

Preface

Marine biology is the scientific study of organisms in the ocean or other marine or brackish bodies of water. Given that in biology many phyla, families and genera have some species that live in the sea and others that live on land, marine biology classifies species based on the environment rather than on taxonomy. Marine biology differs from marine ecology as marine ecology is focused on how organisms interact with each other and the environment, and biology is the study of the organisms themselves.

Marine life is a vast resource, providing food, medicine, and raw materials, in addition to helping to support recreation and tourism all over the world. At a fundamental level, marine life helps determine the very nature of our planet. Marine organisms contribute significantly to the oxygen cycle, and are involved in the regulation of the Earth's climate. Shorelines are in part shaped and protected by marine life, and some marine organisms even help create new land.

Marine biology covers a great deal, from the microscopic, including most zooplankton and phytoplankton to the huge cetaceans (whales) which reach up to a reported 48 meters (125 feet) in length.

The habitats studied by marine biology include everything from the tiny layers of surface water in which organisms and abiotic items may be trapped in surface tension between the ocean and atmosphere, to the depths of the oceanic trenches, sometimes 10,000 meters or more beneath the surface of the ocean. It studies habitats such as coral reefs, kelp forests, tidepools, muddy, sandy and rocky bottoms, and the open ocean (pelagic) zone, where solid objects are rare and the surface of the water is the only visible boundary.

A large proportion of all life on Earth exists in the oceans. Exactly how large the proportion is unknown, since many ocean species are still to be discovered. While the oceans comprise about 71 per cent of the Earth's surface, due to their depth they encompass about 300 times the habitable volume of the terrestrial habitats on Earth.

Many species are economically important to humans, including food fish. It is also becoming understood that the well-being of marine organisms and other organisms are linked in very fundamental ways. The human body of knowledge regarding the relationship between life in the sea and important cycles is rapidly growing, with new discoveries being made nearly every day. These cycles include those of matter (such as the carbon cycle) and of air (such as Earth's respiration, and movement of energy through ecosystems including the ocean). Large areas beneath the ocean surface still remain effectively unexplored.

Marine biology is a branch of oceanography and is closely linked to biology. It also encompasses many ideas from ecology. Fisheries science and marine conservation can be considered partial offshoots of marine biology (as well as environmental studies).

Microscopic life undersea is incredibly diverse and still poorly understood. For example, the role of viruses in marine ecosystems is barely being explored even in the beginning of the 21st century.

—Author

Contents

1 Introduction

Simply put, marine biology is the study of life in the oceans and other saltwater environments such as estuaries and wetlands. All plant and animal life forms are included from the microscopic picoplankton all the way to the majestic blue whale, the largest creature in the sea—and for that matter in the world.

The study of marine biology includes a wide variety of disciplines such as astronomy, biological oceanography, cellular biology, chemistry, ecology, geology, meteorology, molecular biology, physical oceanography and zoology and the new science of marine conservation biology draws on many longstanding scientific disciplines such as marine ecology, biogeography, zoology, botany, genetics, fisheries biology, anthropology, economics and law.

Like all scientific disciplines, the study of marine biology also follows the scientific method. The overriding goal in all of science is to find the truth. Although following the scientific method is not by any means a rigid process, research is usually conducted systematically and logically to narrow the inevitable margin of error that exists in any scientific study, and to avoid as much bias on behalf of the researcher as possible. The primary component of scientific research is characterization by observations. Hypotheses are then formulated and then tested based on a number of observations in order to determine the degree to which the hypothesis is a true statement and whether or not it can be accepted or rejected. Testing is then often done by experiments if hypotheses can produce predictions based on the initial observations.

The essential elements of the scientific method are iterations and recursions of the following four steps:

1. Characterization (observation)
2. Hypothesis (a theoretical, hypothetical explanation)
3. Prediction (logical deduction from the hypothesis)
4. Experiment (test of all of the above)

These steps are all used in the study of marine biology, which includes numerous sub fields including:

- *Microbiology:* The study of microorganisms, such as bacteria, viruses, protozoa and algae, is conducted for numerous reasons. One example is to understand what role microorganisms play in marine ecosystems. For example, bacteria are critical to the biological processes of the ocean, as they comprise 98 per cent of the ocean's biomass, which is the total weight of all organisms in a given volume. Microbiology is also important to our understanding of the food chain that connects plants to herbivorous and carnivorous animals. The first level in the food chain is primary production, which occurs at the microbial level. This is an important biological activity to understand as primary production drives the entire food chain.

  Scientists also study marine microbiology to find new organisms that may be used to help develop medicines and find cures for diseases and other health problems.
- *Fisheries and Aquaculture:* Fisheries and aquaculture to protect biodiversity and to create sustainable seafood sources because of the world's dependence on fish for protein. There are many areas of study in this.

  The ecology of fisheries includes the study of their population dynamics, reproduction, behaviour, food webs, and habitat.

- Fisheries management includes studies on the impact of overfishing, habitat destruction, pollution and toxin levels, and ways to increase populations for sustainability as seafood.
- Aquaculture includes research on the development of individual organisms and their environment. The objective is most often to develop the knowledge needed to cultivate certain species in a designated area in open water or in captivity in order to meet consumer demand. Technological advances have enabled seafood 'farms' to produce high-demand products that traditional commercial fisheries cannot meet. This is a controversial area however, and an issue that will become of greater importance as our fish stocks continue to decline.
- *Environmental marine biology:* includes the study of ocean health. It is important for scientists to determine the quality of the marine environment to ensure water quality is sufficient to sustain a healthy environment. Coastal environmental health is an important area of environmental marine biology so that scientists can determine the impact of coastal development on water quality for the safety of people visiting the beaches and to maintain a healthy marine environment. Pollutants, sediment, and runoff are all potential threats to marine health in coastal areas. Offshore marine environmental health is also studied. For example, an environmental biologist might be required to study the impact of an oil spill or other chemical hazard in the ocean. Environmental biologists also study Benthic environments on the ocean bottom in order to understand such issues as the chemical makeup of sediment, impact of erosion, and the impact of dredging ocean bottoms on the marine environment.
- *Deep-sea ecology:* It advances in technology of equipment needed to explore the deep sea have opened the door to the study of this largely unknown space in the sea. The biological characteristics and processes in the deep-sea environment are of great interest to scientists. Research

includes the study of deep ocean gases as an alternate energy source, how animals of the deep live in the dark, cold, high pressure environment, deep sea hydrothermal vents and the lush biological communities they support.

- *Ichthyology:* Ichthyology is the study of fishes, both salt and freshwater species. There are some 25,000+ species of fishes including: bony fishes, cartilaginous fishes, sharks, skates, rays, and jawless fishes. Ichthyologists study all aspects of fish from their classification, to their morphology, evolution, behaviour, diversity, and ecology. Many ichthyologists are also involved in the field of aquaculture and fisheries.
- *Marine mammology:* This is the field of interest to most aspiring marine biologists. It is the study of cetaceans—families of whales and dolphins, and pinnipeds (seals, sea lions, and the walrus). Their behaviours, habitats, health, reproduction, and populations are all studied. These are some of the most fascinating creatures in the sea; therefore, this is an extremely competitive field, and difficult to break into because the competition for research funding is also quite heavy.

  One area of research currently being conducted on whales is the impact of military sonar on their health and well-being. The scientific community believes that high frequency sound waves cause internal damage and bleeding in the brains of whales, yet the military denies this claim. Military sonar can also interfere with the animal's own use of sonar for communication and echolocation. More research is needed; however, in recent years science has proven the claims to be valid and the military has begun limiting its use of sonar in specific areas.
- *Marine ethology:* The behaviour of marine animals is studied so that we understand the animals that share the planet with us. This is also an important field for help in understanding how to protect endangered species, or how to help species whose habitats are threatened by

man or natural phenomena. The study of marine animal behaviour usually falls under the category of ethology because most often marine species must be observed in their natural environment, although there are many marine species observed in controlled environments as well. Sharks are most often studied in their natural habitat for obvious reasons.

Life in the sea has been a subject of fascination for thousands of years. One of the most important reasons for the study of sea life is simply to understand the world in which we live. The oceans cover 71 per cent (and rising) of this world, and yet we have only scratched the surface when it comes to understanding them. Scientists estimate that no more than 5 per cent of the oceans have been explored. Yet, we need to understand the marine environment that helps support life on this planet, for example:

Health of the oceans/planet

Climate change

Pollution (toxicology, dumping, runoff, impact of recreation, blooms)

Coral reefs

Invasive species...

Human health

Air quality

Dissolution of carbon dioxide...

Sustainability and biodiversity

Overfishing

Endangered species

Impacts on the food chain...

Research and product development

Pharmaceuticals

Biomedical applications

Alternate energy sources

Study of Marine Biology

Advances in technology have opened up the ocean to exploration from the shallows to the deep sea. New tools for marine research are being added to the list of tools that have been used for decades such as:

- *Trawling:* It has been used in the past to collect marine specimens for study, except that trawling can be very damaging to delicate marine environments and it is difficult to collect samples discriminately. However when used in the midwater environment, trawls can be every effective at collecting samples of elusive species with a wide migratory range.
- *Plankton nets:* Plankton nets have a very fine weave to catch microscopic organisms in seawater for study.
- *Remotely operated vehicles (ROVs):* It have been used underwater since the 1950s. ROVs are basically unmanned submarine robots with umbilical cables used to transmit data between the vehicle and researcher for remote operation in areas where diving is constrained by health or other hazards. ROVs are often fitted with video and still cameras as well as with mechanical tools for specimen retrieval and measurements.
- *Underwater habitats:* The National Oceanic and Atmospheric Administration (NOAA) operates beneath the surface where researchers can live and work underwater for extended periods.
- *Fiber optics:* Fiber optic observational equipment uses LED light (red light illumination) and low light cameras that do not disturb deep-sea life to capture the behaviours and characteristics of these creatures in their natural habitat.
- *Satellites:* Satellites are used to measure vast geographic ocean data such as the temperature and colour of the ocean. Temperature data can provide information on a variety of ocean characteristics such as currents, cold upwelling, climate, and warm water currents such as the

Gulf Stream. Satellites are also used for mapping marine areas such as coral reefs and for tracking marine life tagged with sensors to determine migratory patterns.

- *Sounding:* Sounding hydrophones, the microphone's counterpart, detect and record acoustic signals in the ocean. Sound data can be used to monitor waves, marine mammals, ships, and other ocean activities.
- *Sonar:* Sonar similar to sounding, sonar is used to find large objects in the water and to measure the ocean's depth (bathymetry). Sound waves last longer in water than in air, and are therefore useful to detect underwater echoes.
- *Computers:* It sophisticated computer technology is used to collect, process, analyze, and display data from sensors placed in the marine environment to measure temperature, depth, navigation, salinity, and meteorological data. NOAA implemented computer technology aboard its research vessels to standardize the way this data is managed.

Marine Biology *Versus* Biological Oceanography

The difference between the terms 'marine biology' and 'biological oceanography' is subtle, and the two are often used interchangeably. As mentioned above, marine biology is the study of marine species that live in the ocean and other salt-water environments. Biological oceanography also studies marine species, but in the context of oceanography. So a biological oceanographer might study the impact of cold upwellings on anchovy populations off the coast of South America, where a marine biologist might study the reproductive behaviour of anchovies.

Biofuels from the Sea

The use of kelp (*Laminaria digitata*) as a biofuel could provide an important alternative to terrestrial grown biofuels; however the suitability of its chemical composition varies on a seasonal basis. Harvesting the kelp in July when carbohydrate levels are at their highest would ensure optimal sugar release for biofuel production.

Oceans support vast populations of single-celled phytoplankton which, through photosynthesis, remove about half the carbon dioxide produced by burning fossil fuels. One group of phytoplankton, the coccolithophores, are known for their ability to build chalk scales inside their cells and secrete them, forming a protective armor. A new study has revealed the mechanism which achieves this, and that this process may be directly affected by the increasing levels of dissolved carbon dioxide in the oceans.

Importance of Marine Biology

Marine biology is the scientific study of organisms in the ocean or other marine or brackish bodies of water. Given that in biology many phyla, families and genera have some species that live in the sea and others that live on land, marine biology classifies species based on the environment rather than on taxonomy. Marine biology differs from marine ecology as marine ecology is focused on how organisms interact with each other and the environment, and biology is the study of the organisms themselves.

Marine life is a vast resource, providing food, medicine, and raw materials, in addition to helping to support recreation and tourism all over the world. At a fundamental level, marine life helps determine the very nature of our planet. Marine organisms contribute significantly to the oxygen cycle, and are involved in the regulation of the Earth's climate. Shorelines are in part shaped and protected by marine life, and some marine organisms even help create new land.

Marine biology covers a great deal, from the microscopic, including most zooplankton and phytoplankton to the huge cetaceans (whales) which reach up to a reported 48 metres (125 feet) in length.

The habitats studied by marine biology include everything from the tiny layers of surface water in which organisms and abiotic items may be trapped in surface tension between the ocean and atmosphere, to the depths of the oceanic trenches, sometimes 10,000 metres or more beneath the surface of the ocean. It studies habitats such as coral reefs, kelp forests, tidepools, muddy, sandy and rocky bottoms, and the open ocean (pelagic) zone, where solid objects are rare and the surface of the water is the only visible boundary.

A large proportion of all life on Earth exists in the oceans. Exactly how large the proportion is unknown, since many ocean species are still to be discovered. While the oceans comprise about 71 per cent of the Earth's surface, due to their depth they encompass about 300 times the habitable volume of the terrestrial habitats on Earth.

Many species are economically important to humans, including food fish. It is also becoming understood that the well-being of marine organisms and other organisms are linked in very fundamental ways. The human body of knowledge regarding the relationship between life in the sea and important cycles is rapidly growing, with new discoveries being made nearly every day. These cycles include those of matter (such as the carbon cycle) and of air (such as Earth's respiration, and movement of energy through ecosystems including the ocean). Large areas beneath the ocean surface still remain effectively unexplored.

The marine ecosystem is large, and thus there are many sub-fields of marine biology. Most involve studying specializations of particular animal groups, such as phycology, invertebrate zoology and ichthyology.

Other subfields study the physical effects of continual immersion in sea water and the ocean in general, adaptation to a salty environment, and the effects of changing various oceanic properties on marine life. A subfield of marine biology studies the relationships between oceans and ocean life, and global warming and environmental issues (such as carbon dioxide displacement).

Recent marine biotechnology has focused largely on marine biomolecules, especially proteins, that may have uses in medicine or engineering. Marine environments are the home to many exotic biological materials that may inspire biomimetic materials.

Related Fields

Marine biology is a branch of oceanography and is closely linked to biology. It also encompasses many ideas from ecology. Fisheries science and marine conservation can be considered partial offshoots of marine biology (as well as environmental studies).

Fungi

Over 1500 species of fungi are known from marine environments. These parasitize marine algae or animals, or are saprobes on algae, corals, protozoan cysts, sea grasses, wood and other substrata, and can also be found in sea foam. Spores of many species have special appendages which facilitate attachment to the substratum. A very diverse range of unusual secondary metabolites is produced by marine fungi.

Microscopic Life

Microscopic life undersea is incredibly diverse and still poorly understood. For example, the role of viruses in marine ecosystems is barely being explored even in the beginning of the 21st century.

The role of phytoplankton is better understood due to their critical position as the most numerous primary producers on Earth. Phytoplankton are categorized into cyanobacteria (also called blue-green algae/bacteria), various types of algae (red, green, brown, and yellow-green), diatoms, dinoflagellates, euglenoids, coccolithophorids, cryptomonads, chrysophytes, chlorophytes, prasinophytes, and silicoflagellates.

Zooplankton tend to be somewhat larger, and not all are microscopic. Many Protozoa are zooplankton, including dinoflagellates, zooflagellates, foraminiferans, and radiolarians. Some of these (such as dinoflagellates) are also phytoplankton; the distinction between plants and animals often breaks down in very small organisms. Other zooplankton include cnidarians, ctenophores, chaetognaths, molluscs, arthropods, urochordates, and annelids such as polychaetes. Many larger animals begin their life as zooplankton before they become large enough to take their familiar forms. Two examples are fish larvae and sea stars (also called starfish).

Invertebrates

As on land, invertebrates make up a huge portion of all life in the sea. Invertebrate sea life includes Cnidaria such as jellyfish and sea anemones; Ctenophora; sea worms including the phyla Platyhelminthes, Nemertea, Annelida, Sipuncula, Echiura, Chaetognatha, and Phoronida; Mollusca including shellfish, squid, octopus; Arthropoda including Chelicerata and Crustacea; Porifera; Bryozoa; Echinodermata including starfish; and Urochordata including sea squirts or tunicates.

Plants and Algae

Plant life is widespread and very diverse under the ocean. Microscopic photosynthetic algae contribute a larger proportion of the worlds photosynthetic output than all the terrestrial forests combined. Most of the niche occupied by sub plants on land is actually occupied by macroscopic algae in the ocean, such as *Sargassum* and kelp, which are commonly known as seaweeds that creates kelp forests. The non algae plants that survive in the sea are often found in shallow waters, such as the seagrasses (examples of which are eelgrass, *Zostera*, and turtle grass, *Thalassia*). These plants have adapted to the high salinity of the ocean environment. The intertidal zone is also a good place to find plant life in the sea, where mangroves or cordgrass or beach grass might grow. Microscopic algae and plants provide important habitats for life, sometimes acting as hiding and foraging places for larval forms of larger fish and invertebrates.

Fish

Fish anatomy includes a two-chambered heart, operculum, swim bladder, scales, fins, lips, eyes and secretory cells that produce mucous. Fish breathe by extracting oxygen from water through their gills. Fins propel and stabilize the fish in the water.

Well known fish include: sardines, anchovy, ling cod, clownfish (also known as anemonefish), and bottom fish which include halibut or ling cod. Predators include sharks and barracuda.

Reptiles

Reptiles which inhabit or frequent the sea include sea turtles, sea snakes, terrapins, the marine iguana, and the saltwater crocodile. Most extant marine reptiles, except for some sea snakes, are oviparous and need to return to land to lay their eggs. Thus most species, excepting sea turtles, spend most of their lives on or near land rather than in the ocean. Despite their marine adaptations, most sea snakes prefer shallow waters nearby land, around islands, especially waters that are somewhat sheltered, as well as near estuaries. Some extinct marine reptiles, such as ichthyosaurs, evolved to be viviparous and had no requirement to return to land.

Seabirds

Seabirds are species of birds adapted to living in the marine environment, examples including albatross, penguins, gannets, and auks. Although they spend most of their lives in the ocean, species such as gulls can often be found thousands of miles inland.

Marine Mammals

There are five main types of marine mammals:

1. Cetaceans include toothed whales (Suborder Odontoceti), such as the Sperm Whale, dolphins, and porpoises such as the Dall's porpoise. Cetaceans also include baleen whales (Suborder Mysticeti), such as the Gray Whale, Humpback Whale, and Blue Whale.
2. Sirenians include manatees, the Dugong, and the extinct Steller's Sea Cow.
3. Seals (Family Phocidae), sea lions (Family Otariidae - which also include the fur seals), and the Walrus (Family Odobenidae) are all considered pinnipeds.
4. The sea otter is a member of the family mustelidae, which includes weasels and badgers.

5. The polar bear (Family Ursidae) is sometimes considered a marine mammal because of its dependence on the sea.

Marine Habitats

Marine habitats can be divided into coastal and open ocean habitats. Coastal habitats are found in the area that extends from the shoreline to the edge of the continental shelf. Most marine life is found in coastal habitats, even though the shelf area occupies only seven per cent of the total ocean area. Open ocean habitats are found in the deep ocean beyond the edge of the continental shelf.

Alternatively, marine habitats can be divided into pelagic and demersal habitats. Pelagic habitats are found near the surface or in the open water column, away from the bottom of the ocean. Demersal habitats are near or on the bottom of the ocean. An organism living in a pelagic habitat is said to be a pelagic organism, as in pelagic fish. Similarly, an organism living in a demersal habitat is said to be a demersal organism, as in demersal fish. Pelagic habitats are intrinsically shifting and ephemeral, depending on what ocean currents are doing.

Marine habitats can be modified by their inhabitants. Some marine organisms, like corals, kelp and seagrasses, are ecosystem engineers which reshape the marine environment to the point where they create further habitat for other organisms.

Intertidal and Shore

Intertidal zones, those areas close to shore, are constantly being exposed and covered by the ocean's tides. A huge array of life lives within this zone.

Shore habitats span from the upper intertidal zones to the area where land vegetation takes prominence. It can be underwater anywhere from daily to very infrequently. Many species here are scavengers, living off of sea life that is washed up on the shore. Many land animals also make much use of the shore and intertidal habitats. A subgroup of organisms in this habitat bores and grinds exposed rock through the process of bioerosion.

Reefs

Reefs comprise some of the densest and most diverse habitats in the world. The best-known types of reefs are tropical coral reefs which exist in most tropical waters; however, reefs can also exist in cold water. Reefs are built up by corals and other calcium-depositing animals, usually on top of a rocky outcrop on the ocean floor. Reefs can also grow on other surfaces, which has made it possible to create artificial reefs. Coral reefs also support a huge community of life, including the corals themselves, their symbiotic zooxanthellae, tropical fish and many other organisms.

Much attention in marine biology is focused on coral reefs and the El Niño weather phenomenon. In 1998, coral reefs experienced the most severe mass bleaching events on record, when vast expanses of reefs across the world died because sea surface temperatures rose well above normal. Some reefs are recovering, but scientists say that between 50 per cent and 70 per cent of the world's coral reefs are now endangered and predict that global warming could exacerbate this trend.

Open Ocean

The open ocean is relatively unproductive because of a lack of nutrients, yet because it is so vast, in total it produces the most primary productivity. Much of the aphotic zone's energy is supplied by the open ocean in the form of detritus. The open ocean consists mostly of jellyfish and its predators such as the mola mola.

Deep Sea and Trenches

The deepest recorded oceanic trenches measure to date is the Mariana Trench, near the Philippines, in the Pacific Ocean at 10,924 m (35,838 ft). At such depths, water pressure is extreme and there is no sunlight, but some life still exists. A white flatfish, a shrimp and a jellyfish were seen by the American crew of the bathyscaphe *Trieste* when it dove to the bottom in 1960.

Other notable oceanic trenches include Monterey Canyon, in the eastern Pacific, the Tonga Trench in the southwest at

10,882 m (35,702 ft), the Philippine Trench, the Puerto Rico Trench at 8,605 m (28,232 ft), the Romanche Trench at 7,760 m (24,450 ft), Fram Basin in the Arctic Ocean at 4,665 m (15,305 ft), the Java Trench at 7450 m (24,442 ft), and the South Sandwich Trench at 7,235 m (23,737 ft).

In general, the deep sea is considered to start at the aphotic zone, the point where sunlight loses its power of transference through the water. Many life forms that live at these depths have the ability to create their own light known as bio-luminescence.

Marine life also flourishes around seamounts that rise from the depths, where fish and other sea life congregate to spawn and feed. Hydrothermal vents along the mid-ocean ridge spreading centres act as oases, as do their opposites, cold seeps. Such places support unique biomes and many new microbes and other lifeforms have been discovered at these locations.

An active research topic in marine biology is to discover and map the life cycles of various species and where they spend their time. Marine biologists study how the ocean currents, tides and many other oceanic factors affect ocean lifeforms, including their growth, distribution and well-being. This has only recently become technically feasible with advances in GPS and newer underwater visual devices.

Most ocean life breeds in specific places, nests or not in others, spends time as juveniles in still others, and in maturity in yet others. Scientists know little about where many species spend different parts of their life cycles. For example, it is still largely unknown where sea turtles and some sharks travel. Tracking devices do not work for some life forms, and the ocean is not friendly to technology. This is important to scientists and fishermen because they are discovering that by restricting commercial fishing in one small area they can have a large impact in maintaining a healthy fish population in a much larger area far away.

The history of marine biology may have begun as early as 1200 BC when the Phoenicians began ocean voyages using celestial navigation. References to the sea and its mysteries abound in Greek mythology, particularly the Homeric poems 'The Iliad' and 'The Odyssey'. However, these two sources of ancient history mostly refer to the sea as a means of transportation and food source.

It wasn't until the writings of Aristotle from 384-322 BC that specific references to marine life were recorded. Aristotle identified a variety of species including crustaceans, echinoderms, mollusks, and fish. He also recognized that cetaceans are mammals, and that marine vertebrates are either oviparous (producing eggs that hatch outside the body) or viviparous (producing eggs that hatch within the body). Because he is the first to record observations on marine life, Aristotle is often referred to as the father of marine biology.

Early Expedition

The modern day study of marine biology began with the exploration by Captain James Cook (1728-1779) in 18th century Britain. Captain Cook is most known for his extensive voyages of discovery for the British Navy, mapping much of the world's uncharted waters during that time. He circumnavigated the world twice during his lifetime, during which he logged descriptions of numerous plants and animals then unknown to most of mankind. Following Cook's explorations, a number of scientists began a closer study of marine life including Charles Darwin (1809-1882) who, although he is best known for the Theory of, contributed significantly to the early study of marine biology. His expeditions as the resident naturalist aboard the HMS *Beagle* from 1831 to 1836 were spent collecting and studying specimens from a number of marine organisms that were sent to the British Museum for cataloguing. His interest in geology gave rise to his study of coral reefs and their formation. His experience on the *HMS Beagle* helped Darwin formulate his theories of natural selection and evolution based on the similarities he found in species specimens and fossils he discovered in the same geographic region.

The voyages of the HMS *Beagle* were followed by a 3-year voyage by the British ship HMS *Challenger* led by Sir Charles Wyville Thomson (1830-1882) to all the oceans of the world during which thousands of marine specimens were collected and analyzed. This voyage is often referred to as the birth of oceanography. The data collected during this trip filled 50 volumes and served as the basis for the study of marine biology across many disciplines for many years. Deep sea exploration was a benchmark of the *Challenger's* voyage disproving British explorer Edward Forbes'.

The *Challenger* was well equipped to explore deeper than previous expeditions with laboratories aboard stocked with tools and materials, microscopes, chemistry supplies, trawls and dredges, thermometres, devices to collect specimens from the deep sea, and miles of rope and hemp used to reach the ocean depths. The end product of the *Challenger's* voyage was almost 30,000 pages of oceanographic information compiled by a number of scientists from a wide range of disciplines. The "Report of the Scientific Results of the Exploring Voyage of H.M.S. Challenger during the years 1873-76" reported, in addition to the fact that life does exist below 550 m/1,800 feet, findings such as:

- 4,717 new species;
- The first systematic plot of currents and temperatures in the ocean;
- A map of bottom deposits much of which has remained current to the present;
- An outline of the main contours of the ocean basins; and
- The discovery.

The report is an important work still used by scientists today. In addition to the report, Sir Thomson also wrote a book about the voyage in 1877 titled *"The Voyage of the Challenger"*. He also wrote one of the early marine biology textbooks *"The Depths of the Sea"* in 1877.

The Institutions

These expeditions were soon followed by marine laboratories established to study marine life. The oldest marine station in the world, was established in Concarneau, France founded by the College of France in 1859. Concarneau is located on the northwest coast of France. The station was originally established for the cultivation of marine species, such as Dover sole, because of its location near marine estuaries with a variety of marine life. Today, research is conducted on molecular biology, biochemistry, and environmental studies.

In 1871, Spencer Fullerton Baird, the first director of the US Commission of Fish and Fisheries (now known as the National Marine Fisheries Service), began a collection station in Woods Hole, Massachusetts because of the abundant marine life there and to investigate declining fish stocks. This laboratory still exists now known as the, and is the oldest fisheries research facility in the world. Also at Woods Hole, the was established in 1888 by Alpheus Hyatt, a student of Harvard naturalist Louis Agassiz who had established the first seaside school of natural history on an island near Woods Hole. MBL was designed as a summer programme for the study of the biology of marine life for the purpose of basic research and education. The Woods Hole Oceanographic Institute was created in 1930 in response to the National Academy of Science's call for "the share of the United States of America in a worldwide programme of oceanographic research" and was funded by a $3 million grant by the Rockefeller Foundation.

An independent biological laboratory was established in San Diego in 1903 by University of California professor Dr. William E. Ritter, which became part of the University of California in 1912 and was named the Scripps Institution of Oceanography after its benefactors. Scripps has since become one of the world's leading institutions offering a multi-disciplinary study of oceanography.

Deep Sea Exploration

Technology brought the study of marine biology to new heights during the years following the HMS *Challenger* expedition. In 1934 William Beebe (1877-1962) and descended

923 m/3,028 ft below the surface off the coast of Bermuda in a bathysphere designed and funded by Barton. This depth record was not broken until 1948 when Barton made a bathysphere dive to 1,372 m/4,500 ft. During the interim, Beebe was able to observe deep sea life in its own environment rather than in a specimen jar. Although he was criticized for failing to publish results in professional journals, his vivid descriptions of the bathysphere dives in the books he published inspired some of today's greatest oceanographers and marine biologists.

In 1960, a descent was made to 10,916 m/35,813 ft in the Challenger Deep of the Marianna trench—the deepest known point in the oceans, 10,924 m/35,838 ft deep at its maximum, near 11° 22′N 142° 36′E—about 200 miles southwest of Guam. The dive was made in the bathyscape *Trieste* built by Auguste Piccard, his son Swiss explorer Jean Ernest-Jean Piccard and U.S. Navy Lieutenant Don Walsh. The descent took almost five hours and the two men spent barely twenty minutes on the ocean floor before undertaking the 3 hour 15 minute ascent.

The *Trieste's* first dive was made in 1953. In the years following, the bathyscape was used for a number of oceanographic research projects, including biological observation, and in 1957 she was chartered and later purchased by the U.S. Navy. The Navy continued to use the bathyscape for oceanographic research off the coast of San Diego, and later used the *Trieste* for a submarine recovery mission off the U.S. east coast. The bathyscape was retired following the U.S. Navy's commission of the *Trieste II*, and is currently on exhibit at the Washington Moval Historical Centre.

The scientists Rachel Carson (1907-1964) was a scientist and writer who brought the wonders of the sea to people with her lyrical writings and observations about the sea. Although she was a biologist for the US Fish and Wildlife Service, she devoted her spare time to translating science into writings that would infect the reader with her sense of wonder and respect for nature. She published an article in

Atlantic Monthly in 1937 titled *'Undersea'* which was followed by a book in 1941 titled *'Under the Sea-Wind'*. These publications described the sea and the life within it from a scientist's point of view, but in the words of a naturalist. In 1951, she published *'The Sea Around Us'* a prize-winning bestseller on the history of the sea. The success of this book allowed her to resign from federal service and write full-time. Shortly after, her focus turned to the negative impact of pesticides, a cause to which she remained devoted to by fighting to raise public awareness until her death in 1964.

Inspired by the work of William Beebe, Dr. Sylvia Earle (1935) began her work as an oceanographer at the tender age of 3 when she was knocked off her feet by a wave. She was fascinated by the ocean and its creatures at a very early age growing up near the shore in New Jersey and later in Florida on the Gulf of Mexico. She began her studies with marine botany based on her belief that vegetation is the foundation of any ecosystem. Although she struggled to balance her studies and starting a family, Earle earned her Ph.D., from Duke University, becoming well known in the marine science community for her detailed studies of aquatic life. Early in her career, and while she was four months pregnant, Earle traveled 30.5 m/100 ft below the surface in a submersible. This was the first of many submersible dives she would make during her career. Her experience living in an underwater marine habitat earned her celebrity status in the scientific community. In 1969, the Smithsonian Institute released a call for proposals that was circulated in the marine science community for those interested in conducting research while living in an underwater habitat. Earle submitted a proposal describing her intention to use the opportunity to study the ecology of marine plants and fishes in great detail by combining her observations with those of the ichthyologists on board. Unfortunately, the other applicants were male, and the review board deemed Earle's cohabitation with them inappropriate. Her request to be a part of the Tektite I mission was rejected; however, the Smithsonian later proposed an which Earle became a part of. The Tektite II mission received a lot of attention at the time (1970) because of its all female crew.

Following her experience aboard the underwater habitat, Earle developed an interest in deep sea exploration, and in 1979 she broke the record for deep diving at 381 m/1,250 ft below the surface in a special suit called the *Jim suit* designed to withstand the pressure. Her record has not been broken. Earle decided to test the *Jim suit* as part of her research on a book published by National Geographic *'Exploring the Deep Frontier'*, and out of her frustration that scuba diving techniques only scratched the surface of the ocean. Following this adventure, Earle started two companies that manufacture deep sea exploration vehicles. The continued advancements in the the technology of these vehicles has helped open up areas in the deep sea previously unexplored. During the 1990s, Earle served as Chief Scientist for the National Oceanic and Atmospheric Administration (NOAA). She is currently an Explorer-in-Residence with National Geographic, and, in addition to her research, remains committed to raising awareness on marine environmental issues.

Dr. Robert Ballard (1942) also a deep-sea explorer, may be best known for finding the Titanic using technologies he helped to develop, including the *Argo/Jason* remotely operated vehicles and the technology that transmits video images from the deep sea. His earlier deep sea explorations led to the first discovery of hydrothermal vents during an exploration in a manned submersible of the Mid-Ocean Ridge. Ballard founded the Woods Hole Oceanographic Institution's Deep Submergence Laboratory and spent 30 years there working on the use of manned submersibles. Ballard has devoted a great deal of time to furthering the field of deep sea exploration. He created a distance-learning programme with more than one million students enrolled, taught by more than 30,000 science teachers worldwide. He also founded the Institute for Exploration located in Mystic, Connecticut for the study of deep-water archaeology which led to the discovery of the largest number of ancient ships ever found in the deep sea. Currently, he is a National Geographic Society Explorer-in-Residence Professor of Oceanography at the University of Rhode Island's Graduate School of Oceanography, and Director of the Institute for Archaeological Oceanography.

The Future

Today, the possibilities for ocean exploration are nearly infinite. In addition to scuba diving, rebreathers, fast computers, remotely-operated vehicles (ROVs), deep sea submersibles, reinforced diving suits, and satellites, other technologies are also being developed. But interdisciplinary research is needed to continue building our understanding of the ocean, and what needs to be done to protect it. In spite of ongoing technological advances, it is estimated that only 5 per cent of the oceans have been explored. Surprisingly, we know more about the moon than we do the ocean. This needs to change if we are to ensure the longevity of the life in the seas—and they cover 71 per cent of the earth's surface. Unlike the moon, they are our backyard. Without a detailed collective understanding of the ramifications of pollution, overfishing, coastal development, as well as the long-term sustainability of ocean oxygen production and carbon dioxide and monoxide absorption, we face great risks to environmental and human health. We need this research so that we can act on potential problems—not react to them when it is already too late.

Fortunately, thanks to the work of past and present ocean explorers, the public is increasingly aware of these risks which encourage public agencies to take action and promote research. Already the US Commission on Ocean Policy favors multi-disciplinary research to shape ocean policy. The efforts of public agencies using a multi-disciplinary approach, together with the efforts provided by numerous private marine conservation organisations that work on issues such as advocacy, education, and research, will help drive the momentum needed to face the challenges of preserving the ocean.

2 Marine Science

Marine science, is the branch of earth science that studies the ocean. It covers a wide range of topics, including marine organisms and ecosystem dynamics; ocean currents, waves, and geophysical fluid dynamics; plate tectonics and the geology of the sea floor; and fluxes of various chemical substances and physical properties within the ocean and across its boundaries. These diverse topics reflect multiple disciplines that oceanographers blend to further knowledge of the world ocean and understanding of processes within it: biology, chemistry, geology, meteorology, and physics as well as geography.

Humans first acquired knowledge of the waves and currents of the seas and oceans in pre-historic times. Observations on tides are recorded by Aristotle and Strabo. Early modern exploration of the oceans was primarily for cartography and mainly limited to its surfaces and of the creatures that fishermen brought up in nets, though depth soundings by lead line were taken.

Although Juan Ponce de León in 1513 first identified the Gulf Stream, and the current was well-known to mariners, Benjamin Franklin made the first scientific study of it and gave it its name. Franklin measured water temperatures during several Atlantic crossings and correctly explained the Gulf Stream's cause. Franklin and Timothy Folger printed the first map of the Gulf Stream in 1769-1770.

When Louis Antoine de Bougainville, who voyaged between 1766 and 1769, and James Cook, who voyaged from 1768 to 1779, carried out their explorations in the South Pacific, information on the oceans themselves formed part of the reports. James Rennell wrote the first scientific textbooks about currents in the Atlantic and Indian oceans during the late 18th and at the beginning of 19th century. Sir James Clark Ross took the first modern sounding in deep sea in 1840, and Charles Darwin published a paper on reefs and the formation of atolls as a result of the second voyage of HMS *Beagle* in 1831-6. Robert FitzRoy published a report in four volumes of the three voyages of the *Beagle*. In 1841-42 Edward Forbes undertook dredging in the Aegean Sea that founded marine ecology.

As first superintendent of the United States Naval Observatory (1842-1861) Matthew Fontaine Maury devoted his time to the study of marine meteorology, navigation, and charting prevailing winds and currents. His *Physical Geography of the Sea*, 1855 was the first textbook of oceanography. Many nations sent oceanographic observations to Maury at the Naval Observatory, where he and his colleagues evaluated the information and gave the results worldwide distribution.

The steep slope beyond the continental shelves was discovered in 1849. The first successful laying of transatlantic telegraph cable in August 1858 confirmed the presence of an underwater 'telegraphic plateau' mid-ocean ridge. After the middle of the 19th century, scientific societies were processing a flood of new terrestrial botanical and zoological information.

In 1871, under the recommendations of the Royal Society of London, the British government sponsored an expedition to explore world's oceans and conduct scientific investigations. Under that sponsorship the Scots Charles Wyville Thompson and Sir John Murray launched the Challenger expedition (1872-1876). The results of this were published in 50 volumes covering biological, physical and geological aspects. 4417 new species were discovered.

Other European and American nations also sent out scientific expeditions (as did private individuals and institutions). The first purpose built oceanographic ship, the 'Albatros' was built in 1882. The four-month 1910 North Atlantic expedition headed by Sir John Murray and Johan Hjort was at that time the most ambitious research oceanographic and marine zoological project ever, and led to the classic 1912 book (*The Depths of the Ocean*).

Oceanographic institutes dedicated to the study of oceanography were founded. In the United States, these included the Scripps Institution of Oceanography in 1892, Woods Hole Oceanographic Institution in 1930, Virginia Institute of Marine Science in 1938, Lamont-Doherty Earth Observatory at Columbia University, and the School of Oceanography at University of Washington. In Britain, there is a major research institution: National Oceanography Centre, Southampton which is the successor to the Institute of Oceanography. In Australia, CSIRO Marine and Atmospheric Research, known as CMAR, is a leading centre. In 1921 the International Hydrographic Bureau (IHB) was formed in Monaco.

In 1893, Fridtjof Nansen allowed his ship 'Fram' to be frozen in the Arctic ice. As a result he was able to obtain oceanographic data as well as meteorological and astronomical data. The first international organisation of oceanography was created in 1902 as the International Council for the Exploration of the Sea.

The first acoustic measurement of sea depth was made in 1914. Between 1925 and 1927 the 'Meteor' expedition gathered 70,000 ocean depth measurements using an echo sounder, surveying the Mid atlantic ridge. The Great Global Rift, running along the Mid Atlantic Ridge, was discovered by Maurice Ewing and Bruce Heezen in 1953 while the mountain range under the Arctic was found in 1954 by the Arctic Institute of the USSR. The theory of seafloor spreading was developed in 1960 by Harry Hammond Hess. The Ocean

Drilling Project started in 1966. Deep sea vents were discovered in 1977 by John Corlis and Robert Ballard in the submersible 'Alvin'.

In the 1950s, Auguste Piccard invented the bathyscaphe and used the 'Trieste' to investigate the ocean's depths. The nuclear submarine Nautilus made the first journey under the ice to the North Pole in 1958. In 1962 there was the first deployment of FLIP (Floating Instrument Platform), a 355 foot spar buoy.

Then, in 1966, the U.S. Congress created a *National Council for Marine Resources and Engineering Development*. NOAA was put in charge of exploring and studying all aspects of Oceanography in the USA. It also enabled the National Science Foundation to award *Sea Grant College* funding to multi-disciplinary researchers in the field of oceanography.

From the 1970s, there has been much emphasis on the application of large scale computers to oceanography to allow numerical predictions of ocean conditions and as a part of overall environmental change prediction. An oceanographic buoy array was established in the Pacific to allow prediction of El Niño events.

1990 saw the start of the World Ocean Circulation Experiment (WOCE) which continued until 2002. Geosat seafloor mapping data became available in 1995.

In 1942, Sverdrup and Fleming published 'The Ocean' which was a major landmark. 'The Sea' (in three volumes covering physical oceanography, seawater and geology) edited by M.N. Hill was published in 1962 while the "Encyclopedia of Oceanography" by Rhodes Fairbridge was published in 1966.

Connection to the Atmosphere

The study of the oceans is linked to understanding global climate changes, potential global warming and related biosphere concerns. The atmosphere and ocean are linked because of evaporation and precipitation as well as thermal flux (and solar insolation). Wind stress is a major driver of ocean currents while the ocean is a sink for atmospheric carbon dioxide.

Our planet is invested with two great oceans; one visible, the other invisible; one underfoot, the other overhead; one entirely envelopes it, the other covers about two thirds of its surface.

Branches

The study of oceanography is divided into branches:

- *Biological oceanography*, or *marine biology*, is the study of the plants, animals and microbes of the oceans and their ecological interaction with the ocean.
- *Chemical oceanography*, or *marine chemistry*, is the study of the chemistry of the ocean and its chemical interaction with the atmosphere.
- *Geological oceanography*, or *marine geology*, is the study of the geology of the ocean floor including plate tectonics and paleoceanography.
- *Physical oceanography*, or *marine physics*, studies the ocean's physical attributes including temperature-salinity structure, mixing, waves, internal waves, surface tides, internal tides, and currents.

These branches reflect the fact that many oceanographers are first trained in the exact sciences or mathematics and then focus on applying their interdisciplinary knowledge, skills and abilities to oceanography.

Data derived from the work of Oceanographers is used in marine engineering, in the design and building of oil platforms, ships, harbours, and other structures that allow us to use the ocean safely.

Oceanographic data management is the discipline ensuring that oceanographic data both past and present are available to researchers.

Oceanic Climate

An oceanic climate, also called marine west coast climate, maritime climate, Cascadian climate and British climate for

Köppen climate classification *Cfb* and subtropical highland for Köppen *Cfb* or *Cwb*, is a type of climate typically found along the west coasts at the middle latitudes of some of the world's continents. This climate has cool summers and warm winters, with a narrow annual temperature range. It typically lacks a dry season, as precipitation is more evenly dispersed through the year. It is the predominant climate type across much of Europe, coastal northwestern North America, portions of southern South America and Africa, southeast Australia, New Zealand, as well as isolated locations elsewhere.

Properties

Climates near the ocean have moderately cool summers and comparatively warm winters, they are generally characterized by a narrower annual range of temperatures than are encountered in other places at a comparable latitude, and generally do not have the extremely dry summers of Mediterranean climates. Oceanic climates are most dominant in Europe, where they spread much farther inland than in other continents.

Similar climates in thermal range are also found in tropical highlands even at considerable distance from any coastline. Generally, they fall into Köppen climate classification *Cfb* or *Cwb*. The narrow range of temperatures results from the slight thermal range of temperatures between seasons characteristic of tropical lowlands. Altitudes are high enough that some places have at least one month cooler than 18° C (64° F) and do not qualify for grouping in the true tropical climates. This variation of the oceanic climate is termed 'subtropical highland climate'. Unlike the norm in true oceanic climates, subtropical highland climates may have a marked winter drought. Agricultural potential in both oceanic climates and subtropical highland climates are similar.

Precipitation

Precipitation is both adequate and reliable throughout the year in oceanic climates, except in certain tropical highland areas, which would have tropical savanna or steppe climates (with a dry season in winter) if not for the high altitude making them cooler (Koppen *Cwb*). Under some variations of the Koeppen classification system, parts of the Pacific Northwest and south-central Chile are sometimes considered as having a Mediterranean climate (Koppen 'Csb') due to a drying trend in the summer. However despite the 'Csb' designation, these areas are generally considered oceanic as opposed to 'Mediterranean'.

In most areas with an oceanic climate, for the majority of the year precipitation comes in the form of rain. However during the winter, despite its C classification, the majority of areas with this climate see some snowfall annually. Outside of Australia, South Africa and tropical highland locations, most areas with an oceanic climate experiences at least one snowstorm per year. In the poleward locations of the oceanic climate zone ('subpolar oceanic climates', described in greater detail below), snowfall is more frequent and commonplace.

Temperature

Overall temperature characteristics vary among oceanic climates; those at the lowest latitudes are nearly subtropical from a thermal standpoint, but more commonly a mesothermal regime prevails, with cool, but not cold, winters and warm, but not hot, summers. Summers are also cooler (often much cooler) than in areas with a humid subtropical climate. Average temperature of warmest month must be less than 22°C (72°F) and that of the coldest month warmer than -3°C (27°F) although American scientists prefer 0°C (32°F) in the coldest month. Poleward of the latter is a zone of the aforementioned subpolar oceanic climate, with long but relatively mild winters and cool and short summers (average temperatures of at least 10°C (50°F) for one to three months). Examples of this climate include parts of coastal Iceland in the Northern Hemisphere and extreme southern Chile and Argentina in the Southern Hemisphere.

The British Isles experience a typically maritime climate, with prevailing south-westerly winds from the Atlantic Ocean. The annual average temperature range in the British Isles is only about 14°C (57°F). Although the west coast of Alaska experiences a maritime climate, the absence of an equally significant warm Pacific current in the upper-mid latitudes means that these regions are generally colder in winter, with more precipitation falling as snow. Typical oceanic climates are also found in the Netherlands, Belgium, most of France, western Germany, northern Spain, etc.

All mid-latitude oceanic climates are classified as humid. Some rainshadow climates with thermal régimes similar to those of oceanic climates but steppe-like (*BSk*) or even desert-like (*BWk*) scarcity of precipitation include lowland valleys of Washington and Oregon to the east of the Cascade Range, Patagonia in southern Argentina, and the Atacama Desert in northern Chile. Another example are coastal areas in southeast Western Australia.

Under Koeppen-Geiger, many areas generally considered to have Oceanic climates are classified as cool summer, dry-summer subtropical (*Csb*). These areas are not usually associated with a typical Mediterranean climate, and include much of the Pacific Northwest, southern Chile, parts of west-central Argentina, and northwestern Spain (Galicia) and northern Portugal. Many of these areas would be classified Oceanic (*Cfb*), except dry-summer patterns meet Koeppen's *Cs* thresholds, and cities such as Concepción, Chile; Seattle, Washington; Portland, Oregon; Victoria, British Columbia; and Vancouver, British Columbia can be classified as *Csb*.

The only noteworthy area of Maritime Climate at or near sea-level within Africa is in South Africa from Mossel Bay on the Western Cape coast to Plettenberg Bay, with additional pockets of this climate inland of the Eastern Cape and KwaZulu-Natal coast. Interior southern Africa, elevated portions of eastern Africa, and Mozambique also share this climate type. It is usually warm most of the year with no pronounced rainy season, but slightly more rain in autumn and spring. The only significant areas where this climate is found in Asia is on the Black Sea coast in northern Turkey, in small pockets along or near the Caspian Sea in Azerbaijan and in small pockets along or near the Tsugaru Strait in northern Japan. The oceanic climate is prevalent in a good portion of western Europe and the European part of northern Turkey. The oceanic climate is prevalent in the more southerly locations of Oceania. A mild Maritime climate is in existence in New Zealand, the island of Tasmania, Australia, southern parts of Victoria and New South Wales, Australia. It can also be found along the western areas of the south coast of Western Australia. The oceanic climate is found in isolated pockets in South America. It exists in central Argentina, southern Chile and parts of Brazil, Ecuador and Colombia. The oceanic climate exists in an arc spreading across the north-western coast of North America, largely in the Pacific Northwest. It includes the western parts of Washington and Oregon, the Alaskan panhandle, western portions of British Columbia, and north-western California.

Subtropical Highland Variety (Cwb)

The Subtropical Highland variety of the oceanic climate exists in elevated portions of the world that are either within the tropics or subtropics, though it is typically found in mountainous locations in some tropical countries. Despite the latitude, due to the higher altitudes of these regions, it tends to share characteristics with oceanic climates, though it also tends to experience noticeably drier weather during the 'low-sun' season.

In locations outside the tropics, other than the drying trend in the winter, Subtropical Highland climates tend to be essentially identical to an oceanic climate, complete with mild summers, noticeably cooler winters and in some instances, some snowfall. In the tropics, a Subtropical Highland climate tends to feature spring-like weather year-round. Temperatures here remain relatively constant throughout the year and snowfall is seldom seen. Areas with this climate feature monthly averages below 22°C (72°F) but above -3°C (27°F) (or 0°C (32°F) using American standards). At least one month's average temperature is below 18°C (64°F). Without the elevation, many of these regions would likely feature either tropical or humid subtropical climates. These regions usually carry a *Cwb* or *Cfb* designation.

This type of climate exists in parts of east, south and south-eastern Africa, some mountainous areas across southern Europe, sections of mountainous Latin America, some mountainous areas across Southeast Asia, higher elevations of the southern Appalachians, and parts of the Himalayas. It also occurs in a few areas of Australia, although the summers there are hotter and drier than is typical of the Subtropical Highland Climate, with maximums sometimes exceeding 40°C (104°F)

Subpolar Variety (Cfc)

Areas with Subpolar Oceanic climates feature an oceanic climate but are usually located closer to Polar regions. As a result of its location, these regions tend to be on the cool end of oceanic climates. Snowfall tends to be more common here than in other oceanic climates. Subpolar Oceanic climates are less prone to temperature extremes than Subarctic climates or Humid continental climates, featuring milder winters than these climates. Subpolar Oceanic climates feature only one to three months of average monthly temperatures that are at least 10°C (50°F). Like oceanic climates, none of its average monthly temperatures fall below -3°C (26.6°F). It typically carries a *Cfc* designation. This variant of an oceanic climate is found in parts of coastal Iceland, Faroe Islands, northwestern coastal areas of Norway reaching to 70°N on some islands, southern islands of Alaska and northern parts of the Alaskan Panhandle, the far south of Chile and Argentina and Mountainous areas of Europe, including the Scottish Highlands and uplands near the coast of southwestern Norway. The classifications used to this regime are Cfc.

Csb Problematics

Despite the fact that dry summers is a feature which differentiates Csb areas from oceanic climates, some areas of Csb climate are typically considered 'Oceanic' as opposed to 'Mediterranean'. Technically, this version of the Oceanic climate meets Koppen's minimum precipitation threshold limit of 30 millimetres (1.2 in) (or 40 millimetres (1.6 in) under Koppen-Geiger), resulting in a *Csb* designation for this zone.

Nevertheless, due to the higher annual cumulation of precipitations than in Csa areas, scientists such as Trewartha has decided to include areas with more than 900 mm of precipitation in the oceanic climate (Do under the classification). This is especially the case with Northwestern coasts of USA, some sections of coastal Chile or Galicia, and where the athmospheric conditions are less hot in summer and wetter in the year. Nevertheless, those regions experience several Mediterranean features:

- A higher yearly sunshine bright than the typical oceanic domain. For example, La Coruna or Seattle have at least 2000 hours of sunshine, while the values of the typical Cfb regions are far below (almost always below 2000 hours).
- Some areas of this category remain relatively warm in summer (temperature of the hottest month in Galicia are generally above 19ºC), when it often falls under 18ºC in the Cfb areas (about 15ºC or 16ºC in the Northwestern coasts of Europe).
- A vegetation which is partially adapted to xeric conditions. So the cork oak, a typically acidophilus Mediterranean species, and which is widely distributed in Portugal and in southern-half of Galicia. In contrast, beech or birch, widely distributed in the Cfb area, are not common in Iberia, mostly confined to the Pyrenees and the Cantabrian mountains. Douglas fir which is the typical species of the Pacific Northwestern forests, is very well adapted to the summer drought.
- Forest fires are regular in those regions due to the summer-drought.

Ocean

An ocean (from Greek 'okeanos' Oceanus) is a major body of saline water, and a principal component of the hydrosphere. Approximately 71 per cent of the Earth's surface (~3.6×108 km^2) is covered by ocean, a continuous body of water that is customarily divided into several principal oceans and smaller seas.

More than half of this area is over 3,000 metres (9,800 ft) deep. Average oceanic salinity is around 35 parts per thousand (%) (3.5%), and nearly all seawater has a salinity in the range of 30 to 38 per cent. Scientists estimate that 230,000 marine species are currently known, but the total could be up to 10 times that number.

Though generally described as several 'separate' oceans, these waters comprise one global, interconnected body of salt water sometimes referred to as the World Ocean or global ocean. This concept of a continuous body of water with relatively free interchange among its parts is of fundamental importance to oceanography.

The major oceanic divisions are defined in part by the continents, various archipelagos, and other criteria. These divisions are (in descending order of size):

- Pacific Ocean, which separates Asia and Australia from the Americas
- Atlantic Ocean, which separates the Americas from Eurasia and Africa
- Indian Ocean, which washes upon southern Asia and separates Africa and Australia
- Southern Ocean, sometimes considered an extension of the Pacific, Atlantic and Indian Oceans, which encircles Antarctica.
- Arctic Ocean, sometimes considered a sea of the Atlantic, which covers much of the Arctic and washes upon northern North America and Eurasia.

The Pacific and Atlantic may be further subdivided by the equator into northern and southern portions. Smaller regions of the oceans are called seas, gulfs, bays, straits and other names.

Geologically, an ocean is an area of oceanic crust covered by water. Oceanic crust is the thin layer of solidified volcanic basalt that covers the Earth's mantle. Continental crust is thicker but less dense. From this perspective, the earth has three oceans: the World Ocean, the Caspian Sea and Black Sea. The latter two were formed by the collision of Cimmeria with Laurasia. The Mediterranean Sea is at times a discrete ocean, because tectonic plate movement has repeatedly broken its connection to the World Ocean through the Strait of Gibraltar. The Black Sea is connected to the Mediterranean through the Bosporus, but the Bosporus is a natural canal cut through continental rock some 7,000 years ago, rather than a piece of oceanic sea floor like the Strait of Gibraltar.

Despite their names, smaller landlocked bodies of saltwater that are not connected with the World Ocean, such as the Aral Sea, are actually salt lakes.

The ocean has a significant effect on the biosphere. Oceanic evaporation, as a phase of the water cycle, is the source of most rainfall, and ocean temperatures determine climate and wind patterns that affect life on land. Life within the ocean evolved 3 billion years prior to life on land. Both the depth and distance from shore strongly influence the amount and kinds of plants and animals that live there.

The area of the World Ocean is 361 million square kilometres (139 million square miles) Its volume is approximately 1.3 billion cubic kilometres (310 million cu mi). This can be thought of as a cube of water with an edge length of 1,111 kilometres (690 mi). Its average depth is 3,790 metres (12,430 ft), and its maximum depth is 10,923 metres (6.787 mi) Nearly half of the world's marine waters are over 3,000 metres (9,800 ft) deep. The vast expanses of deep ocean (anything below 200 metres (660 ft)) cover about 66 per cent of the Earth's surface. This does not include seas not connected to the World Ocean, such as the Caspian Sea.

The total mass of the hydrosphere is about 1,400,000,000,000,000,000 metric tons (1.5×1018 short tons) or 1.4×1021 kg, which is about 0.023 per cent of the Earth's total mass. Less than 3 per cent is freshwater; the rest is saltwater, mostly in the ocean.

A common misconception is that the oceans are blue primarily because the sky is blue. In fact, water has a very slight blue colour that can only be seen in large volumes. While the sky's reflection does contribute to the blue appearance of the surface, it is not the primary cause. The primary cause is the absorption by the water molecules of red photons from the incoming light, the only known example of colour in nature resulting from vibrational, rather than electronic, dynamics.

Sailors and other mariners have reported that the ocean often emits a visible glow, or luminescence, which extends for miles at night. In 2005, scientists announced that for the first time, they had obtained photographic evidence of this glow. It may be caused by bioluminescence.

Ocean travel by boat dates back to prehistoric times, but only in modern times has extensive underwater travel become possible.

The deepest point in the ocean is the Mariana Trench, located in the Pacific Ocean near the Northern Mariana Islands. Its maximum depth has been estimated to be 10,971 metres (35,994 ft) (plus or minus 11 metres; see the Mariana Trench article for discussion of the various estimates of the maximum depth.) The British naval vessel, Challenger II surveyed the trench in 1951 and named the deepest part of the trench, the 'Challenger Deep'. In 1960, the Trieste successfully reached the bottom of the trench, manned by a crew of two men.

Much of the ocean bottom remains unexplored and unmapped. A global image of many underwater features larger than 10 kilometres (6.2 mi) was created in 1995 based on gravitational distortions of the nearby sea surface.

Depths and Zones

Oceanographers divide the ocean into regions depending on physical and biological conditions of these areas. The pelagic zone includes all open ocean regions, and can be divided into further regions categorized by depth and light abundance. The photic zone covers the oceans from surface level to 200 metres down. This is the region where photosynthesis can occur and therefore is the most biodiverse. Since plants require photosynthesis, life found deeper than this must either rely on material sinking from above or find another energy source; hydrothermal vents are the primary option in what is known as the aphotic zone (depths exceeding

200 m). The pelagic part of the photic zone is known as the epipelagic. The pelagic part of the aphotic zone can be further divided into regions that succeed each other vertically according to temperature.

The mesopelagic is the uppermost region. Its lowermost boundary is at a thermocline of 12°C (54°F), which, in the tropics generally lies at 700-1,000 metres (2,300-3,300 ft). Next is the bathypelagic lying between 10 and 4°C (50 and 39°F), typically between 700-1,000 metres (2,300-3,300 ft) and 2,000-4,000 metres (6,600-13,000 ft) Lying along the top of the abyssal plain is the abyssalpelagic, whose lower boundary lies at about 6,000 metres (20,000 ft). The last zone includes the deep trenches, and is known as the hadalpelagic. This lies between 6,000-11,000 metres (20,000-36,000 ft) and is the deepest oceanic zone.

Along with pelagic aphotic zones there are also benthic aphotic zones. These correspond to the three deepest zones of the deep-sea. The bathyal zone covers the continental slope down to about 4,000 metres (13,000 ft). The abyssal zone covers the abyssal plains between 4,000 and 6,000 m. Lastly, the hadal zone corresponds to the hadalpelagic zone which is found in the oceanic trenches.

The pelagic zone can also be split into two subregions, the neritic zone and the oceanic zone. The neritic encompasses the water mass directly above the continental shelves, while the oceanic zone includes all the completely open water. In contrast, the littoral zone covers the region between low and high tide and represents the transitional area between marine and terrestrial conditions. It is also known as the intertidal zone because it is the area where tide level affects the conditions of the region.

Climate Effects

World map with coloured, directed lines showing how water moves through the oceans. Cold deep water rises and warms in the central Pacific and in the Indian, while warm water sinks and cools near Greenland in the North Atlantic and near Antarctica in the South Atlantic.

A summary of the path of the thermohaline circulation/ Great Ocean Conveyor. Blue paths represent deep-water currents, while red paths represent surface currents

Ocean currents greatly affect the Earth's climate by transferring heat from the tropics to the polar regions, and transferring warm or cold air and precipitation to coastal regions, where winds may carry them inland. Surface heat and freshwater fluxes create global density gradients that drive the thermohaline circulation part of large-scale ocean circulation. It plays an important role in supplying heat to the polar regions, and thus in sea ice regulation. Changes in the thermohaline circulation are thought to have significant impacts on the Earth's radiation budget. Insofar as the thermohaline circulation governs the rate at which deep waters reach the surface, it may also significantly influence atmospheric carbon dioxide concentrations.

For a discussion of the possibilities of changes to the thermohaline circulation under global warming, see shutdown of thermohaline circulation.

It is often stated that the thermohaline circulation is the primary reason that the climate of Western Europe is so temperate. An alternate hypothesis claims that this is largely incorrect, and that Europe is warm mostly because it lies downwind of an ocean basin, and because atmospheric waves bring warm air north from the subtropics.

The Antarctic Circumpolar Current encircles that continent, influencing the area's climate and connecting currents in several oceans.

One of the most dramatic forms of weather occurs over the oceans: tropical cyclones (also called 'typhoons' and 'hurricanes' depending upon where the system forms).

Lifeforms native to oceans include:

- Radiata
- Fish
- Cetacea such as whales, dolphins and porpoises
- Cephalopods such as octopus and squid

- Crustaceans such as lobsters, clams, shrimp and krill
- Marine worms
- Plankton
- Echinoderms such as brittle stars, starfish, sea cucumbers and sand dollars.
- Economy
- The oceans are essential to transportation: most of the world's goods move by ship between the world's seaports.
- Oceans are also the major supply source for the fishing industry. Some of the more major ones are shrimp, fish, crabs and lobster.
- Ancient oceans

Genesis of an Ocean

Continental drift continually reconfigures the oceans, joining and splitting bodies of water. Ancient oceans include:

- Bridge River Ocean, the ocean between the ancient Insular Islands and North America.
- Iapetus Ocean, the southern hemisphere ocean between Baltica and Avalonia.
- Panthalassa, the vast world ocean that surrounded the Pangaea supercontinent.
- Rheic Ocean
- Slide Mountain Ocean, the ocean between the ancient Intermontane Islands and North America.
- Tethys Ocean, the ocean between the ancient continents of Gondwana and Laurasia.
- Khanty Ocean, the ocean between Baltica and Siberia.
- Mirovia, the ocean that surrounded the Rodinia supercontinent.
- Paleo-Tethys Ocean, the ocean between Gondwana and the Hunic terranes.
- Poseidon Ocean
- Proto-Tethys Ocean

- Pan-African Ocean, the ocean that surrounded the Pannotia supercontinent.
- Superocean, the ocean that surrounds a global supercontinent.
- Ural Ocean, the ocean between Siberia and Baltica.

Earth is the only known planet with liquid water on its surface and is certainly the only one in our own solar system. However, a layer of liquid water thick enough to decouple the crust from the mantle is thought to be present under the surfaces of the moons Titan, Europa and, with less certainty, Callisto and Ganymede. A similar magma ocean is thought to be present on Io. Geysers have been found on Saturn's moon Enceladus, though these may not involve bodies of liquid water. Other icy moons and trans-neptunian objects may also have internal oceans, or have once had internal oceans that have now frozen. The planets Uranus and Neptune may also possess large oceans of liquid water under their thick atmospheres, though their internal structure is not well understood

There is currently much debate over whether Mars once had an ocean in its northern hemisphere, and over what happened to it; recent findings by the Mars Exploration Rover mission indicate Mars had long-term standing water in at least one location, but its extent is not known.

Astronomers believe that Venus had liquid water and perhaps oceans in its very early history. If they existed, all later vanished via resurfacing.

Liquid hydrocarbons are thought to be present on the surface of Titan, though lakes may be a more accurate term. The Cassini-Huygens space mission initially discovered only what appeared to be dry lakebeds and empty river channels, suggesting that Titan had lost what surface liquids it might have had. Cassini's more recent fly-by of Titan offers radar images that strongly suggest hydrocarbon lakes near the colder polar regions. Titan is thought to have a subterranean water ocean under the ice and hydrocarbon mix that forms its outer crust.

Beyond the solar system, the planet Gliese 581 c is at the right distance from its sun to support liquid surface water. However, its greenhouse effect would make it too hot for oceans to exist on the surface. On Gliese 581 d the greenhouse effect may bring temperatures suitable for surface oceans. Astronomers dispute whether HD 209458 b has water vapour in its atmosphere. Gliese 436 b is believed to have 'hot ice'. Neither of these planets are cool enough for liquid water—but if water molecules exist there, they are also likely to be found on planets at a suitable temperature. GJ 1214 b, detected by transit, found evidence that this planet has oceans made of exotic form of ice VII, making up 75 per cent of all the planet's mass.

The original concept of 'ocean' goes back to notions of Mesopotamian and Indo-European mythology, imagining the world to be encircled by a great river. Okeanos in Greek, reflects the ancient Greek observation that a strong current flowed off Gibraltar and their subsequent assumption that it was a great river. (Compare also Samudra from Hindu mythology and Jörmungandr from Norse mythology.)

Artworks which depict maritime themes are known as marine art, a term which particularly applies to common styles of European painting of the 17th to 19th centuries.

3 Marine Taxonomy

The science of taxonomy classifies species into evolutionary relationships to help identify organisms and name species. Taxonomy is also referred to as scientific classification.

Today's classification system was developed by Carl Linnaeus as an important tool for use in the study of biology and for use in the protection of biodiversity. Without very specific classification information and a naming system to identify species' relationships, scientists would be limited in attempts to accurately describe the relationships among species. Understanding these relationships helps predict how ecosystems can be altered by human or natural factors.

Preserving biodiversity is facilitated by taxonomy. Species data can be better analyzed to determine the number of different species in a community and to determine how they might be affected by environmental stresses. Family, or phylogenetic, trees for species help predict environmental impacts on individual species and their relatives.

Linnaean Taxonomic System

Carl Linnaeus was born in 1707 and died in 1778. He created the entire category of systematic zoology and botany as well as a classification scheme—still used by biologists today. His masterpiece was the Systema Naturae. Linnaeus invented the classification system to establish consensus on plant and animal names and to understand complex evolutionary relationships between organisms. The Linnaean taxonomic system begins with the most general category of Domain or Kingdom and becomes increasingly specific until it ends with a specific genus and species name derived from Greek and/or Latin roots.

Based on concepts introduced by his scientist predecessors, Linnaeus developed his system so that each species had a Latin double name. The first name is the genus and the second is the species name. This two-word naming system is called binomial nomenclature. The name is always italicized with the genus capitalized and the species in lowercase letters.

There are eight general taxonomic groupings, starting with the most general and ending at the most specific. The groupings are: Domain, Kingdom, Phylum (or Division for plants), Class, Order, Family, Genus and Species. In some cases, subgroups are included for accuracy such as subclass, superorder, suborder, and infraorder to name a few. The naming of life can become incredibly complex. When the species grouping is not specific enough, subspecies categories are added. Domains are also sometimes added above the kingdom level, if a high level of generality is needed. On the other hand, if more detail is needed, tribes can be added between family and genus categories and sections or series can be added between genus and species categories.

The five Kingdoms are Monera, Protista, Fungi, Plantae, and Animalia. Under each Kingdom, Phylums are listed and under each Phylum there are many Classes (and so on). With over 10,000 species, Kingdom Monera consists of unicellular bacteria and cyanobacteria. Kingdom Monera is also the only kingdom made up of prokaryotic cells or cells without nuclei and organelles not surrounded by a membrane. The other four kingdoms consist of eukaryotes or cells with nuclei and organelles bound by a membrane. Kingdom Protista consists of 250,000 species of single celled protozoans and macroscopic algae. There are 100,000 species in Kingdom Fungi and they are usually either heterotrophic haploid or dikaryotic cells. There are 250,000 species in Kingdom Plantae and they all are autotrophic forms of plants that keep the embryo on the female part of the plant. With over 1,000,000 species, Kingdom Animalia consists of multicellular animals that lack a cell wall (plant cells have a rigid cell wall) and form a blastula early in life.

To demonstrate how an organism is classified, let us use the classification of the commonly named "the blue whale". The information provided by this common name is not enough to put the whale into any evolutionary relationship with other organisms. Scientists however, call the blue whale by its scientific name—*Balaenoptera musculus*. An example of how scientists would classify and name a blue whale is as follows:

- All whales are animals because they have more than one cell, eat food and originate from a fertilized egg—so they first are categorized into the most general category—Kingdom Animalia.
- Whales are placed into the Phylum Chordata (the category below Kingdom) because they have a spinal cord and gill pouches. In fact, humans are also in Phylum Chordata.
- Because they are warm-blooded, produce milk for their young and have a heart with four chambers, whales are in the Class Mammalia.
- At the 'Order' category, whales begin to be distinguished from humans and other land mammals. Whales are classified as cetaceans because they live in the water all year round. The suborder is Mysticeti due to the baleen plates in the mouths of whales, helping them to filter in food.
- Blue whales have folds around their throat that expand to take in large volumes of water when feeding. Because not all whales have this characteristic, blue whales are placed into the Family 'Balaenidae'.
- Within the Family is another group of species more immediately related to each other. The "Genus" for blue whales is *Balaenoptera*.

- The definition of a species includes many factors, especially the requirement that individuals must be able to successfully breed with each other. The species name for blue whales is *musculus*, meaning that in addition to other common traits, whales of the species *musculus* are able to breed with each other and provide viable (living) offspring. The final scientific name is *Balaenoptera musculus* with the genus capitalized and the species name in lower case letters and both italicized.

Phylogenetic Trees

A phylogenetic tree is similar to a family tree except that it shows evolutionary relationships between species rather than relationships between individuals. Phylogenetic trees contain a lot of information and can reveal how far back in time a species began, along with the most recent common ancestors between species. DNA analysis is used to provide information to support the construction of phylogenetic trees. Every 'node' on a phylogenetic tree is referred to as a taxonomic unit and represents a common ancestor. Scientists can zoom in on a particular part of a phylogenetic tree, omitting the 'root' of the tree in order to focus on a particular segment. A rooted tree is simply the bigger, zoomed-out picture.

The Science of Classification

Taxonomists are responsible for the discovery of new species, analysis and compilation of collected data, and the release of new information to the public, including other scientists. The research requires valuable identification skills, the ability to categorize and recognize species relationships, an understanding of ecosystems and ecology, knowledge of species distribution, and the ability to determine keystone species. They must also be able to submit data and explain the synthesis clearly for people in communities.

Scientists have relied on Linnaeus's system of classification for the last two hundred years. After Darwin's time, it became clear that another dimension could be added to the phylogenetic tree so taxonomic groups would represent the principle of common descent. Related taxa (or categories) were moved to occupy what can be visualized as a bunch of leaves on a particular branch. These relatively new and helpful groupings are referred to as monophyletic groups.

A new development in taxonomy is the revelation that using a cladogram can make it easier to view evolutionary relationships. A cladogram is basically an isolated branch of the phylogenetic tree turned sideways with each line indicating the amount of time between the ancestor and the species. Each "clade" represents a monophyletic group. Because it is only a short branch of the entire tree it is not usually necessary to refer to the more general Linnaean form of classification.

Taxonomy is becoming more important as scientists struggle to identify species in order to understand the subtle relationships and complex reactions of ecosystems threatened by human pursuits. The study of taxonomy provides a solid foundation for the research needed for the conservation of marine life.

The World Register of Marine Species

As of 22 March, 2012:

212,906 accepted species; of which 192,888 are checked (91%)

361,601 species names including synonyms

447,277 taxa (infraspecies to kingdoms).

The aim of a World Register of Marine Species (WoRMS) is to provide an authoritative and comprehensive list of names of marine organisms, including information on synonymy. While highest priority goes to valid names, other names in use are included so that this register can serve as a guide to interpret taxonomic literature.

The content of World Register of Marine Species (WoRMS) is controlled by taxonomic experts, not by database managers. WoRMS has an editorial management system where each taxonomic group is represented by an expert who has the authority over the content, and is responsible to control the quality of the information. Each of these main taxonomic editors can invite several specialists of smaller groups within their area of responsibility.

This register of marine species grew from the European Register of Marine Species (ERMS), and its combination with several other species registers maintained at the Flanders Marine Institute (VLIZ). Rather than building separate registers for all projects, and to make sure taxonomy used in these different projects is consistent, we developed a consolidated database called 'Aphia'. The WoRMS is an idea that is being developed, and will combine information from Aphia

Oceans support vast populations of single-celled phytoplankton which, through photosynthesis, remove about half the carbon dioxide produced by burning fossil fuels. One group of phytoplankton, the coccolithophores, are known for their ability to build chalk scales inside their cells and secrete them, forming a protective armor. A new study has revealed the mechanism which achieves this, and that this process may be directly affected by the increasing levels of dissolved carbon dioxide in the oceans.

4 Phytoplankton and Marine Plants

The plant kingdom is made up of multicellular, photosynthetic eukaryotes. These multicellular organisms contain specialized cells that perform different tasks. Algae are some of the simplest aquatic plants, often referred to as seaweed in the marine environment. Marine algae are abundant throughout the ocean and can either float freely or cling to substrate such as rocks and reefs. The majority of seaweeds are classified as red algae (~6,000 species). There are also brown algae (~1,750 species) and green algae (~1,200 species). None of the algae species are known to be poisonous.

Phytoplankton

Phytoplankton are microalgae that form an essential component of the marine food chain. These single-celled plants provide nourishment to many marine species and they also play an important role in regulating the amount of carbon in the atmosphere. There are two main types of the larger phytoplankton species: Diatoms and Dinoflagellates. Smaller phytoplankton categorized as nanoplankton and picoplankton.

Diatoms

The cell walls of diatoms are made of silica formed into their characteristic 'pillbox' shape. Diatoms are composed of two valves or *frustules*, one on top of the other, within which the living matter of the diatom is found. Diatoms are either found singly where each individual lives in a single box, or found in chains. Diatoms reproduce by dividing in half. One half is attached to the top valve, the other is attached to the bottom valve. Once the division takes place, each half creates a new valve to form another whole. The new valve is secreted in the old valve, therefore the average size of each diatom is reduced with every new generation. It is thought that as many as 50,000 species of diatoms have inhabited the earth. They occur in both fresh and salt water.

Dinoflagellates

Dinoflagellates are the other primary form of large phytoplankton with about 2,000 species. Unlike diatoms, dinoflagellates are mobile through the use of a flagella. Also unlike diatoms, they do not have an external skeleton made of silica, however they are protected by cellulose.

Dinoflagellates are typically solitary and do not form chains like diatoms. Like the diatom they reproduce through fission. Once divided, each half retains half of the original cellulose armor and replaces the missing half to form a new whole. Some dinoflagellates can produce toxins that are released into seawater. When there are large blooms, a phenomenon known as red tide occurs. In some cases increased levels of dinoflagellate toxin may cause other marine life to die. The symbiotic algae found in many corals, or zooxanthellae, are actually a non-mobile species of dinoflagellate. Dinoflagellates have strong bioluminescence and have been a source of fascination for sailors and other mariners as their ships pass through waves which become lit up by these organisms at night.

Algae

As mentioned earlier, algae are photosynthetic eukarotes that are either unicellular, colonial, or multicellular. Algae with at least some multicellular members are grouped into three Divisions of the plant kingdom: Division Rhodophyta (red algae), Division Phaeophyta (brown algae) and Division Chlorophyta (green algae). These three groups are thought to have evolved from different groups of unicellular ancestors. Red and brown algae species are most commonly marine; green algae are found in abundance in both marine and freshwater.

Phylum Rhodophyta (Red Algae)

Red algae grow as single-celled plants or plants that grow as filaments, branched plants, broad flat plates, and ruffled plants. They come in a variety of sizes, but most red algae are small. All species attach to substrate such as rock or coral and sometimes to an animal shell or even another algae species.

Class Phaeophycea (Brown Algae)

Brown algae contain the largest and most complex algae plants. Pacific kelp are a brown algae species. There are no unicellular or colonial forms of brown algae. Brown algae stores food reserves as a substance called laminarin, similar to a lesser known species of gold algae in the division Chrysotphyta. Brown and gold algae also have in common the presence of flagellated cells of both sperm and motile spores. Brown algae are commonly found attached to substrate in cool, shallow waters near the shore in temperate and subpolar regions. Some forms of brown algae have developed adaptations to survive life on the coast where they may be pounded by surf or submerged then exposed with the tide. Large brown algae are used as shelter for some bottom-dwelling animals. They also provide serve as substrate for other algae that grow as epiphytes, or plants that grow on other plants.

- *Alaria esculenta* (babberlocks)
- *Ascophyllum nodosum* (asco, sea whistle, bladderwrack)
- *Fucus serratus* (serrated wrack)
- *Fucus spiralis* (spiralled wrack)
- *Fucus vesiculosus* (bladderwrack)
- *Laminaria saccharina* (sugar kelp)
- *Laminaria hyperborea* (kelp, May weed)
- *Laminaria digitata* (kelp)
- *Laminaria ochroleuca* (kelp)
- *Macrocystis pyrifera* (giant Pacific kelp)

Chlorophyta (green algae) is the most biodiverse of the algaes with species that grow in a variety of forms and in a variety of habitats. They are typically small and simple, with many single-celled species, some that form branched filaments, hollow balls of cells, or broad, flat sheets. Some species attach to sandy shores by secreting a calcareous cement rather than holdfasts that might shift with the sand and become unstable.

- *Ulva compressa*
- *Ulva rigida*

Seagrasses

Seagrasses, unlike seaweed, are flowering plants that live submerged in the marine environment. There are an estimated 50 species of seagrasses worldwide, most of which are found in the tropics. Seagrass beds grow in shallow waters forming thick beds that provide an important habitat for marine life in temperate and tropical seas. These habitats vary in size and abundance from isolated patches to a continuous area that grows for miles. In waters with a lot of wave activity, beds tend to be patchy. In calmer waters, seagrass beds tend to carpet the seafloor.

Seagrasses typically grow as long, thin leaves with air channels that grow up from a creeping rhizome. Seagrasses are found from the mid-intertidal region to depths of 50 m. Most species grow in soft substrates, such as sand, and form a dense mat of entwined rhizomes and roots that not only secure the plant, but also stabilize sediment. They also absorb wave motion and slow currents.

Kelp Beds: Forests of the Sea

As mentioned previously, Pacific kelp is a large species of brown algae. Kelps grow throughout the cold temperate regions of the world. They are known as kelp beds where there is no surface canopy and kelp forests where they form a canopy.

Like other algae species, kelps attach to the substrate using a holdfast. The holdfast extends into a stem or trunk ending in broad, flat blades. A gas-filled pneumatocyst is found beneath the blade, which floats the kelp at the surface. They take up nutritents generated by the constantly moving seawater.

Macrocystis and *Nereocystis* are the two genera that make up most kelp forests on the Pacific coast of North America. These enormous kelps grow upward through the water column to 20-30 m in length. These plants grow toward the surface where they can spread their blades to obtain sunlight, which often blocks sunlight from other organisms. Beneath the canopy, an 'understory' of algae is found, which forms another layer.

Kelps grow extremely quickly under the right conditions. Growth rates of 6 cm/day have been recorded in *Nereocystis luetkanan* and *Macrocystis pyrifera* has been recorded at 50 cm/day on the California coast. Surprisingly, despite this rapid growth rate and high rate of productivity, relatively few marine species graze directly on the kelp.

5

Zooplankton

Plankton is composed of the phytoplankton ('the plants of the sea') and *zooplankton* (zoh-plankton) which are typically the tiny animals found near the surface in aquatic environments. Like phytoplankton, zooplankton are usually weak swimmers and usually just drift along with the currents. Plankton are comprised of two main groups, permanent members of the plankton, called holoplankton (such as diatoms, radiolarians, dinoflagellates, foraminifera, amphipods, krill, copepods, salps, etc.), and temporary members (such as most larval forms of sea urchins, sea stars, crustaceans, marine worms, some marine snails, most fish, etc.), which are called meroplankton. Along with phytoplankton, zooplankton are key components of marine ecosystems forming the base of most marine food webs.

Taxonomy

Zooplankton are classified by size and/or by developmental stage. Size categories include: *picoplankton* that measure less than 2 micrometres, *nanoplankton* measure between 2-20 micrometres, *microplankton* measure between 20-200 micrometres, *mesoplankton* measure between 0.2-20 millimetres, *macroplankton* measure between 20-200 millimetres, and the *megaplankton*, which measure over 200 millimetres (almost 8 inches). There are two categories used to classify zooplankton by their stage of development:

meroplankton and *holoplankton*. Meroplankton are actually larvae that eventually change into worms, mollusks, crustaceans, coral, echinoderms, fishes, or insects. Holoplankton remain plankton for their entire life cycle and include pteropods, chaetognaths, larvaceans, siphonophores, and copepods.

Meroplankton and holoplankton are a component of almost every taxonomic group. However, the most common plankton are protists, nanoplanktonic flagellates, cnidarians, ctenophores, rotifers, chaetognatha, veliger larvae, copepods, cladocera, euphausids, krill and tunicates. Protists produce energy by photosynthesis and form the base of marine food webs as primary producers. Protozoa are also protists and are similar to animals. Protozoa make up a huge part of micro and nanozooplankton, such as amoebas, ciliates, and flagellates. These animals do not photosynthesize energy. Some amoebas such as those classified as Foraminifera and Actinopoda have hard skeletons, usually larger than 2 millimetres in diametre, that help form deep-sea sediment.

Nanoplanktonic Flagellates

Zooplankton also include the nanoplanktonic flagellates that help keep bacteria populations under control. They are characterized by either a long tail used for swimming (flagellates) or by hair-like structures called cilia (ciliates). Some dinoflagellates have a net-like structure called a protoplasmic net—used to capture and eat prey that are typically larger in size than bacteria. Some dinoflagellate species are also responsible for harmful fish kills and the infamous red tides. Ciliates are capable of catching bacteria, other protists and phytoplankton.

Mixotrophs are an amazing organism that are half plant and half animal. Mixotrophs have the ability to ingest other organisms through phagocytosis (phago: 'to eat' + cytosis: 'cells' = the process of engulfing other cells for ingestion) but also contain functional photosynthetic structures.

Cnidarians

Cnidaria is a phylum that contains the colonial siphonophores and the scyphozoans—also known as the true jellyfish. Both of these animals are predators and have stinging tentacles. They are not found often in fresh water and in the ocean they inhabit the layers closer to the surface. Comb jellies or ctenophores were previously classified under Cnidaria but have recently been distinguished from other jellyfish because they lack the characteristic stinging cells of other jellyfish known as nematocysts. Comb jellies effectively keep copepod zooplankton levels in check through.

Phylum Rotifera

There are about 2,375 species of rotifers in freshwater and only 125 in the ocean. Most of the rotifers are non-motile (not able to move) but about 100 species are holoplanktonic. Rotifers eat bacteria, detritus, other rotifers, algae or protozoa. Rotifers are highly efficient reproducers. They are able to reproduce asexually (without a mate) when environmental conditions are good, and sexually when environmental conditions are stressful. This ability allows rotifers to conserve energy in good conditions and adapt to their environment in stressful conditions. Adaptation is possible through sexual reproduction because a variety of offspring are produced, allowing the individuals best suited to the environment to survive.

Chaetognatha

The chaetognatha or Arrow worms are mostly holoplanktonic and are abundant worldwide. These transparent worms are approximately cm long and have fins on the sides of their bodies.

Marine Gastropods

Another type of zooplankton include the larvae of benthic mollusks usually found in coastal waters, such as marine gastropods including heteropods or pteropods.

Polychaeta

The Polychaeta or polychaetes are a class of annelid worms, generally marine. Each body segment has a pair of fleshy protrusions called parapodia that bear many bristles, called chaetae, which are made of chitin. *Polychaeta* means 'many-bristled' (as opposed to the Oligochaeta which are 'few-bristled'), and indeed the polychaetes are sometimes referred to as. More than 10,000 species are described in this class. Common representatives include the lugworm (*Arenicola marina*) and the sandworm or clam worm *Nereis*.

Copepods (Phylum Arthropoda, Subphylum Crustacea, Order Copepoda)

Most macrozooplankton are copepods found in marine and freshwater ecosystems. Copepods swim using an antenna and frontal structures on their bodies. They eat phytoplankton and detritus, and occasionally other zooplankton smaller in size.

Cladocerans (Phylum Arthropoda, Subphylum Crustacea, Order Cladocera)

Claudocera are planktonic crustaceans found in coastal waters. They swim using an antenna, like copepods, but instead of using their first antenna—they use the second antenna. They appear to have two sections to their body but it's only an illusion caused by a folded outer shell. Cladocerans eat phytoplankton and other zooplankton. Like many species of zooplankton, cladocerans migrate to the surface at night. This is referred to as 'diurnal migration'.

Krill

Krill, classified under Euphausids, are found all over the world. They can be 3 cm large and are an important source of food for many types of whales. In cold waters, krill often feed on diatoms, a type of phytoplankton. In warmer water they prefer to eat other animals. More on krill (*Euphausia superba*).

Insect Larvae

The larvae of the midge *Chaoborus* is the only widely known insect larvae classified as plankton. *Chaoborus* comes up during the night to float with other plankton and eats many types of zooplankton in lakes.

Tunicates

Some tunicates are planktonic, such as the holoplanktonic classes Appendicularia and Thaliasia. Both are filter feeders; Appendicularia consumes small food particles using a mucous filter. Other types of tunicates are benthic and are only planktonic during their larval stages.

Adaptations

All species of plankton have been forced to develop certain structural adaptations to be able to float in the water column. Adaptations include: flat bodies, lateral spines, oil droplets, floats filled with gases, sheaths made of gel-like substances, and ion replacement. The flat body and spines allow some species of plankton to resist sinking by increasing the surface area of their bodies while minimizing the volume. All other adaptations keep plankton from sinking quickly to the bottom. Zooplankton have also adapted mechanisms to deter fish (their heaviest predator) including: transparent bodies, bright colours, bad tastes, red colouring in deeper water, and cyclomorphosis. Cyclomorphosis occurs when predators release chemicals in the water that signal zooplankton, such as rotifers or cladocerans, to increase their spines and protective shields.

Night Swimming

Many types of zooplankton migrate deeper into the water during the day and come up at night. The migration of species appears to be dependent on location rather than particular species types. All plankton migrate differently based on factors like age, sex and the season. The amount of light is probably the major factor in the extent of migratory behaviour. It seems that zooplankton move around most in low light and least in higher light situations. It's possible that zooplankton migrate to lower levels during the day so they are less visible to predators relying on vision. At night, zooplankton can sneak up to the surface and snack on phytoplankton relatively safely. The lower metabolism occurring in colder waters during the day may also be a factor in the migration of zooplankton. This way, zooplankton can save energy by feeding in the cooler, night waters. The fact that different species of zooplankton have varying migration times may be the result of a partitioning of resources.

Communities of Zooplankton

Specific species of zooplankton occupy particular marine habitats. Each species is uniquely adapted to factors like light, temperature, turbulence, and salinity in its environment. Zooplankton on one side of the Gulf Stream are different species from those on the other side. These characteristics of different species of zooplankton can sometimes help scientists distinguish one water mass from another.

Zooplankton are also sensitive to their environment and like phytoplankton—a change in zooplankton concentration can indicate a subtle environmental change. Zooplankton are highly responsive to nutrient levels, temperatures, pollution, food that is not nutritious, levels of light, and increases in predation As well as providing an essential link in the marine food chain (which is an understatement), the diversity of species, amount of biomass and abundance of zooplankton communities can be used to determine the health of an ecosystem.

Other factors that influence the distribution of zooplankton include predation, reproduction, community interactions and the amount of available resources. Zooplankton can also be predators of algae or protozoa causing the sizes of these organisms to change through evolution. When light concentrations in boreal or temperate areas increase in the spring, phytoplankton communities increase in number. Because zooplankton feed on phytoplankton, the numbers of zooplankton increase in response during the spring. However, the reaction of zooplankton is dependent on the species type as well, so sometimes the zooplankton numbers increase only in the summer with another spike in the fall.

Zooplankton are also affected by levels of pH, heavy metals, calcium, and aluminum. Nutrients like nitrogen and phosphorus will affect the prey of zooplankton (like algae, protozoa and bacteria), indirectly affecting zooplankton survival. Scientists are still putting together pieces of the zooplankton puzzle. Some questions include how nutrient levels found in algae can influence the growth and behaviour of zooplankton. Another question important to marine and human life is how toxins and pollution will affect this crucial link in the food chain.

Zooplankton can use specialized adaptations that allow them to hide from predators in areas of the ocean where oxygen levels are so low almost nothing can survive — but they may run into trouble as these areas expand under climate change.

Marine shallow water sandy bottoms on the surface appear desert-like and empty, but in the interstitial space between the sand grains a diverse fauna flourishes. One of the strangest members of this interstitial fauna is Paracatenula, a several millimetres long, mouth and gut-less flatworm, which is found from tropical oceans to the Mediterranean.

6 Marine Invertebrates

Animals that lack backbones are known as *invertebrates*. Over 98 per cent of species on Earth are invertebrates that rely on other strategies than a backbone for support such as hydrostatic pressure, exoskeletons, shells, and in some, even glass spicules. Some invertebrate phyla have only one species, while others like include more than 83 per cent of all described animal species with over a million species. The most common marine invertebrates are sponges, cnidarians, marine worms, lophophorates, mollusks, arthropods, echinoderms and the hemichordates.

Sponges

There are between 9,000 and 15,000 species of sponges classified under the Phylum Porifera. Sponges are relatively simple animals that originated with the first animal life in the Precambrian times.

The anatomy of a typical sponge is organized so that flagella inside the sponge pull water into small holes (ostia) in the body and expel waste through larger holes (oscula). Sponge species have a variety of body plans that provide structure, including support by organic fibers (Class Demospongiae - 90 per cent of sponge species), calcareous spicules (Class Calcarea ~400 species), and siliceous spicules (Class Hexactinellida) or combinations of these.

The body plan of a sponge has adapted to filter small food particles from the passing water allowing them to reside in most habitats, including polar shelves and submarine caverns that often contain very few nutrients.

Like other animals, sponges were found to also grow extremely slowly in cold waters such as those of the Antarctic. Age estimates based on growth rates of one glass sponge (*Scolymastra joubini*) in the Ross Sea were between 15,000 and 23,000 years, which means that specimen appears to be the longest-lived animal on earth yet recorded. Sponges are often studied by scientists to find clues about the first life forms on Earth with more than one cell.

Sponges are hermaphroditic and are able to reproduce both and asexually. Most sponges usually reproduce by sexual reproduction, where sperm cells (spermatocytes) develop from choanocytes (collar cells) and eggs develop from. When environmental conditions are favorable, spermatocytes are ejected in out-going currents and the eggs, once fertilized inside the sponge in some sponges, develop into flagellated larva that swim about as plankton until they find a suitable place to settle and grow into adults. Asexual reproduction occurs when favorable environmental conditions deteriorate and includes both *regeneration* (regenerating from fragments), *budding* (groups of cells differentiate into small sponges that are then released externally or expelled through the central canal (oscula)), or the formation of *gemmules* ("survival pods" of unspecialized cells that remain dormant until conditions improve and then either form completely new sponges or re-colonize the skeletons of their parents).

Sponges are eaten by chitons, snails, nudibranchs,, fish, and insects. They provide a home to sea anemones, polychaetes, octopuses, copepods, zoanthids, shrimps, brittle stars, amphipods, barnacles, and fish. There are numerous between animals and sponges.

Sponges that are composed of organic fibers (demosponges) have been used by humans for thousands of years for cleaning and other purposes. Sponge diving has declined significantly due to overfishing and most sponges these days are now synthetic.

Cnidarians

The Phylum Cnidaria ('Ny-DARE-eeya') consists of about 10,000 species of 'simple' animals found only in marine habitats and includes Class Anthozoa (corals and sea anemones), Class Hydrozoa (hydrozoans), Subphylum Medusozoa: Class Cubozoa (box jellyfish), Class Scyphozoa (jellyfish), and Class Staurozoa which contains Order Stauromedusae (stalked jellyfish). Phylum Cnidaria may also contain and Family Tetraplatidae. Species in cnidaria have special stinging cells called cnidocytes. Cnidarians evolved during the and are some of the earliest multicellualr life forms known.

Most cnidarians have a very basic body plan which includes a digestive cavity with one opening. This opening functions as both the mouth and anus for the organism. The only true organs in cnidarians are the. Most cnidarians are symmetrical, an observation referred to as 'radial symmetry'. Cnidarians also have an ectoderm (tissue that covers the outer body surfaces) and an endoderm (inner layer of cells forming the gastrointestinal and respiratory tracts, and inner organs). The ectoderm is connected to the endoderm by a gel-like substance known as the mesoglea. Cnidarians use a nerve net and very basic receptors for impulses to move. Oxygen is taken in directly from the water through the tissues.

Organisms in cnidaria capture and kill their prey using cnidocysts, or stinging cells, around their mouth which send out stinging barbs which immobilize their prey and help protect against predators. Once prey is captured the tentacles move it into the central gastrovascular cavity where it is digested. Waste is then expelled back through the mouth.

The four classes of cnidarians are the Anthozoa, the Hydrozoa, the Scyphozoa, and the Cubozoa. Anemones, corals, and sea fans are in class Anthozoa, which was the first to diverge throughout evolution. Portuguese man-o-wars and obelia are examples of animals in Hydrozoa, jellyfish are in class Scyphozoa, and box jellies are in class Cubozoa.

Cnidarian species have a variety of life-cycles. Some alternate between being free-swimming medusae and asexual polyps depending on their environment. In some groups like Anthozoa, organisms never make it to the free-swimming medusae stage, but instead live their whole lives as a non-moving polyp. Organisms in the groups Scyphozoa and Cubozoa spend most of their lives in the medusal stage. Medusae can measure anywhere from a few millimeters to 30 meters long including the tentacles. Some, like the Siphonophores, are individuals but can live in colonies and appear as one organism.

Marine Worms

Marine worms can be placed into more than ten different phyla and come in a variety of colours, shapes, and sizes. Marine worms are often confused with other animals with thin and long bodies. Most marine worms are grouped into the Annelids, a group that includes the Polychaetes (bristle worms), Oligochaetes, Hirudinae, and the *Eunice aphroditois*. Polychaetes are most often found near the shoreline and swim or crawl using a pair of legs found on each segment of their body. The Oligochaetes, which include earthworms, are mainly found on land and the subclass Hirudinae include leeches that usually live in freshwater environments. Some marine worm species, such as the bearded fire worm, can deliver a nasty burning sting to humans when handled.

The body structure of an annelid consists of a front end with a prostomium, also referred to as a significantly defined head. Most annelids have two pairs of eyes, three antennae, a pharynx or proboscis used to eat food and tentacle-like cirri for probing the surrounding area. An example of the biodiversity of worm species is the Sipunculid also known as the peanut worm. This worm digs itself into a hole underneath rocks, eats organic material, has no segments and looks like a peanut when it pulls its proboscis into itself.

In general, marine worms live underneath rocks near the edge of the ocean, in algae, or anywhere there is mud or sand. Species of marine worms can be ringed, segmented, or flat and include tube-digging worms, burrow-dwelling worms, ribbon worms, and peanut worms.

Some common annelids include the tube-making *Galeoloaria*, the stinging fireworm, the short scale worm, and the huge *Eunice aphroditois*. Tube worms actually make a tube with a hard shell and retreat into the shell when threatened. The Christmas tree worm has many brightly coloured feather-like tentacles shaped somewhat like a Christmas tree that is used to filter food from the water.

Lophophorates

Lophophorates are characterized by a special feeding organ called a lophophore which is an extension of the body wall into a tentacled structure that surrounds the mouth and is either U-shaped or circular. The lophophore is used to trap floating food particles in passing currents (called suspension feeding). Tentacles surrounding the mouth are usually hollow and the mouth is usually located inside the lophophore. The anus is on the same side of the body but on the outside of the lophophore. Lophophorates include the phyla Phoronida, Bryozoa (Ectoprocta), and Brachiopoda and are related to the Mollusca and Annelida phyla. Many lophophorates have tubes, shells, or exoskeletons for protection. They are usually sessile (non-moving), benthic (sea floor dwellers), and live in salt water, although there are a few freshwater lophophorates in the Phylum Bryozoa.

Phylum Bryozoa contains Class Gymnolaemata (marine bryozoans) and Class Phylactolaemata (freshwater bryozoans ~50 species) and are tiny though visible colonial animals that look a bit like tiny coral colonies that also build skeletons of calcium carbonate (although some species lack calcification and instead are mucilaginous (made of slime)). Members of the Phylum Bryozoa are known as 'moss animals' or 'sea mats' and they generally prefer warm, tropical waters, but are known to occur worldwide. There are about 8,000 living species, with many times that known from the fossil record. Fossil bryozoans are common throughout the world in sedimentary rocks representing shallow marine habitats, especially in rocks of Paleozoic age.

Bryozoans are usually found on hard substrates such as rocks, shells, wood, blades of kelp, and ships which can become heavily encrusted with bryozoans. Some bryozoan colonies also form colonies directly on marine sediments. Bryozoans have been found at depths of 8,200 m (27,000 ft) though most inhabit shallower warmer waters. Most bryozoans are sessile though a few are able to creep about and some non-colonial bryozoans live and move about in the spaces between sand grains. One species appears to make its living while floating in the Southern Ocean.

Almost all bryozoans are colony-forming animals often with millions of individuals in each colony. The colonies range from millimeters to meters in size, but the individuals that make up the colonies (called zooids) are tiny, usually less than a millimeter long. In each colony, different individuals or zooids assume different functions. Some gather food for the colony (autozooids) while others have specialized for different functions (heterozooids) such as kenozooids which provide structural support and vibracula which have long whiplike structures that they use to clear debris away from the surface of the colony. There is only a single known solitary species, *Monobryozoon ambulans*, which does not form colonies.

Bryozoan skeletons grow in a variety of shapes and patterns: mound-shaped, lacy fans, branching twigs, and even corkscrew-shaped. Their skeletons have numerous tiny openings, each of which is the home of a zooid. They also have a coelomate body with a looped alimentary canal or gut, opening at the mouth and terminating at the anus. They feed with a specialized, ciliated structure called a lophophore, which is a crown of tentacles surrounding the mouth. Their diet consists of small microorganisms, including diatoms and other unicellular algae. In turn, bryozoans are preyed on by grazing organisms such as sea urchins and fish. Bryozoans do not have any defined respiratory, or circulatory systems due to their small size. However, they do have a simple nervous system and a hydrostatic skeletal system. Several studies have been undertaken on the crystallography of bryozoan skeletons, revealing a complex fabric suite of oriented calcite or aragonite crystallites within an organic.

The tentacles of the bryozoans are ciliated, and the beating of the cilia creates a powerful current of water which drives water together with entrained food particles (mainly phytoplankton) towards the mouth.

Because of their small size, bryozoans have no need of a blood system. Gaseous exchange occurs across the entire surface of the body, but particularly through the tentacles of the lophophore.

Bryozoans can reproduce both sexually and asexually. All bryozoans, as far as is known, are hermaphroditic (meaning they are both male and female). Asexual reproduction occurs by budding off new zooids as the colony grows, and is the main way by which a colony expands in size. If a piece of a bryozoan colony breaks off, the piece can continue to grow and will form a new colony. A colony formed this way is composed entirely of clones genetically identical individuals) of the first animal, which is called the ancestrula.

One species of bryozoan, *Bugula neritina*, is of current interest as a source of cytotoxic chemicals, bryostatins, under clinical investigation as anti-cancer agents.

The closest relations of the Bryozoa appear to be the brachiopods.

Mollusks

Animals classified under the phylum Mollusca are extremely diverse in form, but all have a fairly simple body plan. Familiar mollusks include oysters, chitons, clams, snails, slugs, octopus, and squid. Most mollusks have a soft body and a hard or "calcareous" shell. Many mollusca use mucous and cilia to eat, move, and reproduce. There are more than 110,000 species in phylum Mollusca, more than every other phylum except Arthropoda. With a few exceptions, all living species of mollusks are categorized underGastropoda or Bivalvia. Another important class is Cephalopoda. Some scientists have determined that there is more biomass from marine mollusks than any other animal on earth.

Mollusks reproduce through external fertilization where the eggs and sperm are released into the water. In some more complex mollusks, fertilization can take place internally after long courtship rituals and mollusk dances. Many of the more sophisticated snails are hermaphroditic. Some go through phases where they alternate gender, others are both female and male at the same time.

Almost all mollusks living in freshwater are gastropods although a few bivalves can be found in brackish water. Some species of mollusks have adapted to living on land but can only live in humid environments. Terrestrial mollusks must have the ability to regulate their temperature, breathe air, make larger eggs, and maintain moisture levels by conserving water. Snails that live in the littoral zone of the ocean often show similar adaptations as terrestrial or land living snails. Snails in the class Pulmonata have adapted to living on land so well that they can be found at high altitudes. Other snails in Pulmonata that once could breathe air have gone back to living in the water.

Mollusks can be found in all habitats of the ocean. Some bivalves like the Protobranchiates, are even found in waters 9,000 m or 29,500 ft deep. The more advanced cephalopods could be viewed as the most sophisticated invertebrates. Animals like squid, cuttlefish, and octopuses have relatively 'huge' brains and move about using their arms, fins, and siphons (in a manner similar to jet propulsion).

Arthropods

Arthropoda is the largest phylum in the taxonomic system and is composed of insects, crustaceans, and arachnids. Nearly 4/5 of all living animals are arthropods.

This ancient phylum dates back to the earliest days of the Cambrian period.

Arthropods are characterized by a segmented body plan with a head, abdomen, and thorax and legs or appendages on every segment with a rigid exoskeleton made out of chitin. Arthropods use their appendages to feed, as sensory mechanisms, and for locomotion. Aquatic arthropods use gills for respiration.

Although spiders are possibly the most familiar arthropod, lobsters, crabs, barnacles, and shrimp in the class Crustacea are also in this phylum.

Arthropods are most closely related to the Annelida, or segmented worms. The five main subgroups of the phylum are the Trilobita, Myriapoda, Chelicerata, Crustacea, and the Hexapoda.

Echinoderms

The Echinoderms lack a head and have five-point radial symmetry. These fascinating animals live only in marine environments. They have an endoskeleton made out of calcareous plates, which is often protected by spines. The plates that make up the endoskeleton often support the spines and enclose the coelom, an anatomical feature used for movement, respiration, collecting food, and as a sensory mechanism. The coelom also houses the reproductive organs and alimentary canal.

Echinoderms can be found in all oceans in all zones with approximately 6,000 described species.

The two main subphylums in phylum Echinodermata are Eleutherozoa and Pelmatozoa.

Subphylum Eleutherozoa conatins the superclasses Asterozoa and Cryptosyringida.

Superclass Asterozoa contains the sea stars/starfishes in Class Asteroidea and the extinct Class Somasteroidea.

Superclass Cryptosyringida contains Class Echinoidea (heart urchins, sand dollars, and sea urchins), Class Holothuroidea (sea cucumbers), and Class Ophiuroidea (basket stars, brittlestars, and snake stars).

Subphylum Pelmatozoa contains the Class Crinoidea (feather stars and sea lillies).

Mature echinoderms have five points that face outward from the center of the body with a mouth underneath and the anus on top. There are exceptions to this plan however; some echinoderms lack an anus and others, like the crinoids, have both the mouth and the anus on the same side of the body. Scientists refer to the side of the body with the mouth as the oral side and the side with the anus as the aboral side. Crinoids, ophiuroids, and holothuroids have tube feet to help collect food particles floating towards their body. Other types of echinoderms like asteroids are carnivorous and will surround or throw their stomach over their prey. Some echinoids even have teeth used to chew and dismantle plants and small animals.

Most echinoderms reproduce sexually producing larvae that feed on phytoplankton until they reach maturity. Some species of echinoderms develop their offspring in embryonic sacs located on the outside of their bodies.

Echinoderms have fascinating water-vascular systems that likely originated from some sort of respiratory system that evolved to include food gathering and movement. They accomplish these tasks through the use of their numerous hollow tube feet that resemble tentacles. There are two rows of tube feet on the outside of the body that fill with seawater so that when the animal expands or contracts, water is drawn into the feet. Once filled, the feet extend outward allowing the animal to walk. Suckers located at the tips of the tube feet are often used to grab prey or to hold onto solid objects when the echinoderm wants to remain attached to something.

The most familiar echinoderm known to humans is probably the sea star, categorized in the superclasses Asterozoa and Cryptosyringida. There are two classes of sea stars which include Asteroidea and Ophiuroidea. True sea stars and sun stars in are in Class Asteroidea while brittle stars and basket stars are in Class Ophiuroidea.

Echinoderms in the class Asteroidea have arms that are smoothly connected to the body; echinoderms in Ophiuroidea have arms that shoot out from a disk-like center. Both are able to regenerate their limbs when one is broken off. In some cases, a lost limb can generate a whole new sea star. The small bumps on top of the sea star are referred to as dermal branchiae and are used to absorb oxygen from the water for respiration. Pedicellaria are small appendages used to keep foreign bodies off of the sea star. The madreporite is a hard opening on the aboral side of the sea star used to regulate and filter sea water.

Sea stars also have an eye-like structure at the end of each arm, called the eyespot, used to detect light.

Hemichordates

Hemichordates are a relatively small phylum. These creatures are extremely important to the study of the evolution of vertebrates. They are characterized by a body divided into three main areas: the preoral lobe, the collar, and the trunk. Hemichordates are partial chordates and are closely related to the first chordates. According to DNA analysis, hemichordates are closely related to echinoderms, which is also apparent during observations of hemichordate and echinoderm larval stages. Hemichordates have gill slits, a structure that resembles a notochord but is called the stomochord, a dorsal nerve cord, and a reduced ventral nerve cord.

There are three classes of hemichordates which include Enteropneusta, Pterobranchia, and Graptolithina. The most well-known class is the Enteropneusta or 'acorn worms'. Acorn worms have gill slits, burrow into the sediment, and likely feed on dirt and detritus. They can reach up to 2.5 m or 8 ft in length but most are actually quite small. In the Pterobranchia class, there are only a few species notably different from the acorn worms. Pterobranchs live in colonies connected by stem-like stolons. Each tiny individual is referred to as a zooid and has one gill slit. The Graptolithina are most well-known in the fossil record showing up in the Ordovician and Silurian times.

7 Marine Vertebrates

Marine vertebrates, classified under the Kingdom Animalia, Phylum Chordata and Subphylum Vertebrata, are among the most structurally complex organisms. The seven main superclasses and classes in Vertebrata are:

- **Agnatha** (jawless fishes)
  - Class Cephalaspidomorphi (lampreys)
  - Class Myxini (hagfishes)
- **Gnathostomata**

  Pisces (formerly Osteichthyes (now a synonym)) (bony fishes)

  Class Actinopterygii (ray-finned fishes)

  Class Elasmobranchii (formerly Chondrichthyes) (cartilaginous fishes: sharks, rays and skates)

  Class Holocephali (cartilaginous fishes: chimaeras, ratfishes)

  Class Sarcopterygii (lobe-finned fishes: lungfishes, coelacanths)

  Tetrapoda

  Class Aves (birds)

  Class Mammalia (mammals)

  Class Reptilia (reptiles)

Superclasses Agnatha and Pisces are all a form of fish. Superclass Agnatha contains the 105 species of jawless fish such as lampreys and hagfish.

Superclass Pisces contains at least 27,712 species of bony fishes including Class Actinopterygii which contains well over 20,000 species of ray-finned fishes, Class Elasmobranchii with at least 928 species of sharks, rays and skates, Class Holocephali with at least 928 species of chimaeras, and Class Sarcopterygii which contains the lobe-finned fishes such as lungfishes and coelacanths.

Under Superclass Tetrapoda, important marine classes include Class Aves (the birds) containing at least 9,842 species, Class Mammalia (all mammals) with at least 4,835 species, and Class Reptilia (the reptiles) which contains at least 3,082 species, which are all have species common in both terrestrial and marine environments.

Superclass Agnatha

This superclass includes the 'primitive' jawless fish such as lampreys and hagfish in the Classes Cephalaspidomorphi (lampreys), Myxini (hagfishes), and Pteraspidomorphi (fossil jawless vertebrates).

Class Chondrichthyes

This class consists of cartilaginous fish such as sharks and rays. instead, their skeletal structure is made up of cartilage. This class contains some of the first marine species to develop paired fins. They all have 5-7 gill slits and they lack swim bladders. Their large livers hold a large volume of oil that aids in buoyancy. Because they lack a swim bladder, most sharks must swim constantly to avoid sinking. Constant swimming also aids in maintaining the flow of water and oxygen over the gills through their mouths. Their skin is covered in denticles rather than scales giving it a rough sandpaper-like feel. They reproduce through internal fertilization.

Class Osteichthyes

There are tens of thousands of species of bony fishes found in both marine and freshwater environments. Note that the plural form of fish ('fishes') is used when referring to more than one species of fish. Bony fishes come in all shapes and sizes and live in all marine zones. They range in size from the that measure up to 3 m to the stout infant fish, which measures about 7 mm. Most fish are slightly endothermic, meaning that they are able to regulate the temperature of their bodies, but not to the extent seen with mammals. Endothermic bony fishes belong to the Suborder Scombroidei which includes about 122 species such as albacores, bonitos, cutlassfishes, frostfishes, hairtails, kingfishes, scabbardfishes, seerfishes, tuna, and wahoo. Endothermy uses a lot of energy but results in greater muscle control, better nerve signals, and improved digestion.

Marine Reptiles (Class Reptilia)

Reptiles are vertebrates in the Class Reptilia, which includes four orders: Testudines (turtles, terrapins, and tortoises), Squamata (lizards, worm lizards, and snakes), Crocodilia (crocodiles, alligators, gavials, and caimans), and Rhynchocephalia (two species of lizard-like tuataras). The majority of marine reptiles are sea turtles and sea snakes, as well as the marine iguana, and the saltwater crocodile. In general a reptile is an animal that has very strong, dry skin sometimes covered with scales. Reptiles are cold-blooded or, use lungs to breathe, and have tough skin without feathers or hair. Although reptiles are most commonly found in tropical and desert environment, they are also found in lakes, ponds, oceans, and even on top of mountains. Because they cannot regulate their internal body temperature, they are not found in extremely cold climates.

The more than 260 species of turtles and tortoises almost all have a protective shell surrounding their body. They range in size from the huge leatherback sea turtle (whose shell consists of bones beneath thick skin), which can reach up to 2.4 m in length and can weigh 907 kg to the smallest bog turtle that measures only 11.4 cm at most. Turtles that live in water have a lighter, flatter shell than the terrestrial species.

Lizards are the most common reptile with more than 2,700 species. Lizards usually have four legs with claws, however there are exceptions such as the worm lizard that usually has no appendages at all. Lizards range from a few inches to nearly 10 feet long, are typically insectivores, and inhabit trees, shrubs, or rocks. Some lizards will eat other vertebrates and others only eat plants. The Galapagos Islands are home to the, the only iguana of the 416 known species that ventures into the ocean.

Snakes are basically reptiles with no appendages. There are about 2,000 species of snakes in the world measuring between 10 cm to m in length. Snakes are thought to have evolved from lizards. Unlike other reptiles, snakes lack outside ears and have eyes covered with permanent transparent scales. Snakes have adapted to almost all habitats in the world and can also be found on lakeshores and even in ocean waters. Sea snakes have evolved to be extensively adapted to a fully aquatic life, except for the genus *Laticauda*, which retains ancestral characteristics that allows limited movement on land. Sea snakes are found in warm coastal waters from the Indian to the Pacific Oceans. All have paddle-like tails and most have laterally compressed bodies. However, unlike fish, they do not have gills and must come to the surface regularly to breathe. Nevertheless, they are among the most completely aquatic of all air-breathing vertebrates. Among this group are also species with some of the most potent venoms of all snakes. Most sea snakes will bite only when provoked, while others are much more aggressive at certain times of the year. Currently there are of sea snakes.

The Crocodilians are comprised of and include alligators, crocodiles and caimans. Crocodilians can measure anywhere from 1.2 m to 6.2 m long in the saltwater crocodile. Crocodilians are usually found in tropical waters, although some alligators live in temperate climates especially in the US and China. Crocodilians have long flattened tails that enable them to swim efficiently through water. They breathe through nostrils located at the top of their head.

All reptiles have a sophisticated brain, central nervous system, and lungs. Some snakes only have one lung. Reptiles also have a three chambered heart with the exception of crocodiles, which have four chambers like mammals or birds. The digestive system of reptiles differs from other vertebrates in that waste, including that from the urinary system, the sexual organs, and the digestive system, empties into a holding tank called the cloaca. In the cloaca, water can be reabsorbed into the body to be used again.

The tough skin of reptiles helps protect the animal from desiccation or drying out. Many species use the tough skin as a form of protection from other animals and for protection during mating rituals. Some reptiles have the ability to change colour for camouflage, communication, or sexual attraction. They reproduce through internal fertilization. Most reptiles lay eggs, although some lizards and snakes give birth to live young. Reptile eggs contain yolk and protein and are protected by a leathery or hard shell, which allows carbon dioxide and water to be exchanged while protecting the embryo from drying out or being consumed by bacteria. have been known to lay 150 eggs multiple times every season. Sea turtles lay their eggs in the sand and then leave them to hatch alone. The large number of eggs is necessary because many hatchlings do not survive. They are vulnerable to predation by birds, snakes, mammals, and sharks. Their nesting areas are also vulnerable to coastal development and eggs are vulnerable to human consumption. Sea turtles that do reach maturity can live up to 120 years in the wild. Alligators also have a long life span up to 70 years.

Marine Birds (Class Aves)

Marine birds are characterized by a variety of adaptations to marine conditions. These adaptations include the ability of feathers to resist water, the presence of salt glands, curved bills, and webbed feet. Many marine birds are able to dive into the water to capture prey and some birds, like penguins, are able to swim into deeper water.

The preening gland releases waxes and water repellant fats that create a protective shield on the bird to prevent water from saturating the feathers. This protective shield also keeps the bird insulated and, when combined with feathers made out of keratin, the birds are essentially waterproof. Salt glands allow marine birds to drink salt water and expel the excess salt from their bodies. Salt glands work by condensing salt from the blood into the sinuses allowing the bird to sneeze out the excess. Some marine birds push out salt directly from salt glands.

Seabirds have a wide variety of eating mechanisms. Cormorants and Anhingas use their curved bills to puncture fish. Many marine birds dig into the sand for prey. Some have a distensible pouch such as those found in, frigatebirds, and cormorants. This pouch is located between the two parts of the lower mandible and is used to drain sea water from around the fish before it is eaten. Frigatebirds are known to snatch fish from other birds. Flamingos have a beak that can filter small invertebrates, algae, and other small organisms from water; their long bills and long legs enable them to stand in shallow water while they search for food.

Many birds will fly directly above the surface and look for fish swimming below. Black skimmers fly close to the surface and pluck fish near the surface of the water. Gulls and terns higher to find fish and plummet from the air to snatch them out of the water. are an unusual but very familiar marine bird that dives down into the ocean to look for fish.

As well as having a multitude of hunting strategies and bill adaptations, marine birds also have many different types of legs and feet. If a bird has very short legs with webbed feet, it is probably a very powerful swimmer. Webbed feet are referred to as *totipalmate* feet (having webbing connecting all four toes) and partially webbed feet are referred to as *palmate* feet. Birds that do a lot of swimming often rely upon what is called countercurrent exchange to keep the cold blood flowing up and away from their feet and from shocking their body. The arteries in these birds run very close to veins so that they are warm enough to allow the bird to swim in very cold water. Many marine birds also have very well developed eyesight and an amazing sense of smell. Birds in the Order

Procellariiformes, called the 'tubenoses' (albatrosses (13 species), diving-petrels (4 species), shearwaters and petrels (66 species), and storm-petrels (21 species)) can smell food up to 30 km away.

Marine birds are important to ecosystems for many reasons including their ability to move seeds throughout the environment and their predatory roles. They are also some of the most well-known and loved creatures of the sea. From the folkloric albatross to the march of the penguins, sea birds have fascinated humans for generations. However, they are threatened greatly by loss of habitat, oil spills, entanglement in fishing nets or garbage, and the disruption in migration due to global warming.

Marine Mammals (Class Mammalia)

Marine mammals are vertebrates that have hair or fur, blubber, are warm blooded, use lungs to breathe air, bear live young, and produce milk through mammary glands. Marine mammals are very similar to land mammals with the exception of a thick layer of blubber instead of thick fur for insulation. They also typically have long bodies, which allow them to move swiftly through the water. Although they breathe air for oxygen, they are able to stay underwater for long periods of time because of their ability to hold extra oxygen in their muscles and blood. Many marine mammals have an excess amount of blood and can direct it to the most important organs when necessary during deep dives. They can also slow their heartbeat for more efficient oxygen use when diving.

The four most common groups of marine mammals include:

1. Pinnipeds (Family Otariidae (sea lions and fur seals), Family Phocidae (seals), Family Odobenidae (walruses).
2. Carnivores [Family Ursidae (polar bears) and Family Mustelidae (sea otters)].
3. Cetaceans (Suborder Mysticeti (baleen whales) and Suborder Odontoceti (toothed whales such as sperm whales, orca, dolphins, and porpoises).

4. Sirenians (Family Dugongidae (2 species of dugongs) and Family Trichechidae (3 species of manatees).

Whales are divided into the baleen whales (Suborder Mysticeti) and the toothed whales (Suborder Odontoceti - sperm whales, dolphin, porpoises, beaked whales, belugas, narwhals, etc.). Both types of whales have highly developed senses, blubber to keep warm and long bodies enabling them to swim quickly. Baleen whales have instead of teeth composed of rigid fibers that act like a filter to catch zooplankton and phytoplankton. The upper jaws of baleen whales are long and flat. Toothed whales such as sperm whales and dolphins use teeth to catch prey like fish, octopus, and squid. Dolphins have larger brains than porpoises and porpoises have more rounded rostrums, triangular-shaped dorsal fins and spade-like teeth.

There are three families of pinnipeds which include the Family Otariidae (sea lions and fur seals),, and Family Odobenidae (walruses). Although pinnipeds have blubber, they are warm blooded. They can live on land or in water. Seals can live out at sea for months at a time only returning to land for the mating season and to molt. Seals are found all over the world in coastal areas. The fur seals and sea lions are part of the eared seal family Otariidae. These animals have large flippers in the front, tiny ear lobes and webbed back legs that can rotate around. For this reason, eared seals are capable of moving quite easily when in water or on land. With no ears, short flippers and no rotation of the back flippers, true seals of the Phocidae family are easily distinguishable from the eared seals mostly because they look very awkward when trying to move on land. Walruses have a little hair on their body, long tusks and short thick whiskers. They are also quite a bit larger than other pinnipeds.

In the Order Sirenia, there are three species of manatees and two species of. Although dugongs have many of the characteristics of other marine mammals, they have a higher blubber ratio. Dugongs and manatees are gentle animals with large front flippers. Manatees are characterized by a round tail and can be found in Southeast U.S. coastal waters and in the coastal and inland waterways of Central America and along the northern coast of South America. Dugongs have a dolphin-like tail and are found discontinuously in coastal waters of east Africa from the Red Sea to northernmost South Africa, northeastern India, along the Malay peninsula, around the northern coast of Australia to New Guinea and many of the island groups of the South Pacific.

Polar bears are the largest of all carnivores that live on land and are found throughout the arctic on sea ice, islands, and coastlines. These amazing predators often feed on, bearded, harp, and hooded seals. The skin of polar bears is black with a layer of dense underfur and a layer of outer fur called guard hairs that are actually transparent. Polar bears are also protected from extreme temperatures with a thick (10 cm) layer of blubber.

8 Coral Reefs

Coral reefs are a precious resource in the ocean because of their beauty and biodiversity. Coral reefs provide shelter for a wide variety of marine life, they provide humans with recreation, they are a valuable source of organisms for potential medicines, they create sand for beaches, and serve as a buffer for shorelines. Coral reefs are built by millions of coral polyps, small colonial animals resembling overturned jellyfish that use excess carbon dioxide in the water from the atmosphere and turn it into limestone.

Corals are in fact animals that fall under the phylum Cnidaria and the class Anthozoa. They are relatives of jellyfish and anemones. Corals can exist as individual polyps, or in colonies and communities that contain hundreds to hundreds of thousands of polyps. For example, brain corals consist of colonies of many individual polyps; each individual polyp averages 1-3 mm in diameter. Corals can be divided into two groups: hard coral and soft coral. Hard corals, also known as stony coral, produce a rigid skeleton made of calcium carbonate ($CaCO_3$) in crystal form called aragonite, with reef-building capabilities. Alternatively, soft corals, including sea fans, do not produce a rigid calcium carbonate skeleton and do not form reefs, though they may be present in a reef ecosystem.

Most reef-building corals have a mutually beneficial relationship with a microscopic unicellular algae called *zooxanthellae* that lives within the cells of the coral's gastrodermis. As much as 90 per cent of the organic material the algae manufacture photosynthetically is transferred to the host coral tissue. In addition to the symbiotic relationship with algae, most corals capture and consume live prey ranging from microscopic zooplankton to small fish, depending on coral size. Using its tentacles that extend outside it body, the coral uses its *nematocysts*, or stinging cells, to stun and kill its prey before passing it to its mouth. Once the food has been digested, the waste is expelled from the same opening.

Corals are unique in that they are capable of reproducing both sexually and asexually. Sexual reproduction is the more common method and can be performed in two ways: *broadcast spawning* or *brooding*. Broadcast spawning consists of both male and female coral expelling massive amounts of gametes (eggs and sperm) into the water column during synchronized events. Brooding is similar to broadcast spawning, except only the male gametes are released into the water column. Coral sperm is negatively buoyant once released and hopefully will be carried by ocean currents to female coral where they will fertilize the egg cells of the female coral.

The Variety of Coral Reefs

Coral reefs can be found in both shallow and deep waters and are classified into two main categories:

Hard Corals

Scleractinia, also called Stony corals, are exclusively marine animals; they are very similar to sea anemones but generate a hard skeleton. They first appeared in the Middle Triassic and replaced tabulate and rugose corals that went extinct at the end of the Permian. Much of the framework of coral reefs is formed by scleractinians. There are two groups of Scleractinia: Colonial corals found in clear, shallow tropical waters; they are the world's primary reef-builders and solitary corals which are found in all regions of the oceans and do not build reefs. Some live in temperate, polar waters, or below the photic zone down to 6,000 m.

Soft Corals

The Alcyonacea, or the soft corals are an order of corals which do not produce calcium carbonate skeletons and so are neither reef-building corals nor do they lay new foundations for future corals. Instead they contain minute, spiney skeletal elements called sclerites. Aside from their scientific utility in species identification, sclerites give these corals some degree of support and give their flesh a spiky, grainy texture that deters predators.

Unlike stony corals, most soft corals thrive in nutrient-rich waters with less light intensity. Almost all utilize zooxanthella as a major energy source. However, most will readily eat any free floating food, such as brine shrimp, out of the water column.

Sea Fans

A gorgonian, also known as sea whip or sea fan (soft coral), is an order of sessile colonial cnidarian found throughout the oceans of the world, especially in the tropics and subtropics. Gorgonians are similar to the sea pen, another soft coral. Individual tiny polyps form a colonies that are normally erect, flattened, branching, and reminiscent of a fan. Others may be whiplike, bushy, or even encrusting. A colony can be several feet high and across but only a few inches thick. They may be brightly coloured, often purple, red, or yellow.

In 1999, a deep coral reef m below the surface was discovered by the United States Geological Survey (USGS) Centre for Coastal and Wetland Studies near Pulley Ridge, an underwater barrier island west of the Dry Tortugas National Park off the southern coast of Florida. The Pulley Ridge reef absorbs more light by increasing surface area and growing flat rather than the usual vertical growth seen in shallower coral reefs. Other deep water reefs include the Darwin Mounds and the Mingulay reef complex. More is known about shallow water coral reefs in tropical zones than deep-water reefs discovered recently, however much research into these unique ecosystems is being conducted.

Tropical Coral Reefs

Tropical coral reefs are biotic reefs formed in tropical waters by live organisms such as calcareous algae (including red algae) and corals. In contrast, abiotic reefs are formed by the deposit of sand and other materials in shallow water. Organisms responsible for building tropical (biotic) coral reefs can only grow at 20-, so although coral reefs live in all oceans, most are found between the Tropic of Capricorn and the Tropic of Cancer. The best growing habitat for coral reefs is a clear-water photic zone less than 50 m deep where light shines down and microscopic algae can best provide photosynthesis for the corals.

Corals can be found throughout the oceans, from deep, cold waters to shallow, tropical waters. Shallow coral reefs have optimal growth rates in warm water ranging from 70-85° F (21-29° C). Coral reefs can be found at depths exceeding 91 m (300 ft), but reef-building corals generally grow best at depths shallower than 70 m (230 ft). The most prolific reefs occupy depths of 18-27 m (60-90 ft), though many of these shallow reefs have been degraded. Corals also need salt water to survive, so they also grow poorly near river openings with fresh water runoff. Other factors influencing coral distribution are availability of hard-bottom substrate, the availability of food such as plankton, and the presence of species that help control macroalgae, like urchins and herbivorous fish.

The wide array of coral reef forms includes the Apron reef, the Fringing reef, the Barrier reef, the Patch reef, the Ribbon reef, the Table reef and the Atoll reef. The Apron and Fringe reef both reach down and out from the shore point or peninsula although the Apron reef is typically not as steep as the Fringe reef. Barrier reefs, like the Great Barrier Reef, are separated from the shore by lagoons. An Atoll reef surrounds a lagoon in a circular or uninterrupted fashion and is different from the others because there is no island in the middle.

A Critical Situation

Coral reefs are extremely sensitive to changes in light, temperature (bleaching), overfishing, damaging fishing practices, pollution, and excess sediment from development and erosion. Reefs in Southeast Asia are most at risk of damage due to these factors. Human activity is one of the greatest threats to coral reefs, particularly the destruction of mangrove forests that naturally absorb sediment and nutrients that can suffocate coral reefs with silt and algae blooms.

Cyanide fishing in the Indonesian and Philippine coral reefs of South Asia stuns and injures valuable fish. Although 85 per cent of the world's aquarium fish are captured with this destructive method, they suffer a 90 per cent mortality rate usually several weeks after they have been poisoned by cyanide. Fishermen in developing countries depend on reef fish for income to provide for their families; however, illegal fishing practices and overfishing is depleting fish stocks in these areas, rapidly threatening the livelihood of these local.

Fishermen hit the coral reefs with crowbars to shake out stunned fish and they also even fish with dynamite, which often destroys every living thing on the reef. Many reefs once teeming with life are now wastelands that even the most vigorous conservation efforts can't begin to restore.

With approximately 85,470 sq km of tropical coral reefs, Indonesia hosts about 33 per cent of the total coral in the world and 25 per cent of all fish species. However, in 2000 it was reported that over 70 per cent of the coral reefs are in bad to fair condition due to fishing practices, out of control tourism, and long periods of bleaching. Coral reefs in the Philippines were found to be 77 per cent less productive from 1966-1986, while the national population doubled in size. If the destruction continues, we will lose about 70 per cent of the world's reefs within 25-40 years.

The effects of El Niño during 1998 and 2004 are an example of the natural factors that influence the growth of coral reefs. During this El Niño, sea temperatures rose and many coral reefs were bleached or obliterated. Coral bleaching occurs when the single-celled algae vital for coral reef survival and known as symbiotic zooxanthellae are rejected from the coral, soft corals, some sponges and even Tridacna clams. The pigment containing organisms are lost as temperature or stress level due to increased light reaches intolerable levels. As temperatures return to normal, some reefs can recover within several weeks or months. However, equilibrium may not be restored due to global warming and the bleaching effect exposes corals to white and black band diseases. There is some evidence that global warming may actually add to the productivity of an ecosystem through an increase in carbon dioxide and higher temperatures, though the validity of this evidence remains to be seen.

· Massive coral bleaching occurred in the Great Barrier Reef of Australia between 1998 and 2002 and in reefs in the Indian Ocean, the Maldives, Sri Lanka, Kenya, Tanzania, and the Seychelles. Most areas in the Great Barrier Reef rebounded with little damage but in some areas approximately 90 per cent of the coral has vanished. The reefs in the Indian Ocean suffered the most damage and 90 per cent of the coral reefs were lost in the remaining five locations. In Indonesia, the damage is less extensive but more diversity is lost in an area significantly more difficult to restore.

Restoration and Conservation

The fish that grow and live on coral reefs are a significant food source for over a billion people worldwide—many of whom live far from the reefs that feed them. Approximately half of all federally managed fisheries in the United States depend on coral reefs and related habitats for a portion of their life cycles. The NOAA National Marine Fisheries Service estimates the annual commercial value of US fisheries from coral reefs to be over $100 million. Reef-based recreational fisheries generate over $100 million annually in the US. Globally, one estimate shows fisheries benefits account for $5.7 billion of the total $29.8 billion global net benefit provided by coral reefs. Sustainable coral reef fisheries in Southeast Asia alone are valued at $2.4 billion per year. These numbers do not take into account the value of deep-sea corals, which are themselves home for many commercially valuable species and thus additional fisheries value.

Part of the problem with the coral reefs in Indonesia was the move made in 1991 to delocalize power in the Indonesian and Philippine governments. The result was a lack of funding and national support for protection of the South Asian reefs. More recently, conservation efforts have included roping off, research and implementation of electrolysis as stimulant for growth, moving reefs to new places and cutting back on harmful fishing practices—all expensive and time consuming endeavors estimated to cost over $100 million dollars. MPAs have been established in regions like Indonesia so that sustainable fisheries can be managed and ecologically important habitats will be protected with a social and biological objective. Laws similar to those found in national parks have been developed to prohibit illegal harvesting of fishes. The hope is that by designating MPAs, coral reefs will be restored, areas will become more beautiful, diversity of life will not be lost and communities will have a sustainable source of income in fishing and tourism. Work is being done to effectively manage MPAs and scientists have found that co-management, the collaboration of local, provincial and national parties, is an effective management strategy. As with many organisations, MPAs will have to overcome challenges that include finding participants, streamlining viewpoints about how effective certain ideas will be and raising enough money to implement change.

An international and non-profit organisation called the Marine Aquarium Council or MAC was created to make the aquarium fish trade more responsible and sustainable through education and to limit harmful fishing practices. By avoiding stock depletion, adding more governmental regulation of reefs, managing reefs better, learning how to take care of fish and food once it is caught and creating a reliable data record, the MAC hopes to avoid a ban on the aquarium industry with a loss of income to the locals and a boom in illegal fishing. Among those involved in the project are researchers, conservationists and industry operators, all who would like to find a sustainable way to meet industry demands through education in the form of international standards and certification plans. MAC hopes that consumers, collectors and retailers will begin to realize how important it is to them and others to sustain their most valuable natural resource—the coral reef.

Other conservation efforts by various organisations include the intricate process of growing coral and coral reefs, a fragile organism that is sensitive to any environmental or biological change. Coral can be grown using a process known as mineral accretion where limestone is stimulated to collect on metal by a safe low voltage current, providing a nice place for baby coral to latch on and grow. The voltage itself can be provided using solar panels or energy from wave action.

Medicines

Many species found in coral ecosystems produce chemical compounds for defense or attack, particularly the slow-moving or stationary species like nudibranchs and sponges. Searching for potential new pharmaceuticals, termed *bioprospecting*, has been common in terrestrial environments for decades. However, bioprospecting is relatively new in the marine environment and is nowhere close to realizing its full potential. Creatures found in coral ecosystems are important sources of new medicines being developed to induce and ease labour; treat cancer, arthritis, asthma, ulcers, human bacterial infections, heart disease, viruses, and other diseases; as well as sources of nutritional supplements, enzymes, and cosmetics. The medicines and other potentially useful compounds identified to date have led to coral ecosystems being referred to as the medicine cabinets of the 21st century by some, and the list of approved and potential new drugs is ever growing.

Tourism and Recreation

Every year, millions of scuba divers and snorkelers visit coral reefs to enjoy their abundant sea life. Even more tourists visit the beaches protected by these reefs. Local economies receive billions of dollars from these visitors to reef regions through diving tours, recreational fishing trips, hotels, restaurants, and other businesses based near reef ecosystems. One estimate places the total global value of coral-reef based recreation and tourism at $9.6 billion of the total global net benefit of coral reefs.

Adaptations to Marine Living 9

Over the last 2,000 million years, plant and animal life on earth has continuously evolved from its simple beginnings in the oceans to the complex existence lived today. It's no accident that protoplasm, a substance found in every living cell, strongly resembles seawater. Although some animals emerged from the sea millions of years ago to fill all available niches on land, some remained in the ocean and evolved and adapted to life beneath the surface.

The ocean covers the majority of the planet, yet it remains a little understood realm as scientists are limited in the study of habitats that lack physical boundaries and can span thousands of miles.

Each form of marine life has become adapted to a specific niche with a relatively narrow variation in salinity, temperature, and light. The high salt content found in the ocean can support the large bodies of giant squids and whales, which has allowed them to evolve without the use of strong limbs for support. Nevertheless, salt water exerts enormous pressure on the air spaces of marine animals at depth (fluids like blood are practically incompressible). For every 33 feet of water, pressure increases by 14.7 pounds per square inch (equal to one atmosphere every 10 metres) which limits our depths significantly unless we use diving craft specifically designed to maintain one atmosphere.

And yet all sorts of other organisms thrive at high pressure. Some of them are even air-breathing surface dwellers like us. Weddell seals and elephant seals can dive up to a mile (sperm whales go much deeper than that). All these animals seem to share the same secret: Instead of fighting the pressure, they let it collapse their lungs completely. Some oxygen remains in their lungs, but they mostly store it in their muscles, where it's needed; their muscle tissue contains much higher concentrations of oxygen-binding myoglobin than ours does.

Moreover, collapsed lungs give deep-diving mammals another big advantage, as a team led by researcher. Once a seal's lungs have collapsed, it becomes heavier than water, and so it sinks. Thus it doesn't have to flap flukes or flippers all the way down; it reaches great depths mostly by gliding effortlessly, saving its oxygen stores for the strenuous climb back to the surface.

The deep seafloor itself, well beyond the range of diving mammals, is inhabited by an incredible diversity of animals. Some of the fish even have lunglike swim bladders to control their buoyancy: They move up in the water column by secreting gas into the bladder and inflating it, and down by reabsorbing gas into their blood. With Jason, the researchers aboard the Knorr have observed such fish hang motionless a few feet above the seafloor. But they've made no effort to bring the fish up to the ship, because they know the results would not be pretty. A swim bladder doesn't collapse at depth because the gas inside is at the same pressure as the water outside—which means if that external pressure suddenly decreases, the bladder will swell catastrophically. When we bring a fish up from depth, its swim bladder is often sticking out of its mouth.

Marine animals must also regulate the interaction of freshwater and saltwater in their bodies. Specially developed kidneys, gills, and body functions help prevent the water from equalizing salt concentrations across membranes through osmosis. Marine animals must also be able to absorb dissolved gases like oxygen from the water needed to release the energy from food. Simple animals, such as anemones or worms, absorb the gases through their skin. Mobile animals use gills, or even lungs to absorb oxygen from the water and air. All animals in the ocean release carbon dioxide into the water as waste, which is then used by plants to produce energy.

Temperatures vary dramatically between the surface and the ocean floor. Marine life has developed many adaptations to the variations in temperature. Many marine mammals have blubber for insulation from the cold, and some fish have an antifreeze-like substance in their blood to keep it flowing. It is interesting to study the dramatically different adaptations in marine life on a vertical scale in the water. Animals and plants living in surface waters have access to high nutrient levels, increased temperatures, reduced pressure, and more light and therefore lack the adaptations of deep sea creatures that must live in highly pressurized, cold, dark waters with scarce nutrients.

Marine life has adapted to an incredible variety of conditions and habitats. Barnacles and mussels have developed mechanisms that allow them to cling to rocks in environments where they might otherwise be easily washed out by strong waves. Brightly-coloured clownfish have adapted symbiotic relationships with anemones to protect both the clownfish and the anemone from predation. Sperm whales and herring gulls have adapted the ability to travel long distances and the ability to survive in a variety of environments.

Although the focus here is primarily on the adaptations of marine body structures, marine adaptations also include symbiosis, camouflage, defensive behaviour, reproductive strategies, contact and communication, and adaptations to environmental conditions like temperature, light and salinity.

Chordate Origins

Animals in the Phylum Chordata include the vertebrates and some of the more primitive nonvertebrates like the protochordates, lancelets, acorn worms, tunicates, and the pterobranchs. The first vertebrates appearing in the fossil record during the Cambrian age were animals that resembled fishes and had respiratory gills formed by pharyngeal gill slits located in a set of pouches. The first purpose of the skeleton and scales were to protect the animal, to add support to the notochord, and to keep the brain protected. Later, a true backbone (rather than a notochord) evolved in marine animals. In all vertebrates, a heart developed to pump blood throughout the capillaries for the exchange of gases and oxygen. The blood in most fish goes from the heart to the gills and from there it is moved to the brain and other important body structures.

The Agnatha, or jawless fish, lived from the Late Cambrian until the end of the Devonian period. These fish were covered in bony armor, an adaptation that helped protect them from other animals. Parasitic lampreys and deep-sea hagfish are descended from the weak swimming, bottom dwelling jawless fish. Later in the Middle Silurian, a fish with jaws and teeth, known as the Gnathostomata vertebrate, evolved. Most fish are descended from this vertebrate, including all of the tetrapods. The jaws were actually adapted from the front elements of the gills and the teeth came from very bony scales near the skin of the mouth of the fish. Once jaws had developed in fish, many new strategies of surviving in the ecosystem became available. During this time, swimming capabilities were enhanced with the development of paired fins.

This was a time of great diversification in the oceans. Four groups of fishes branched out: the Placodermi (extinct now), the Acanthodii (extinct), the Chondrichthyes and the Osteichthyes (more highly evolved bony fishes). The Placodermi had extreme amounts of armor and were highly prevalent carnivores in the Silurian and Devonian periods. The Acanthodii were small filter-feeders. The Chondrichthyes and Osteichthyes classes survived, adapting to many different ocean conditions and branching out further into a vast array of species. Some of the many adaptations are as follows.

Most sharks in the Class Chondrichthyes have to keep swimming, otherwise they will sink to the bottom of the ocean. This characteristic has led to two distinct forms of sharks: the pelagic and benthic forms. The pelagic sharks move constantly through the water and rely on this movement to pass water across the gills for respiration. The benthic forms lie on the bottom and take in water through a pair of holes at the top of their head called spiracles. Rays also can lie on the ocean floor and respire through a spiracle at the top of their head. Rays have a flattened body type that allows them to hide under the mud and dig up crabs and shelled animals. The intestines and livers of sharks and rays are also shorter and larger than bony fish. Rays have developed stingers at the ends of their tails as a form as protection and some even have developed a type of battery that can deliver a strong electric shock. Another important development aiding in the survival of species in the Class Chondrichthyes was the appearance of the lateral line. The lateral line is a sensory organ in pelagic sharks and some fish. This line runs all the way from the head to the tail and functions to triangulate distances so the shark or fish can locate prey with great precision even in total darkness.

The Class Osteichthyes consists of all the bony fish. It is important to note that bony fish are also referred to as Teleost Fishes. Bony fish include many familiar fish like the bass, perch, cod, tuna, halibut—basically any fish with a bony skeleton. The general characteristics of a fish in this class include a longer intestine than sharks and rays, a single gill slit on each side, a mouth at the front of the body, a tail fin that is equal in size on the top and the bottom and external fertilization of eggs. Bony fish produce thousands of eggs, so there is plenty of genetic variation for natural selection to occur and adaptations in bony fishes abound. The flat fish is a good example of some of the stranger adaptations. The young flat fish appears to be a normal fish but as it develops, one eye actually migrates over to the other side of the body so that both eyes are on the same side. After the eye moves, the fish flips over so it looks like both eyes are on the same side but actually the top is just one side of the body. Another example is the male seahorse, which has adapted a pouch and, unlike most male animals, takes care of the young while the female swims away. The remora has developed a plate on its head to latch on to other fish and feed on food the larger fish leaves behind. The mola mola, or ocean sunfish, cannot swim very well, weighs over 2,000 lbs and has been said to be the largest type of zooplankton. This fish reaches a top speed of 3 miles per hour and floats around eating jellyfish. Some freshwater fish have developed the ability to climb trees, squirt water at insects, breathe air and stay out of water for long periods of time.

Reptiles

The reptiles came about as a novel group of terrestrial animals from the amphibians. Reptiles were extremely successful on land and quickly became the dominant animal for the next 150 million years. When mammals evolved, they took over the dominant position leaving the reptiles to crawl back into the ocean. The reptiles that survived include the snakes, turtles and lizards many of which have changed a little so they can live more successfully in salt-water environments. Although crocodiles have also adapted to saltier conditions, they never made a full change and still prefer brackish waters. Reptiles that abandoned the land for the sea include the sea turtles in the Family Cheloniidae, the marine iguana in the Family Iguanidae, and the sea snakes in the Family Hydrophiidae.

The turtles have not changed too much over the last 100 million years. The hard shell characteristic of turtles has been a great help in protection and the prevention of drying out. Land turtles have a problem with their shell being too heavy but when turtles are in the water—the buoyancy of the water lifts the weight of the shell and allows the turtle to move gracefully through the medium. Sea turtles developed longer feet that were more paddle-like allowing the turtle to fly through the water with great speed and agility. Another adaptation of sea turtles to the sea is a hinge in the lower portion of the turtle that allows them to take in much more air and come up for air less often.

Mammals

Marine mammals include the Order Cetacea (porpoises and whales), the (animals like seals), and the Order Sirenia (dugongs, manatees and sea cows). Marine mammals are still warm-blooded and have to keep the temperature of their bodies above that of the ocean. Adaptations that have helped solve this problem include the reduction of surface area and the increase in internal volume, a fatty layer of blubber under very thick skin, and a reduction in the amount of blood going to areas in contact with the cold water. Unlike land animals, marine mammals are also able to dive very deep into the water without getting the bends because as they dive down deeper they exhale instead of inhale like we do. They expel air from their lungs, and therefore do not absorb excess nitrogen. Other adaptations to marine living include: a slower heartbeat during dives, reduced blood flow to non-vital organs, unusually high hemoglobin count in blood, and an unusually high myoglobin count in muscles.

One fundamental difference between cetaceans and fish is the tail. The tails of mammals are horizontal enabling to swim both vertically and horizontally. The tails of most fish are vertical, so the swimming motion is side to side. The streamlined shape observed in both marine fish and marine mammals is an example of biological convergence. The rounded head and tapering body shape allows marine fish and mammals to glide smoothly through the water, wasting little energy due to resistance. Animals that are not streamlined, like the stingray or the globefish, have sacrificed efficient swimming for benefits of camouflage or body armor.

Most of the power generated for swimming in marine animals comes from the tail at the back. Most fish will move their tail from side to side so that water is pushed backwards and around the side and the fish moves forward. Fins at the side of the fish help counteract the tendency of the head to swing from side to side as the tail moves. Fish also have fins on their back, their sides and underneath their bodies. Fish, whales, turtles and even seals have specialized limbs for swimming.

Animals with Shells

About 500 million years ago, animals with hard-shells became prominent in the fossil record in the Phylum Molluska. The evolution of an impenetrable shell was obviously a very helpful trait for an animal to possess because now mollusks are found in almost every known environment. Animals with hard shells are protected from predation and drying out and some can even use their shell to float if necessary among other things. The seven Classes of mollusks are the Polyplacophora (the chitons), Gastropoda (the snails), Bivalvia (the clams), Cephalopoda (octopus and squid), Scaphopoda (the tusk shells) and Aplacophora (small worm-like organisms). There are at least 30,000 species of gastropods and it is the largest taxonomic class.

The chitons are the most primitive animals in the Phylum Molluska. Every chiton shell is made so that it will fit together and bend. Chitons live only in marine environments and are also recognizable by the eight plates that overlap on their back. The gills are located safely under the shell on either side of their foot. The adaptations seen in chitons allow these organisms to survive heavy surf, so they are often found in tide pools.

Organisms in the Class Gastropoda are most commonly known as snails, limpets, abalones, conchs, and whelks. Other gastropods perhaps less familiar include the nudibranchs, slugs, and some pteropods and heteropods. Gastropods can usually be identified by a shell that spirals to the right although some like the nudibranchs do not have a shell and in others the shell twists to the left. In order to fit into this shell, many gastropods have organs that are reduced in size. Although some gastropods have lost their shell throughout evolution, most still have a shell and benefit from the protection. Many gastropods like limpets and abalone will retreat into their shell when disturbed and close off the opening with a special plate called the operculum. There are many different types of shells and most of the variety is a direct result of adaptation to the environment. For example, in rough waters most animals have flat shells to reduce water resistance. Animals that need to crawl into rocks to hide also have flat shells to fit into smaller cracks. Most gastropods move forward with the help of a foot that is very similar to that of a terrestrial snail.

Cephalopods, like octopuses and squid are feared by many, however they are actually quite gentle, delicate and 'intelligent' creatures. Squid and octopuses are the most advanced mollusks. They have highly developed eyesight, the ability to swim quickly and the amazing ability to rapidly change colour using their chromatophores. The female octopus has excellent parenting skills and keeps her eggs safe and clean until they hatch. Most cephalopods have soft bodies with no shell and can walk on ocean floor or swim using a siphon that squirts water in a powerful jet. Some segments of have been recovered indicating that the whole animal may weigh up to 900 kgs and be 18 metres long. Some scientists believe there are may be squid with lengths over 30 metres. Another interesting adaptation in the cephalopods is the development of an inky substance used to block the senses of sight and smell in predators.

10 The Grazers and Predators

Grazers and predators form the backbone of food webs and influence the ecosystem in very different ways. Predation is a top-down force. Grazers on inorganic nutrients like nitrogen and phosphorus like primary producers exert a bottom-up force. Nutrient levels impact the food chain or a given food web depending on how many grazers are present, how many trophic levels exist, and how grazers react to an increase in resources. The number of grazers in the food chain is regulated by the number predators.

Land ecosystems and marine ecosystems share the cyclic flow of energy, the loss of energy from primary production to predators and the interwoven webs of activity. The first obvious difference between the two is that one is on land or 'terrestrial' and the other is in the water. Terrestrial food chains differ from marine food chains because of the latter's dependence on phytoplankton. A simplified example of a marine food chain would start with phytoplankton eaten by copepods eaten by fish eaten by squid eatin by seals eaten by orca.

A food web describes these complex interactions more accurately than a food chain. A food web illustrates the energy transferred between organisms and the hierarchy of organisms occupying different levels based on their prey. Much marine ecological research is based on food webs. There has been much controversy surrounding the accuracy of these illustrations. The basic concept of food webs eventually evolved into two types of food webs in the ocean. The first is based on plankton primary production and the second is based on detritus primary production.

The Importance of Grazers

The older model of a food web in the ocean depicted planktonic algae grazed on by planktonic crustaceans (also known as copepods). The copepods were eaten by fish and invertebrates. Organisms at the top of the food chain were larger animals (predators). Modern food webs have replaced the less accurate food chains and show how important smaller autotrophic and heterotrophic organisms are to primary and secondary production as well as to the carbon and nitrogen cycle. It is now clear that primary production in planktonic food webs is divided between many different sizes of organisms. Cyanobacteria may be just as important to the productivity of ocean ecosystems as phytoplankton. Microbially based food webs formed by the grazing of protozoa like microflagellates and ciliates on smaller autotrophs have also been taken into account.

Now that the classical food chain has been updated, it is clear to scientists that most of the autotrophic production and grazing is actually controlled by microscopic organisms rather than the larger predators in the food web. Macrophytes are algae that can be seen without a microscope commonly studied in salt marshes, mangrove and seagrass ecosystems.

A commonly studied example of a macrophyte-based food web is the salt marsh, where there is abundant primary production based on detritus in the form of decomposed plants and small organic particles.

These particles come mostly from vascular plants and are responsible for feeding many different types of microbes including ciliates, flagellates, bacteria, and other protozoa. Organisms like crustaceans, fish, mollusks, and gastropods rely on these microbes for food energy.

Even the highly productive estuaries are largely dependent on the detritus-based primary production coming from salt marshes in addition to phytoplankton production in the ocean.

Estuaries and marine ecosystems closer to shore contain the largest amounts of primary and secondary production. In the open ocean, there is less production in the same amount of space. Food webs in the water column or at the bottom of the ocean are highly dependent on the primary production occurring above in the photic zone. The most productive areas in the open ocean are found in near upwellings where conditions are favorable for food webs to continue for long periods of time.

Grazers regulate the effects of unwanted algal blooms resulting from phosphorus pollution in marine ecosystems. If there are too many predators in a lake, like largemouth bass, all of the grazers will be eaten and the algal bloom will take over.

There is a delicate balance in ecosystems because fish that eat algae can be depleted if there are too many predators and algae can be depleted if there are no predators to eat the grazers. Although it might be easy to predict how many plants and algae would be produced by an increase in the nutrient supply in a marine ecosystem, the net biomass produced actually depends on many factors including the trophic structure and abundance of predators. In ecosystems lacking nutrients, top-down control of primary production is more powerful and in nutrient-rich ecosystems, bottom-up control is more important.

The Importance of Predators

In marine environments and on land, predators keep grazers from depleting resources. Thus, the role of predators is crucial to the survival of the ecosystem. This theory in ecology is known as 'the world is green' theory but also applies to the oceans. The actual number of trophic levels is important to the impact of grazers on primary production.

The control of primary production by predators at the top of the food web is called the 'trophic cascade'. The trophic cascade is a phenomenon that exists in lakes, subtidal kelp forests, streams, older meadows, the arctic tundra, habitats with coastal shrubs, grassland savannas, soil communities and in the ocean. If the keystone predator is removed from these systems, there will be a loss of species diversity at trophic levels lower in the food web.

The loss of sea otters in an ecosystem near the coast causes dramatic changes in the coastal ecosystems. For example, in areas where sea otters had been removed sea urchin populations have proliferated out of control. The sea urchins grazed freely on benthic algae depleting it from these environments, disrupting the food web by leaving little food for other organisms.

11

Marine Mammals

Description and Behaviour

For generations, whales and other marine mammals have intrigued humans. 2,400 years ago, Aristotle, a Greek scientist and philosopher, recognized that whales are mammals, not fish, because they nurse their young and breathe air like other mammals. There are numerous myths and legends surrounding marine mammals. The Greeks believed that killing a dolphin was as bad as murdering a human. An Amazon legend said that river dolphins came to shore dressed as men to woo pretty girls during fiestas. During the Middle Ages, there were numerous legends surrounding the narwhals' amazing tusk, which was thought to have come from the unicorn.

Marine mammals evolved from their land dwelling ancestors over time by developing adaptations to life in the water. To aid swimming, the body has become streamlined and the number of body projections has been reduced. The ears have shrunk to small holes in size and shape. Mammary glands and sex organs are not part of the external physiology, and posterior (hind) limbs are no longer present.

Mechanisms to prevent heat loss have also been developed. The cylindrical body shape with small appendages reduces the surface area to volume ratio of the body, which reduces heat loss. Marine mammals also have a counter current heat exchange mechanism created by convergent evolution where the heat from the arteries is transferred to the veins as they pass each other before getting to extremities, thus reducing heat loss. Some marine mammals also have a thick layer of fur with a water repellent undercoat and/or a thick layer of blubber that can't be compressed. The blubber provides insulation, a food reserve, and aids with buoyancy. These heat loss adaptations can also lead to overheating for animals that spend time out of the water. To prevent overheating, seals or sea lions will swim close to the surface with their front flippers waving in the air. They also flick sand onto themselves to keep the sun from directly hitting their skin. Blood vessels can also be expanded to act as a sort of radiator.

One of the major behavioural adaptations of marine mammals is their ability to swim and dive. Pinnipeds swim by paddling their flippers while sirenians and cetaceans move their tails or flukes up and down.

Some marine mammals can swim at relatively high speeds. swim up to 35 kph and orcas can reach. The fastest marine mammal, however, is the common dolphin, which reaches speeds up to 64 kph. While swimming, these animals take very quick breaths. For example, the fin whale can empty and refill its huge lungs in less than 2 seconds. During dives the larynx and esophagus close automatically when marine mammals open their mouths to catch prey. Oxygen is stored in hemoglobin in the blood and in myoglobin in the muscles. The lungs are also collapsible so that air is pushed into the windpipe preventing excess nitrogen from being absorbed into the tissues. Decreasing pressure can cause excess nitrogen to expand in the tissues as animals ascend to shallower depths, which can lead to aka 'the bends'. Bradycardia, the reduction of heart rate by 10 to 20 per cent, also takes place to aid with slowing respiration during dives and the blood flow to non-essential body parts. These adaptations allow sea otters to stay submerged for 4 to 5 minutes and dive to depths up to 55 m. Pinnipeds can often stay down for 30 minutes and reach average depths of 150-250 m. One marine mammal with exceptional diving skills is the Weddell seal, which can stay submerged for at least 73 minutes at a time at depths up to 600 m. The length and depth of whale dives depends on the species. Baleen whales feed on plankton near the surface of the water and have no need to dive deeply so they are rarely seen diving deeper than 100 m. Toothed whales seek larger prey at deeper depths and some can stay down for hours at depths of up to 2,250 m.

Marine mammals are often very social animals. Dolphins travel in pods (schools) and catch rides on the bow waves of boats. Marine mammals are also known to help each other when one member of the group is injured. There have been accounts of members of a pod refusing to leave the wounded or dying, a trait often exploited by whalers. Cetaceans (whales and dolphins) often hunt together, often with one leading the pod to act as a scout when entering unfamiliar territory. This close knit socialization is thought to be a factor in some whale strandings when a pod follows one or more members of the group that have become disoriented due to storm, illness, or injury.

Many marine mammals also participate in yearly migrations, either in groups or individually. Toothed whales are an exception and only move about in search of food, but some baleen whales (such as) embark on extremely long migrations, moving from tropical breeding grounds in winter to feeding areas in colder waters during the summer.

Communication

Marine mammals are capable of sophisticated communications because they live in a world dominated by sound, which travels much more efficiently through water than through air. Dolphins communicate with sound to coordinate hunts; humpback whales sing to attract females. Female pinnipeds and their pups recognize each other by their 'voices'. Slapping the surface during breaching can be heard for miles. Whales have no vocal cords; they warble for up to 30 minutes between breaths just by recycling air. They also emit low frequency sounds that can be heard by humans such as grunts, barks, squeaks, chirps, or even moos. These noises are thought to be associated with different moods and are believed to be used as social or sexual cues during communication. They might also serve as a signature to allow one animal to be recognized by another. Certain pods are known to even have dialects than can be distinguished from others.

They send out rapid sound pulses and listen to their echo to find prey and determine their surroundings. It is thought that sperm whales also use echolocation to stun squid with loud clicks. Clicks can be repeated at different frequencies with low frequencies traveling long distances that are highly penetrating. Toothed whales have a structure called the *melon* on their forehead that focuses and directs the sound waves; incoming sounds are received primarily in the lower jaw, which is filled with fat or oil that transmits the sound to the inner ear.

Evolution

About 65 million years ago (mya) when dinosaurs became mostly extinct, marine mammals began to evolve from their land-dwelling ancestors. Their evolution into sea-dwelling mammals is thought to be a result of the availability of new marine food sources and a way to escape from their terrestrial predators. The fossil record for whales is not as extensive as it is for other marine mammals such as otters and pinnipeds, therefore the transition period between land and water is unclear. In 1994, the remains of *Ambulocetus natans* ('the walking whale that swam') dating 49 mya were found in Pakistan in what's left of the Tethys Sea. These whale remains showed that the animal once had strong legs with long feet, similar to modern pinnipeds, that were functional both on land and in the sea. It retained a tail, but lacked flukes, however it is still thought that this animal swam like modern whales by moving the rear portion of its body up and down. In 2001, other fossils were found that linked early cetaceans to hoofed animals (ungulates).

How Scientists Study Marine Mammals

There are a variety of ways that scientists study whales. Whale teeth have rings, a new one for every year like trees. These rings can be examined to determine whether a whale was healthy and how long it lived. DNA fingerprinting can also be used by taking a small piece of skin or muscle to identify individuals. It can even be used to identify relatives. Humpbacks have unique black and white patterns on their tails used for identification. Whales and other marine mammals can also have telltale scratches and scars that can help in identifying individuals. Various tags are used to monitor heart rate, the animal's movements, and how deep and how fast they swim. Recent genetic analysis has led to new separations of species resulting in, for example, three species of right whales.

Otters and Polar Bears

Sea otters are the smallest of all marine mammals. They lack a layer of blubber so they protect themselves from the cold by trapping air in their extremely dense fur. are also considered marine mammals because they are semi-aquatic and rely entirely on the sea for food.

Pinnipeds

There are three Families of pinnipeds. First are the earless, or true seals, which consist of 19 species. Next are the eared seals (Otariidae) which has 14 species including sea lions and fur seals.

This is a diverse group despite its physiological similarities. Pinnipeds vary greatly in size and the way they utilize the marine environment. They consume a variety of different food sources, including fish and cephalopods (squid, cuttlefishes and octopuses), and certain species have also been known to eat krill, and shellfish. Feeding behaviour and diet may differ widely even within a specific population.

Cetaceans

All cetaceans are marine except for four species of. There are two different groups of cetaceans, toothed and baleen.

The toothed whales (sperm whales, and dolphins) hunt fish and have only one blow hole while the have two blow holes and feed on plankton.

There are a number of different subgroups in this category. The 26 species of oceangoing dolphins are in every ocean except the Arctic and Antarctic. are unique in that the males have a tusk. There are 6 species of porpoises and 18 species of, at least one of which has never been seen alive and is only known from two washed up skulls. The sperm whales are the largest of toothed whales. Orca (killer whales) and consist of 6 species and rorquals, the largest of the whales, are comprised of 6 species.

Because of their physiological adaptations to the marine environment, cetaceans have been able to grow to enormous sizes. A bull elephant, the largest land animal, could stand on a blue whale's tongue. The biggest dinosaur was possibly 7 m longer but weighed about 70 tons less than that of a large blue whale. Animals that feed on plankton and don't have to chase their prey, like baleen whales, don't expend much energy on speed and agility and therefore are able to grow to great sizes.

Sirenians

There are three species of manatees and only one species of dugong, which are the only vegetarian marine mammals. These animals are thought to be distantly related to elephants. They have only one pair of front flippers and no rear limbs.

Life History

All mammals are *viviparous,* meaning that their eggs develop inside the female and the embryo derives nutrition from the mother. Whales and pinnipeds usually mate and give birth in the spring, with pregnancies lasting between 12-18 months. Seals usually have a single pup each year. Whales, however reproduce more slowly and generally raise one calf every 1-3 years. Cetacean calves are born tail first to keep them attached to the placenta as long as possible to avoid oxygen deprivation.

Mating can be a social as well as functional activity with marine mammals. With dolphins, sex is used to establish and maintain bonds among the group. and beluga whales both take part in group matings.

Consevation Status

Marine mammals are greatly influenced by their interactions with humans, either directly or indirectly. Fishing takes the lives of at least hundreds of whales, dolphins, and seals every year that drown when they become tangled in fishing nets. Drift nets meant for fish catch anything that goes by, including dolphins, sharks, sea turtles, seals, seabirds, and other marine life. Pollutants also collect (by a process called) in the blubber of these marine mammals and many are also hunted by humans. Seals and sea otters are still sought after for their pelts in some places. Sirenians are exploited for their meat, which apparently tastes like veal, and for their skin and oil-rich blubber.

Whales have had one of the biggest population declines due to human hunting. Whaling can be traced back to Native Americans who hunted gray whales, but large scale whaling didn't occur until the 1600's when Europeans began whaling followed soon after by Americans, who dominated worldwide whaling. Large-scale whaling started from open boats where harpoons were used. The blubber was used to make soap and lamp oil and baleen was used as stays for corsets and other garments. Meat and other valuable whale parts were also sold. In the 1800's fast steamships began to be used for whaling and even the faster whales like the blue and fin whales couldn't escape the devastating harpoons. The low reproductive potential of these whales caused the whale global populations to be drastically reduced. The first species to be depleted was the right whale, so named because it was the 'right' whale to be killed since it floated after being harpooned. Whaling nations even developed factory ships to process whole carcasses. Blue whales were particularly sought after because there was so much oil, about 9,000 gallons, in an average whale. As the blue and right whale populations began to dwindle, whalers moved to the fin whale and then the smaller sei whale. The disappearance of commercially profitable whales forced the whalers to move to smaller, less profitable whales.

Though much progress has been made toward the protection of whales, much more is needed.

Dolphins are quickly replacing the larger whales as the most threatened of all cetaceans. Fisheries are depleting stocks of fish and squid and are therefore hunting dolphins for human food in places such as Peru because it is cheaper than chicken or beef.

Not all interactions between marine mammals and humans are bad, however. Many people believe that encounters with dolphins can be a spiritual experience. It is also believed that they can help children with behavioural disorders. In Southern Brazil a group of fishermen actually work with the dolphins to catch fish by interpreting cues given by the dolphins that reveal the location and abundance of fish; the dolphins are rewarded by the fishermen with an easy catch.

Marine mammals are a diverse group of 120 species of mammal that are primarily ocean-dwelling or depend on the ocean for food. They include the cetaceans (whales, dolphins, and porpoises), the sirenians (manatees and dugong), the pinnipeds (true seals, eared seals and walrus), and several otters (the sea otter and marine otter). The polar bear, while not fully aquatic, is also usually considered a marine mammal because it lives on sea ice for most or all of the year.

Marine mammals evolved from land dwelling ancestors and share several adaptive features for life at sea such as generally large size, hydrodynamic body shapes, modified appendages and various thermoregulatory adaptations. Whales are the largest mammals ever. Different species are, however, adapted to marine life to varying degrees. The most fully adapted are the cetaceans and the sirenians, which cannot live on land.

Despite the fact that marine mammals are highly recognizable charismatic megafauna, many populations are vulnerable or endangered due to a history of commercial use for blubber, meat, ivory and fur. Most species are currently in protection from commercial use.

There are some 120 extant species of marine mammals, generally sub-divided into the five groups bold-faced below. Each group descended from a different land-based ancestor. The morphological similarities between these diverse groups are a result of convergent and parallel evolution. For example, although whales and seals have some similarities in shape, whales are more closely related to deer than they are to seals.

- *Order Sirenia:* Sirenians, belonging to Afrotheria, a group that includes elephants and hyraxes.

  Family Trichechidae: Manatees (3 species, however, only one is actually a marine mammal).

  Family Dugongidae: Dugong (1 species).
- *Order Cetacea:* Cetaceans, belonging to Cetartiodactyla, a group that includes hippopotamuses, deer, and pigs.
- *Suborder Mysticeti:* Baleen whales (14 or 15 species).

  Suborder Odontoceti: Toothed whales (around 73 species).

  Suborder Archaeoceti:
- *Pakicetus*
- *Ichthyolestes*
- *Ambulocetus*
- *Himalayacetus*
- *Kutchicetus*
- *Remingtonocetus*
- *Rodhocetus*
- *Maiacetus*
- *Protocetus*
- *Dorudon*

Order Carnivora

- *superfamily Pinnipedia,* belonging to Caniformia descended from a bear-like ancestor

Family Phocidae: true seals (around 20 species)
Family Otariidae: eared seals (around 16 species)
Family Odobenidae: walrus (1 species)
Family Mustelidae, belonging to Caniformia and most closely related to other otters and weasels
Sea otter (Enhydra lutris)
Marine otter (Lontra felina)
Family Ursidae, belonging to Caniformia
Polar bear (Ursus maritimus), most closely related to other bears, particularly the brown bear
Order Desmostylia
Order Pilosa
Thalassocnus

Several groups of marine mammals existed in the past that are not alive today. In addition to the ancestors of the modern day whales, seals, and manatees, there existed desmostylians, cousins of the manatees, and Kolponomos, a genus of clam-eating marine bears not related to the modern polar bear.

Adaptations

Since mammals originally evolved on land, their spines are optimized for running, allowing for up-and-down but only little sideways motion. Therefore, marine mammals typically swim by moving their spine up and down. By contrast, fish normally swim by moving their spine sideways. For this reason, fish mostly have vertical caudal (tail) fins, while marine mammals have horizontal caudal fins.

Some of the primary differences between marine mammals and other marine life are:

- Marine mammals breathe air, while most other marine animals extract oxygen from water.
- Marine mammals have hair. Cetaceans have little or no hair, usually a very few bristles retained around the head or mouth. All members of the Carnivora have a coat of fur or hair, but it is far thicker and more important for

thermoregulation in sea otters and polar bears than in seals or sea lions. Thick layers of fur contribute to drag while swimming, and slow down a swimming mammal, giving it a disadvantage in speed.

- Marine mammals have thick layers of blubber used to insulate their bodies and prevent heat loss. Sea otters and polar bears are exceptions, relying more on fur and behaviour to stave off hypothermia.
- Marine mammals give birth. Most marine mammals give birth to one calf or pup at a time.
- Marine mammals feed off milk as young. Maternal care is extremely important to the survival of offspring that need to develop a thick insulating layer of blubber. The milk from the mammary glands of marine mammals often exceeds 40-50 per cent fat content to support the development of blubber.
- Marine mammals maintain a high internal body temperature. Unlike most other marine life, marine mammals carefully maintain a core temperature much higher than their environment. Blubber, thick coats of fur, bubbles of air between skin and water, countercurrent exchange, and behaviours such as hauling out, are all adaptations that aid marine mammals in retention of body heat.

The polar bear spends a large portion of its time in a marine environment, albeit a frozen one. When it does swim in the open sea it is extremely proficient and has been shown to cover 74 km in a day. For reasons like these, some scientists regard it as a marine mammal.

12 Marine Life Species and Interaction

Marine life species interact in a myriad of ways for protection, shelter, food, and more. Competition, symbiosis, commensalims, and parasitism are all categories in which these interactions occur.

Competition

There are two types of competition: *(i)* Interference or contest competition; *(ii)* Exploitation or scramble competition.

Interference competition occurs when one species keeps resources away from another. Scramble competition occurs when one species depletes a resource before another organism has a chance to use it. Competition is intensified when resources are limited and can occur within species or between species. When population sizes increase, competition is increased and organisms die, grow more slowly, and reproduction decreases. Some species will resort to resource partitioning where resources are divided among individuals for survival. Species may also adapt to new niches rather than expend energy on competing for resources.

Species with similar needs cannot live in the same place sustainably for an extended period of time. This principle is referred to as Gause's competitive exclusion principle. Some organisms adapt to conditions by helping each other survive through a mechanism known as symbiosis.

Symbiosis

Symbiotic relationships are non-competitive and include mutualism, commensalism, parasitism, and mimicry. All types of symbiosis are highly efficient and help to achieve a balance in the ecosystem. Mutualism is a relationship in which both species benefit. Commensalism is a relationship in which one species benefits and there is a neutral impact on the other. The term parasitism is generally used when one species benefits, but the other does not.

The basic types of species interactions are indicated by a (0), (+) or (-) indicating whether the two species involved experience zero effects, positive effects, or negative effects respectively. Commensalism is (+,0), Mutualism is (+,+), and Parasitism is (-,+). However, these are very simplistic descriptions and exceptions to the rule are common.

Mimicry is another symbiotic relationship less common than the others. Mimicry is a relationship in where one species mimics another, typically using colour or pattern. For example, the harmless banded snake eel may imitate a more dangerous sea snake. The Mimic octopus changes shape to resemble a Lionfish, sea snake or a stingray. Camouflage is another form of mimicry and can be seen in seahorses and scorpionfish.

Whenever organisms share resources in the environment there will be competition for food and territory. Organisms are forced to occupy specific niches in the environment in order to avoid wasting energy in competition. Organisms will also avoid competition through cooperative relationships within the ecosystem. Fish are frequently found existing in more than one symbiotic relationship. For example, a fish can have parasites and be cleaned by another organism living on its body. The parasites on the fish are food for the organism cleaning the fish. It is important to note that symbiosis only takes place between two different species.

Commensalism

Commensalism is a symbiotic relationship where one species provides protection for another less mobile or more vulnerable species. The relationship between Clownfish and anemones is a well-known example of commensalism. Clownfish live in the stinging tentacles of sea anemones. They are coated in mucous, which protects them from the anemone's stinging nematocysts. Other animals like crabs and shrimps also seek protection in anemones. The Anemone crab lives in the anemone's tentacles and catches its food without ever leaving the safety of the tentacles. Another example of commensalism can be seen with the Man-of-War fish and the Portuguese Man of War jellyfish.

Cooperation within the sea abounds and sometimes takes a very unusual form. Some Imperial shrimps will actually ride on sea cucumbers, hopping off when they want to feed in certain areas. When the shrimp is ready to go to another area, it will hop back on the cucumber and be taken to the next place without using very much energy. Sometimes Imperial shrimp will ride on other animals like nudibranchs, and these animals offer protection to the shrimp because they are poisonous to other animals. Several species of sea cucumbers host the Pearlfish inside their intestines during the day. At night, the Pearlfish swims out of the anus of the sea cucumber to eat crustaceans. The sea cucumber doesn't seem to mind this odd guest and the Pearlfish is relatively safe during the day.

Parasitism

More often than not, parasites are harmful to the host organism. Ectoparasites live on the outside of the host and endoparasites live on the inside of the host. Ectoparasites are often crustaceans in the order Isopoda or Copepoda. Isopods have adapted strong suckers, flat bodies, and sharp jaws used to attach to their host. They tend to molt in stages so that they remain latched on to the host. Some isopods will attach to the fish and cause no harm. In this case they eat particles of food that float by rather than feed on the host directly.

Mutualism

Mutualism is a symbiotic relationship in which both species benefit. For example, some anemones share a mutualistic relationship with Boxer crabs, *Lybia tesselata*. The

Boxer crab holds the anemone in its claws to use its stinging tentacles to fend off predators. In turn, the anemone consumes the crab's leftovers. There are also fish that spend their entire lives cleaning other fish. Gobies, wrasse and shrimps are well-known cleaners that man cleaning stations near coral reefs where rish go to have parasites, dead skin cells, and mucuous removed from their bodies. Cleaners are recognized as such by a characteristic horizontal line, which allows them to enter a larger fish's mouth to clean it without being eaten. Fish in need of cleaning will often change colour or swim in a vertical position to indicate they need to be cleaned. The colour change may also help cleaners see parasites on the skin of the fish being cleaned.

13 Structures of Marine Ecology

Trophic Levels

All organisms in an ecosystem can be placed in trophic levels depending on what energy source they rely upon and how they provide energy for other organisms in the food web. With the exception of life near hydrothermal vents in the deep ocean, life is always dependent directly or indirectly on the energy from the sun. In every ecosystem, there is an organism at the lowest level that converts energy from the sun into useable energy for other organisms. For example, phytoplankton are photosynthesizers that provide energy for a vast number of primary consumers, which in turn provide energy for secondary consumers and decomposers. Biologists study how energy is used in the food chain, known as the economy of energy.

Energy Flow

The food chain consists of trophic levels, or the levels within the food chain in which energy is transformed. Due to basic principles of thermodynamics, energy is always lost to the environment any time an organism at one trophic level uses the energy from the trophic level below. For example, the energy gained by animals that eat phytoplankton is less than the amount of energy initially available. Every trophic level loses energy, so trophic levels are often illustrated as a triangle with primary producers forming the base.

Components of an Ecosystem

There are four parts to every ecosystem: the abiotic environment (e.g. geology or geography), producers (e.g. phytoplankton), consumers (e.g. shrimp) and decomposers (e.g. bacteria). Energy from the sun and abiotic nutrients such as carbon dioxide or minerals are taken in by producers and transformed into usable energy through photosynthesis. Consumers, like herbivores, are dependent on producers to convert sunlight, water, and carbon dioxide into glucose, which can be then be divided through respiration to recover the sun's energy. Carnivores are secondary consumers if they only prey on herbivores and tertiary consumers if they eat other carnivores. Decomposers, the organisms responsible for decomposing dead animal and plant matter, are able to break down organic waste back into minerals that can be used by producers.

Trophic levels begin wtih phytoplankton, a primary producer capable of transforming inorganic carbon into protoplasm. Zooplankton is the second level because they eat phytoplankton and are a source of energy for crustaceans at the third level. The fourth level is fish that eat crustaceans and the fifth is seals and other animals that eat fish. The more trophic levels present, the less energy is conserved at higher trophic levels.

With a few exceptions, every species fits into the ecosystem as something consumed and something that consumes other things. Many prey are eaten by more than a single predator and most predators have diversified to eat more than one type of prey. The amount of biodiversity in an ecosystem is directly related to its degree of stability. When organisms eat a variety of foods, the loss of one type of prey is not as devastating to the overall ecosystem. Biodiversity can be lost through destruction of habitats, overexploitation, biological activity that upsets the balance of the ecosystem such as an invasive species, and pollution. Biodiversity loss upsets the balance of ecosystems, which is why it's important to ensure its sustainability in the ocean.

Biomass

When biomass is produced through photosynthesis, the amount can be measured in terms of primary production. Areas very important to the production of biomass on Earth are tropical rain forests with 2,000 $g/m^2/yr$; algal beds and reefs with 2000 $g/m^2/yr$; swamps and marshes with 2,500 $g/m^2/yr$; river estuaries with 1,800 $g/m^2/yr$; temperate forests with 1,200 $g/m^2/yr$ and cultivated lands with 600 $g/m^2/yr$. The least amount of biomass production occurs in the desert and frozen areas of the Earth.

Nutritional Groups

Organisms in the food chain are categorized into three basic nutritional groups in reference to what kind of carbon, energy, or electron source is utilized to make energy. Heterotrophic organisms use organic substrates and autotrophic organisms use inorganic substrates to obtain carbon. The reducing equivalent source is how organisms get electrons to reduce for biological processes. Lithotrophic organisms utilize inorganic compounds to get electrons and organotrophic organisms use organic compounds to get electrons necessary for biological processes. It is common to find autotrophic lithotrophic organisms or those that use an inorganic source to obtain electrons and carbon dioxide to obtain carbon. The energy source is how an organism makes ATP, the molecules that fuel biosynthetic pathways for energy. Phototrophic organisms use light energy and chemotrophic organisms, like those found near hydrothermal vents, use energy from chemical sources.

Organisms like the photolithotrophic cyanobacteria, can be any combination of the terms above. Fungi are chemo-organo-heterotrophic and plants are photoautotrophic, names that give significant information about their place in the ecosystem. All animals or 'eukaryotes' are heterotrophic, meaning they feed on organic matter. Certain types of algae can switch from being photolithoautotrophic in the light to chemoorganoheterotrophic in the dark. Trophic levels and the exchange of energy are a powerful example of nature's adaptability and the reason for the protection of biodiversity across ecosystems.

Biotic Structure

Biotic structure describes the way organisms interact within an ecosystem. The opposite of biotic is abiotic, which includes the physical and chemical factors present in the environment. Every organism in a species has a limit of tolerance, zone of stress, and optimum range for the abiotic factors present in its environment. Ecosystems can be simplified into three basic groups of organisms: producers, consumers, and decomposers. Some organisms can be in more than one category.

The definition of an ecosystem is a group of living organisms existing in a network of interactions with each other and their environment. The three feeding relationships are the food chain, the food web, and trophic levels. Non-feeding relationships can be defined as symbiotic or competitive.

Food Chains and Food Webs

Food webs illustrate the relationship between animals and what they feed on in the biotic community. Food webs also show how material and energy is transfered and lost within the ecosystem.

Each organism is a source of energy and material for another organism. The path in which biomass is moved can be illustrated in a food chain or food web. Grouping organisms into trophic levels is helpful when attempting to understand how much energy has been lost from the capture of the energy from the sun or from chemicals by primary producers. Primary producers, or autotrophs, can be any species that produce organic material from energy and/or from inorganic sources to be used by other organisms. In the deep sea, primary producers do not have access to sunlight; therefore, they utilize energy from chemicals and are called chemoautotrophs.

Food Chains

A food chain is different from a food web because it illustrates only one energy and nutrient path in an ecosystem.

Each platform is a trophic level with one organism that begins with one primary producer and ends with a secondary or tertiary consumer. A typical food chain might go like this: algae-copepod-fish-squid-seal-orca. In this example the orca feeds on the seals and the seals feed on the squid which feed on fish which feed on copepods. The base of the food chain is formed by algae which are eaten by copepods.

Food Webs

Food webs are more intricate than food chains and illustrate the feeding relationships between a number of organisms at different trophic levels in an ecosystem. Food chains are useful to illustrate relationships in a simple way, and food webs are more accurate as they can illustrate more relationships. Another aspect evident in a food web is the diversification of prey by predators in order to survive the loss of one species.

Trophic Levels

Trophic levels are the platforms in the food chain that indicate a position for a particular organism. In a very basic way, a trophic level will indicate whether an organism is a foundation species, primary consumer, or secondary consumer. Information about whether the organism eats plants or animals can also be obtained. Most often trophic levels are used to determine how much energy is lost from the primary producers up to the tertiary consumers. For each trophic level in the food chain, energy is lost due to the laws of thermodynamics. Levels can be diagrammed to form a triangle with the apex formed by tertiary consumers, or apex predators. The primary producers yield the most profit from the energy of the sun. By the time this energy has been transferred up to the higher trophic levels much of it has been lost to the environment.

Symbiosis

Symbiosis is a term most often used to describe two organisms living in a close association that benefits both of their survival. For example, clownfish live in sea anemones that have dangerous stinging tentacles, to which the clownfish are immune because they are protected by an outer layer of mucus.

The clownfish is therefore protected by the sea anemone, and in turn, acts as bait to lure fish into the stinging anenome. Another example of symbiosis is the goby fish often found living in a burrow with a shrimp. The shrimp makes a burrow for the fish and even does some housekeeping. The fish in turn warns the blind shrimp of impending danger by touching its tail so they can both swim deeper inside their burrow.

Symbiosis usually involves a symbiont (for example, the smaller clownfish) and a host (the anenome which is larger). A microscopic symbiont like bacteria in a termite's gut is usually called an *endosymbiont*. In ecological terms, symbiosis can mean more than just a mutually beneficial relationship. The four basic types of symbiosis are: *parasitism*, *mutualism*, *commensalism*, and *amensalism*. With parasitism, the relationship is good for one organism and bad for the other. A mutual symbiotic relationship is when both organisms benefit, commensalism is when only one benefits (and the other is indifferent), and amensalism is when one is harmed and the other is indifferent.

Depending on how the symbiotic relationship occurs, it is categorized into ectosymbiosis or endosymbiosis. Since 'ecto' means on the outside, an ectosymbiotic relationship indicates that both organisms are separate. An endosymbiotic relationship is when one organism lives inside the cells of the other organism or simply inside the other organism. Most interactions are more complex than simple categorical interactions of competition, mutualism, parasitism, and commensalism. The type of interactions can also change during the lifetime of an individual organism due to its development and the environment.

Competition

Species better adapted to their environment are able to survive and produce offspring. In biological terms, fitness refers to the number of offspring an organism is able to produce (versus the most well known term indicating greater physical strength). Charles Darwin explained that the competition between species is what results in organisms that are better adapted to their environment. Whenever there are limited resources, species or even organisms within a species are forced to compete in order to survive. Competition occurs in predator-prey relationships when both are trying to survive.

Since Darwin wrote about evolution, some details have been fine-tuned. Scientists no longer believe that competition is the only relationship driving evolution. The symbiotic relationships observed in animals like the blenny and the shrimp are evidence that evolution is driven by cooperation, integration, and mutual dependence instead.

Predators

The common definition of a *predator* is one that hunts and kills other organisms for food. It could be claimed that herbivores are predators due to some similarities in their style of seeking and eating food. For example, an animal that eats part of a plant would be a *herbivore* and one that hunts for single-celled algae might be a herbivore, or predator.

Most predators are carnivores, although some are omnivores meaning they also eat plants. A predator like the great white shark is called an *apex predator* because no other animal (except humans) hunts it for food. A *keystone predator* is one that keeps the entire ecosystem in balance and if it were removed the ecosystem would collapse. Scientists generally use the Volterra-Lotka equations to study predator-prey relationships with a mathematical model.

14 Marine Ecology

Introduction

Marine ecology is the scientific study of marine-life habitat, populations, and interactions among organisms and the surrounding environment including their abiotic (non-living physical and chemical factors that affect the ability of organisms to survive and reproduce) and biotic factors (living things or the materials that directly or indirectly affect an organism in its environment).

Marine ecology is a subset of the study of marine biology and includes observations at the biochemical, cellular, individual, and community levels as well as the study of marine ecosystems and the biosphere.

The study of marine ecology also includes the influence of geology, geography, meteorology, pedology, chemistry, and physics on marine environments. The impact of human activity such as medical research, development, agriculture, fisheries, and forestry is also studied under marine ecology. In some ways, marine ecology is more complex than the relatively straightforward study of a particular organism or environment because of the numerous interconnections, symbiotic relationships, and influence of many factors on a particular environment.

To understand the difference between marine biology and marine ecology, it may be useful to look at a community of organisms. A marine biologist may focus on behavioural relationships between the organisms in one particular species while someone studying ecology would study how the behaviour of one organism influences another. An ecologist would also look at abiotic factors and how they influence that organism. A scientist studying community ecology might study a group of organisms to see how they influence other species and abiotic factors.

The major subcategories of ecology are:

- *Physiological ecology:* The study of how biotic and abiotic factors act on the physiological characteristics of an organism and how the organism adapts to the abiotic and biotic environment.
- *Behavioural ecology:* A subcategory of ecology that studies which ecological and evolutionary dynamics are responsible for the way in which organisms adapt to their environment.
- *Population ecology:* The study of populations of organisms in a particular species and how the populations interact with their environment.
- *Community ecology:* The study of how species react to each other in a community.
- *Landscape ecology:* The study of how organisms interact with a particular landscape.
- *Ecosystem ecology:* The study of how energy and matter flow through ecosystems.
- *Global ecology:* The study of how energy and matter interact in the entire web of life on Earth.

The study of ecology in general includes all of the subcategories listed above as they apply to marine ecology, animal ecology, plant ecology, insect ecology, arctic ecology, tropical ecology and desert ecology.

Earth has been divided by ecologists into four areas: the hydrosphere, the lithosphere, the atmosphere, and the biosphere. The hydrosphere refers to water on the planet, the lithosphere consists of soil and rocks, the atmosphere is the air, and the biosphere refers to all of the life on Earth. The biosphere can be visualized as a thin surface layer on the

Earth from 11,000 m below sea level to 15,000 m above sea level, even though there are no permanent residents living in the atmosphere.

The first life on Earth was formed in the photic zone of the hydrosphere when organisms with more than one cell evolved in the deep ocean benthic zones. After the ozone layer formed, which protects land organisms from harmful UV rays, life began to evolve on land. After the continents separated and reformed, biodiversity began to increase as life began to adapt to new environments. Biodiversity can be observed at the genetic level, the species level, the population level, and the ecological level.

Abiotic elements like carbon, nitrogen and oxygen are present in great quantities in the biosphere. Phosphorus, calcium, and potassium are also present in smaller amounts. All are elements critical to the existence of life. Every element in the ecosystem transforms from mineral to organic forms and back to minerals and is never destroyed. Life depends on energy from the sun and the organisms that are capable of transforming light into chemical energy form the basis for the food chain. The process of photosynthesis converts light into chemical energy, resulting in the production of glucose and oxygen. Other organisms depend on glucose produced by photosynthesis for energy to fuel biological processes such as cellular respiration. During cellular respiration, organisms split glucose back into water and carbon dioxide. The breaking down of glucose releases and utilizes energy from the sun stored by photosynthesizing plants. The oxygen level of the Earth's atmosphere is largely reliant on the amount of photosynthetic activity and respiration going on in the biosphere. A build up of elements in areas with a lot of organisms is prevented by circulation of the atmosphere with global air currents.

The Earth is full of cycles simultaneously occurring and interlaced. Water is cycled through the hydrosphere, lithosphere, atmosphere, and biosphere in relatively predictable movements.

The flow of basic elements and the stability of the Earth's climate and temperature depend on oceanic currents and the vast amount of water stored in the ocean. Ecologists often depend on computer modeling to determine how human activity can influence the intricate cycling of the biosphere.

Every organism is influenced somehow by every part of its environment. An ecosystem is any place or time where organisms interact with their environment. Ecosystems can be divided into the life in the area and the area in which life exists. Biocoenosis is the life in the area and the biotope is the environment by which life is influenced. One form of interaction in the ecosystem is the food chain, a system moving energy and matter through organisms and the environment. A microecosystem is a small system like a fish with parasites. A mesoecosystem could refer to the coral reef in which the fish lives and a macroecosystem might be the area in which the coral reefs are located and how they interact.

Abiotic factors include geographical, climatological and geological influences. Biotopes are determined by certain abiotic factors. Examples of abiotic factors include, water, air, soil, pH, salinity, temperature, amount of light, and even natural catastrophic events.

A grouping of populations of plant, animal, or microscopic organisms is referred to as a *biocenose*. When the number of organisms in a species becomes too small, inbreeding reduces the genetic diversity causing weakness in the species and possible extinction. The stability of a biocenose is also connected to biotic ecological interactions by organisms of the same species or organisms of different species.

Interactions between organisms of the same species are cooperation, competition, territorial divisions, and organisation in the population. These factors are collectively referred to as intraspecific relations. The interaction of organisms of different species is referred to as interspecific relations and can include symbiotic interactions, competition, parasitism, and infectious disease. When two organisms occupy the same ecological niche, competition for resources can occur. It is important to determine whether the interaction is positive for both species, negative for both, or positive for only one species. Another example of an interspecific relation that is negative for one species and positive for the other is predation. Predatory activities form the basis for all food chains. While predation is natural and provides nourishment for the predatory species, in some cases it can upset the balance of the food chain when the prey species is already overexploited.

Biogeochemical cycles are present when minerals and organic materials are used by organisms and sent out as waste. Ecosystems can remain relatively stable when untouched by catastrophic events, detrimental human activities, or other unusual occurrences. Homeostasis, or self-regulation of ecosystems, occurs when supported by natural control mechanisms.

A biome is an ecological area separated from other areas by certain definitive characteristics and relies on the interdependent nature of ecosystems. Water, among other elements, can cycle from one ecosystem to another. Organisms like salmon and freshwater eels often move from one ecosystem to another. The biosphere includes all of the Earth's biomes. An example of a biome is the photic portion of the ocean where sunlight is present and photosynthetic algae can be found. Biomes are divided into ecozones corresponding loosely with the continents and are further divided into ecoregions.

Species are related to each other through the role they play in the food chain as producers, consumers, and decomposers. Producers are photosynthesizing plants, consumers are herbivorous or carnivorous animals, and decomposers are organisms (such as bacteria) that break down organic material into minerals, which are eventually used by producers. There are more producers than consumers. The total amount of living matter in any place is called the biomass. When the biomass of plants increases it is measured as the primary productivity: the biomass produced by consumers and decomposers is measured as the secondary productivity.

Primary and secondary productivity are measurements used by scientists to determine an ecosystem's capacity to support life.

An ecological crisis can take place when species or populations evolve in an unsustainable way. Sometimes the quality of the environment is lost after trauma, like a lack of rain or an increase in the temperature of a region. Other times, too much predation can ruin the balance of an ecosystem, as can be seen with overfishing by humans. Sometimes, too many organisms in one place will cause a poor living environment for others. There are different time scales for ecological crises ranging anywhere from a few months to millions of years. Extinction events can affect many species or just a few individual species. Human activities, like oil spills, can cause local crises as well as global crises like global warming. Even with a local crisis, the loss of a few species can have a disastrous effect on the survival of others in the food chain. A global crisis can result in a loss of nearly all species on Earth. The most common example of such a crisis is the extinction of the dinosaurs. Other examples of well-known ecological crises are the Permian-Triassic extinction event, the Cretaceous-Tertiary Event, Global Warming from the Greenhouse effect, the hole in the ozone layer, desertification and deforestation, and nuclear meltdowns like Chernobyl. Fortunately, nature always prevails and when species disappear, new species evolve.

15 Marine Life Cycles

Life Cycles

A life cycle is defined as the developmental stages that an organism undergoes from its primary stage to the primary stage in its offspring. Life cycles range in complexity from extremely simple—as with unicellular bacteria that begin with fission forming the parent and ends when the parent asexually splits into two daughter cells—to increasingly complex—as with multicellular animals that begin with sexual reproduction and morph through developmental stages where their bodies undergo extreme changes.

The Marine Life Cycle

Although at the surface the ocean can appear calm and quiet, in fact there is an enormous amount of life activity taking place, particularly at certain times of the year. Reproductive strategies abound in the ocean where we have fission, budding, eggs hatching externally, eggs hatching internally, live births, some marine animals are born in freshwater, some are born on land, etc. The marine environment creates unique challenges to the cycle of life, some that have been met with amazing adaptability.

Because of the complexity of marine life, research on marine life cycles is important because it helps document how marine organisms cope with abiotic factors in the marine environment such as ocean currents, tides, light, temperature, and the many other abiotic factors that influence life cycles.

For example, habitat plays an important role in the life cycle of many marine organisms. Some select different habitats for different stages of life such as breeding, nesting, juvenile development, and maturity. Tracking migratory marine life through its life cycle is used to understand how a given species survives in its changing environment.

Simple *versus* Complex Life Cycles

Life cycles are defined as either simple or complex. Many birds and mammals have simple life cycles as they do not undergo major morphological changes through their development.

A Simple Life Cycle

Bladder wrack algae can be used to illustrate a simple life cycle. This life cycle begins when reproductive receptacles form on the plants in autumn. Eggs form on the female while sperm forms on the male. The reproductive organs are fully mature the following summer, and the eggs and sperm are released into the water in great quantities. Females can produce more than one million eggs. The sperm cells find the eggs near the ocean floor, which are then fertilized and a new male or female plant starts to grow.

A Complex Life Cycle

Other types of algae have relatively complex life cycles where more than one generation can occur within a developmental stage and each generation changes radically in appearance. Surprisingly, the simplicity of the organism does not always correspond with the simplicity of the life cycle.

In complex life cycles, the larval or juvenile stages are longer, the developmental stages are more complicated, and the appearance of the organism throughout the developmental stages changes dramatically.

Jellyfish have a complex life cycle that progresses through what is called an alternation of generations where the organism takes two very different physical forms. Jellyfish are commonly recognized in their medusal stage, but they also undergo a polyp stage that occurs during the larval phase. Since jellyfish are either male or female, they reproduce sexually and have gonads found in the lining of their gut. The male transfers sperm by spitting it into the water where it is caught in the mouth of the female where her egg is fertilized.

The embryo develops in 'brood pouches' on the arms of the mouth structure inside the female jellyfish. The tiny larvae called planula swim out of the mouth or pouches into the water column where they attach at the bottom. After they are attached, the larvae become polyps and divide and bud into juvenile jellyfish, known as ephyra, which go on to develop into the adult medusa.

Although they are simple organisms, cnidarians (hydroids, jellyfish, anemones, and corals) alternate between sessile (or stationary) and mobile forms during their complex life cycle. Other simple animals alternate between a female form that reproduces asexually to male and female forms that reproduce sexually. The all female generation has the advantage of rapid reproduction during seasons where nutrients are plentiful.

Life Cycle Pressures

Many multicellular species must overcome ecological and practical obstacles to successfully complete a life cycle. For example, many species release eggs and sperm into the water where they must meet to form what are known as free-spawned fertilized gametes. The fertilized gametes, or zygotes, must then find nutrients for energy to grow into pelagic larvae. They must also find a benthic site to develop then survive as juveniles without being preyed upon by other marine life.

The way an organism copes with pressures throughout its lifecycle will influence how future life cycle strategies of the species are developed. Successful strategies will produce offspring that carry the life cycle strategy in their genetic structure.

Unsuccessful strategies result in the death of offspring, which reduces the likelihood that the strategy will be passed on to the next generation. Marine turtles face enormous pressures throughout their life cycles. They have a particularly long life cycle because they grow very slowly; many take decades to reach adulthood. Juveniles either drift in the ocean currents or live in the same area for years before they return to their nesting beach to breed and lay eggs, often migrating up to 3,000 external link km.

Males and females mate offshore with several partners about a month or two before the eggs are laid. The females store the sperm in their bodies and fertilize between 3-7 clutches (or sets) of eggs each season. At nesting time, the female uses her front flippers to navigate the sandy beach toward her nesting site where she digs a pit for the eggs, still using her front flippers, about 30-60 external link cm deep.

The digging process takes between 30-45 minutes, after which the female spends 10-20 minutes laying hundreds of eggs. She then turns around to use her hind flippers to bury the eggs and returns to sea where she will begin fertilizing the next clutch of eggs. The turtles' sex is determined by the temperature of the nest during incubation. Eggs incubated in warm darkly coloured sand produce mostly females, while eggs laid in cool, white sand take a little longer to hatch and produce mostly in males. In about 7-12 weeks the eggs begin to hatch and begin to emerge at night about 2 days later.

The hatchlings then find their way to the sea where they feed on tiny marine organisms. It is thought that ocean currents and magnetic fields present help guide the hatchlings back to the nesting beach years later when its their time to mate.

Sexual or Asexual

Marine organisms have great variation in their reproductive strategies. The evolution of a variety of life cycles among different species is a direct result of the need to reproduce efficiently and effectively so that genetic information is passed down. Asexual reproduction is an energy efficient method used in cases where resources are plentiful and conditions are stable; however, genetic information varies little from generation to generation. Sexual reproduction requires more energy (competition, mate selection, courtship, fertilization), however offspring are more genetically diverse, which facilitates long-term species survival in a changing environment.

Sponges reproduce both sexually and asexually. Sexual reproduction in sponges occurs when sperm is released into the water where it floats to another sponge containing that eggs, which are then fertilized. The fertilized eggs develop into the larval stage of the sponge. Sponges reproduce asexually through budding, a process where a new sponge is created from a piece of the parent sponge.

As mentioned earlier during a description of a complex life cycle, some types of algae switch between sexual and asexual reproduction. The same species of algae may reproduce asexually using spores in one generation, then switch to sexual reproduction using eggs and sperm.

Seasons and Rhythms

Many animals reproduce seasonally according to the time of year and phase of the moon, which can leave a short window of opportunity for sexual reproduction.

In the West Indies, the breeding ritual of a marine fireworm only takes place in spring or summer at sunset during a full moon before the moon rises. The fireworms emerge from crevices in the ocean floor to swim to the surface where eggs are floating. Because they have such specific breeding requirements, the fire worms only breed three or four days each year. Another organism confined to a short breeding period is the grunion, a fish commonly found on California's southern coast. The grunion comes out to mate at dark when the tide is high. They mate in the waves near the shoreline where the fertilized eggs are buried in the sand for two weeks when the next high spring tide washes the sand away.

Many animals breed seasonally so that the young are born during warmer months when more nutrients are available.

Reproductive Strategies

Simpler animals such as corals are often sessile (permanently attached or fixed; not free-moving), which presents a challenge to fertilization in those that reproduce sexually. One solution is to release clouds containing millions of gametes to increase chances of reproduction.

At certain times of the year, the ocean is full of milky sperm clouds floating in search of eggs to fertilize. Gametes from the female are often larger, making it easier for the smaller more mobile sperm to find. Slow moving and sessile organisms often use hermaphroditism or parasitism as a reproductive strategy. Barnacles, for example, are hermaphroditic. They use extremely long sex organs to reach another for the transfer of sperm.

A wide variety of reproductive strategies exist in complex animals. Mobile animals often attract mates using signals such as pheromones, visual clues, sound, and competitive courtship behaviour. Some species begin life as males and change into females as they mature. Many marine organisms produce large amounts of small eggs that hatch quickly producing large populations and therefore a greater chance for species survival. Other species maintain populations by reproducing multiple times during their life cycle, while other more complex animals, such as large mammals, reproduce less frequently because nursing and raising the young to survive requires time and energy.

Habitat use in Marine Organisms

Many marine species are highly mobile and often migratory; therefore they may rely on a number of different habitats throughout their developmental stages. For example, the South Atlantic peneaid shrimp utilizes marine habitats in deeper ocean waters as its spawning ground and estuarine waters in tidal wetlands for its nursing grounds. Salmon are a well-known known transient marine species. They spawn in freshwater rivers and migrate to the open ocean during the juvenile development stage where nutrients are abundant. Most reef fish, on the other hand, remain in sheltered coral reef ecosystems throughout their life cycles.

Types of Marine Life Cycles

Microscopic Life Cycles

Invertebrates such as jellyfish, sea anemones, ctenophores, sea worms, molluscs, sponges, and tunicates generally reproduce sexually, although some do reproduce asexually. The planktonic environment is extremely important for the life cycles of most of these organisms where they reside during their larval stages. Holoplankton are organisms that remain in the plankton for the duration of their life cycle. Meroplankton remain in the plankton for a portion of their life cycle while releasing larvae into the water column. Both holoplankton and meroplankton species have developed specific characteristics that make their reproduction in this habitat very efficient.

Planktonic and benthic organisms often use sexual reproduction and cling to mates using special appendages during fertilization. Some of the meroplanktonic and holoplanktonic invertebrates release sperm gametes into the water column that the female catches to fertilize her eggs. Other organisms release both sperm and eggs into the water column to form free-spawning gametes. Chemical, mechanical, and environmental cues trigger the release of gametes.

Marine Plant Life Cycles

The life cycle of a plant is multigenerational. Each plant starts with a spore that germinates and develops into an organism, known as a gametophyte that produces its own gametes. When the gametophyte reaches maturity, it can produce its own gametes and its offspring produce spores. These mature offspring are called sporophytes. The life cycle is complete when the sporophyte successfully produces spores. Fungi, protests, and plants have this multigenerational life cycle, which is also referred to as an alternation of generations.

Bacteria versus Multicellular Organisms

Bacteria undergo a haplontic life cycle where a single generation of haploid cells have one set of chromosomes. Many multicellular animals with a one generational life cycle have a diplontic life cycle in which cells have two sets of chromosomes. In diploid organisms each individual sex cell is haploid. When the haploid sperm and the haploid egg are joined, a diploid organism, with two sets of chromosomes, is formed. Plant life cycles are referred to as diplohaplontic because they develop from the gametophyte (haploid generation) to the sporophyte (diploid generation).

Fishes

Fish can have a range of life cycles where all stages of development take place in a small confined area like a pond or a stream to life cycles that take place over thousands of kilometres from streams to oceans and back to streams. The life cycles of Salmoniform fishes encompass almost all of the life cycle types and reproductive strategies. Some fish develop from the egg into the juvenile phase then into the adult phase. Some fish species, particularly those in the deep sea, have larval stages distinctly separate from the juvenile and adult stage. The larvae often look very different from the mature fish. Salmoniform fishes are usually either male or female, but some of the deep sea versions are hermaphroditic, a reproductive strategy common in the deep sea.

Because of the value of salmon and trout fisheries, the life cycles of these two fish are very well documented. The results of this research have been used to identify the origin of salmon captured in ocean water to resolve arguments between nations. This information helps to better manage this valuable commodity.

The reproductive strategies of fishes are varied. Sharks reproduce through internal fertilization and many shark species give birth to live young. Sharks that lay eggs produce large, tough shelled egg sacs often referred to as 'mermaid's purses'. Both sharks that give birth to live young and those that lay eggs produce relatively small numbers of young making it more important to preserve those species that are becoming overfished. Some bony fishes also bear live young, but most reproduce sexually through the fertilization of eggs joined by sperm in the water column. Females lay an enormous number of eggs to ensure fertilization as many eggs are eaten prior to encountering sperm in the water.

Like sharks, marine mammals also reproduce slowly and give birth to a limited number of young. Female whales, for example, give birth to a single calf and nurse for many months, in some species longer than a year. Female whales and their calves form a strong bond during the nursing period, which helps whale species ensure a high rate of survival as the mother protects her young until the calf has reached a level of development where it can survive on its own.

16 Whale

Whale (origin Old English h?æl) is the common name for various marine mammals of the order Cetacea. The term whale sometimes refers to all cetaceans, but more often it excludes dolphins and porpoises, which belong to suborder Odontoceti (toothed whales). This suborder also includes the sperm whale, killer whale, pilot whale, and beluga whale. The other Cetacean suborder Mysticeti (baleen whales), are filter feeders that eat small organisms caught by straining seawater through a comblike structure found in the mouth called baleen. This suborder includes the blue whale, the humpback whale, the bowhead whale and the minke whale. All Cetacea have forelimbs modified as fins, a tail with horizontal flukes, and nasal openings (blowholes) on top of the head.

Whales range in size from the blue whale, the largest animal known to have ever existed at 35 m (115 ft) and 136 tonnes, to various pygmy species, such as the pygmy sperm whale at 3.5 m (11 ft).

Whales collectively inhabit all the world's oceans and number in the millions, with annual population growth rate estimates for various species ranging from 3-13 per cent. For centuries, whales have been hunted for meat and as a source of raw materials. By the middle of the 20th century, however, industrial whaling had left many species seriously endangered, leading to the end of whaling in all but a few countries.

Cetaceans are divided into two suborders:

1. The largest suborder, Mysticeti (baleen whales) are characterized by baleen, a sieve-like structure in the upper jaw made of keratin, which it uses to filter plankton from the water.
2. Odontoceti (toothed whales) bear sharp teeth for hunting. Odontoceti also include dolphins and porpoises.

Both cetaceans and artiodactyl are now classified under the super-order Cetartiodactyla which includes both whales and hippopotamuses. Whales are the hippopotamus's closest living relatives.

All cetaceans, including whales, dolphins and porpoises, are descendants of land-living mammals of the Artiodactyl order (even-toed ungulates). Both are related to the Indohyus (an extinct semi-aquatic deer-like ungulate) from which they split around 54 million years ago. Primitive whales probably first took to the sea about 50 million years ago and became fully aquatic about 5-10 million years later.

Anatomy

Like all mammals, whales breathe air, are warm-blooded, nurse their young with milk from mammary glands, and have body hair.

Beneath the skin lies a layer of fat called blubber, which stores energy and insulates the body. Whales have a spinal column, a vestigial pelvic bone, and a four-chambered heart. The neck vertebrae are typically fused, trading flexibility for stability during swimming.

Features of a Blue Whale

Whales breathe via blowholes; baleen whales have two and toothed whales have one. These are located on the top of the head, allowing the animal to remain mostly submerged whilst breathing. Breathing involves expelling excess water from the blowhole, forming an upward spout, followed by inhaling air into the lungs. Spout shapes differ among species and can help with identification.

Appendages

The body shape is fusiform and the modified forelimbs, or fins, are paddle-shaped. The end of the tail is composed of two flukes, which propel the animal by vertical movement, as opposed to the horizontal movement of a fish tail. Although whales do not possess fully developed hind limbs, some (such as sperm whales and baleen whales) possess discrete rudimentary appendages, which may even have feet and digits. Most species have a dorsal fin.

Dentition

Toothed whales, such as the sperm whale, possess teeth with cementum cells overlying dentine cells. Unlike human teeth, which are composed mostly of enamel on the portion of the tooth outside of the gum, whale teeth have cementum outside the gum. Only in larger whales, where the cementum has been worn away on the tip of the tooth, does enamel show.

Instead of teeth, Baleen whales have a row of plates on the upper side of their jaws that resemble the 'teeth' of a comb.

Ears

The whale ear has specific adaptations to the marine environment. In humans, the middle ear works as an impedance matcher between the outside air's low impedance and the cochlear fluid's high impedance. In aquatic mammals such as whales, however, there is no great difference between the outer and inner environments. Instead of sound passing through the outer ear to the middle ear, whales receive sound through the throat, from which it passes through a low-impedance fat-filled cavity to the inner ear.

Males are called 'bulls', females, 'cows' and newborns, 'calves'. Most species do not maintain fixed partnerships and females have several mates each season.

The female delivers usually a single calf tail-first to minimize the risk of drowning. Whale cows nurse by actively squirting milk, so fatty that it has the consistency of toothpaste, into the mouths of their young. Nursing continues for more than a year in many species, and is associated with a strong bond between mother and calf. Reproductive maturity occurs typically at seven to ten years. This mode of reproduction produces few offspring, but increases survival probability.

Socialization

Whales are known to teach, learn, cooperate, scheme, and even grieve.

Sleep

Unlike most animals, whales are conscious breathers. All mammals sleep, but whales cannot afford to become unconscious for long because they may drown. It is thought that only one hemisphere of the whale's brain sleeps at a time, so they rest but are never completely asleep.

Many whales exhibit behaviours such as breaching and tail slapping that expose large parts of their bodies to the air.

Lifespan

Whale lifespans vary among species and are not well characterized. Whaling left few older individuals to observe directly. Researcher estimated that humpback whales may live as long as 77 years. In 2007, a 19th century lance fragment was found in a bowhead whale off Alaska, suggesting the individual could be between 115 and 130 years old. Aspartic acid racemization in the whale eye, combined with a harpoon fragment, indicated an age of 211 years for another male, which, if true would make bowheads the longest-lived extant mammal species. The accuracy of this technique has been questioned because racemization did not correlate well with other dating methods.

Vocalization

Some species, such as the humpback whale, communicate using melodic sounds, known as whale song. These sounds can be extremely loud, depending on the species. Sperm whales have only been heard making clicks, while toothed whales (Odontoceti) use echolocation that can generate about 20,000 watts of sound (+73 dBm or +43 dBw and be heard for many miles. Whale vocalization is likely to serve many purposes, including echolocation, mating, and identification.

Whales are generally classed as predators, but their food ranges from microscopic plankton to very large animals.

Toothed whales eat fish and squid which they hunt by use of echolocation. Orcas sometimes eat other marine mammals, including whales.

Baleen whales such as humpbacks and blues feed only in arctic waters, eating mostly krill. They imbibe enormous amounts of seawater which they expel through their baleen plates. The water is then expelled and the krill is retained on the plates and then swallowed. Whales do not drink seawater but indirectly extract water from their food by metabolizing fat.

Whale Pump

A recent discovery of a positive influence on the productivity of ocean fisheries has been attributed to whales in what has been termed a 'whale pump'. Whales, they found, carry nutrients such as nitrogen from the depths where they feed back to the surface. This functions as an upward biological pump, reversing the assumption of some scientists that whales accelerate the loss of nutrients to the bottom. They note that this nitrogen input in the Gulf of Maine is 'more than the input of all rivers combined', some 23,000 metric tons each year.

Some species of large whales are listed as endangered by multinational organisations such as CITES along with governments and advocacy groups primarily due to whaling's impacts. They have been hunted commercially for whale oil, meat, baleen and ambergris (a perfume ingredient from the intestine of sperm whales) since the 17th century. At its peak in 1846, the American whaling industry employed more than 70,000 people and 736 vessels. More than 2 million were taken in the early 20th century, and by the middle of the century, many populations were severely depleted.

The International Whaling Commission banned commercial whaling in 1986. The ban is not absolute, however, and some whaling continues under the auspices of scientific research (sometimes not proved or aboriginal rights; current whaling nations are Norway, Iceland and Japan and the aboriginal communities of Siberia, Alaska and northern Canada.

Bycatch

Several species of small whales are caught as bycatch in fisheries for other species. In the Eastern Tropical Pacific tuna fishery, thousands of dolphins drowned in purse-seine nets, until preventive measures were introduced. Gear and deployment modifications, and eco-labelling (dolphin-safe or dolphin-friendly brands of tuna), have contributed to a reduction in dolphin mortality by tuna vessels.

Environmentalists speculate that advanced naval sonar endangers some cetaceans, including whales. In 2003 British and Spanish scientists suggested in Nature that the effects of sonar trigger whale beachings and to signs that such whales have experienced decompression sickness. Responses in Nature the following year discounted the explanation.

Mass beachings occur in many species, mostly beaked whales that use echolocation for deep diving. The frequency and size of beachings around the world, recorded over the last 1,000 years in religious tracts and more recently in scientific surveys, have been used to estimate the population of various whale species by assuming that the proportion of the total whale population beaching in any one year is constant. Beached whales can give other clues about population conditions, especially health problems. For example, bleeding around ears, internal lesions, and nitrogen bubbles in organ tissue suggest decompression sickness.

Following public concern, the U.S. Defense department was ordered by the 9th Circuit Court to strictly limit use of its Low Frequency Active Sonar during peacetime. Attempts by the UK-based Whale and Dolphin Conservation Society to obtain a public inquiry into the possible dangers of the Royal Navy's equivalent (the '2087' sonar launched in December 2004) failed as of 2008. The European Parliament has requested that EU members refrain from using the powerful sonar system until an environmental impact study has been carried out.

Whales were little understood for most of human history as they spend up to 90 per cent of the lives underwater, only surfacing briefly to breathe. They also include the largest animals on the planet, so it is not surprising that many cultures, even those that have hunted them, hold them in awe and feature them in their mythologies.

In China, Yu-kiang, a whale with the hands and feet of a man was said to rule the ocean.

In the Tyrol region of Austria it was said that if a sunbeam were to fall on a maiden entering womanhood, she would be carried away in the belly of a whale.

Paikea, the youngest and favourite son of the chief Uenuku from the island of Mangaia in the present day Cook Islands in New Zealand was said by the Kati Kuri people of Kaikoura to have come from the Pacific Islands on the back of a whale many centuries before. The novel and movie Whale Rider follow the trials of a girl named Paikia, who lives in such a culture.

The whale features in Inuit creation myths. When 'Big Raven', a deity in human form, found a stranded whale, he was told by the Great Spirit where to find special mushrooms that would give him the strength to drag the whale back to the sea and thus return order to the world.

The Tlingit people of northern Canada said that the Orcas were created when the hunter Natṣihlane carved eight fish from yellow cedar, sang his most powerful spirit song and commanded the fish to leap into the water.

In Icelandic legend a man threw a stone at a fin whale and hit the blowhole, causing the whale to burst. The man was told not to go to sea for twenty years but in the nineteenth year he went fishing and a whale came and killed him.

In East African legend King Sulemani asked God that He might permit him to feed all the beings on earth. A whale came and ate until there was no corn left and then told Sulemani that he was still hungry and that there were 70,000 more in his tribe. Sulemani then prayed to God for forgiveness and thanked the creature for teaching him a lesson in humility.

Some cultures associate divinity with whales, such as among Ghanaians and Vietnamese, who occasionally hold funerals for beached whales, a throwback to Vietnam's ancient sea-based Austro-asiatic culture. The whale is a revered creature to Vietnamese fishermen. They are respectfully addressed as 'Lord'. If one finds a stranded whale corpse, one is in charge of holding the funeral for the 'Lord' as if it was one's own parent.

Blue Whale

The blue whale (Balaenoptera musculus) is a marine mammal belonging to the suborder of baleen whales (called Mysticeti). At 30 metres (98 ft) in length and 180 metric tons (200 short tons) or more in weight, it is the largest animal ever known to have existed.

Long and slender, the blue whale's body can be various shades of bluish-grey dorsally and somewhat lighter underneath. There are at least three distinct subspecies: *B.m. musculus* of the North Atlantic and North Pacific, *B.m. intermedia* of the Southern Ocean and *B.m. brevicauda* (also known as the pygmy blue whale) found in the Indian Ocean and South Pacific Ocean. *B.m. indica,* found in the Indian Ocean, may be another subspecies. As with other baleen whales, its diet consists almost exclusively of small crustaceans known as krill.

Blue whales were abundant in nearly all the oceans on Earth until the beginning of the twentieth century. For over a century, they were hunted almost to extinction by whalers until protected by the international community in 1966. A 2002 report estimated there were 5,000 to 12,000 blue whales worldwide, located in at least five groups. More recent research into the Pygmy subspecies suggests this may be an underestimate. Before whaling, the largest population was in the Antarctic, numbering approximately 239,000 (range 202,000 to 311,000). There remain only much smaller (around 2,000) concentrations in each of the North-East Pacific, Antarctic, and Indian Ocean groups. There are two more groups in the North Atlantic, and at least two in the Southern Hemisphere.

Blue whales are rorquals (family Balaenopteridae), a family that includes the humpback whale, the fin whale, Bryde's whale, the sei whale and the minke whale. The family Balaenopteridae is believed to have diverged from the other families of the suborder Mysticeti as long ago as the middle Oligocene. However, it is not known when the members of those families diverged from each other.

The blue whale is usually classified as one of eight species in the genus Balaenoptera; one authority places it in a separate monotypic genus, Sibbaldus, but this is not accepted elsewhere. DNA sequencing analysis indicates that the blue whale is phylogenetically closer to the sei whale (Balaenoptera borealis) and Bryde's whale (Balaenoptera brydei) than to other Balaenoptera species, and closer to the humpback whale (Megaptera) and the gray whale (Eschrichtius) than to the minke whales (Balaenoptera acutorostrata and Balaenoptera bonaerensis). If further research confirms these relationships, it will be necessary to reclassify the rorquals.

There have been at least 11 documented cases of blue/fin hybrid adults in the wild. Arnason and Gullberg describe the genetic distance between a blue and a fin as about the same as that between a human and a gorilla. Researchers working off of Fiji believe they photographed a hybrid humpback/blue whale.

The first published description of the blue whale comes from Robert Sibbald's Phalainologia Nova (1694). In September 1692, Sibbald found a blue whale that had stranded in the Firth of Forth—a male 78-feet-long—which had 'black, horny plates' and 'two large apertures approaching a pyramid in shape'.

The specific name musculus is Latin and could mean 'muscle', but it can also be interpreted as 'little mouse'. Linnaeus, who named the species in his seminal Systema Naturae of 1758, would have known this and may have intended the ironic double meaning. Herman Melville called this species sulphur-bottom in his novel Moby-Dick due to an orange-brown or yellow tinge on the underparts from diatom films on the skin. Other common names for the blue whale have included Sibbald's rorqual (after Sibbald, who first described the species), the great blue whale and the great northern rorqual. These names have now fallen into disuse. The first known usage of the term blue whale was in Melville's Moby-Dick, which only mentions it in passing and does not specifically attribute it to the species in question. The name was really derived from the Norwegian blåhval, coined by Svend Foyn shortly after he had perfected the harpoon gun; the Norwegian scientist G.O. Sars adopted it as the Norwegian common name in 1874.

Authorities classify the species into three or four subspecies: B. m. musculus, the northern blue whale consisting of the North Atlantic and North Pacific populations, B. m. intermedia, the southern blue whale of the Southern Ocean, B. m. brevicauda, the pygmy blue whale found in the Indian Ocean and South Pacific, and the more problematic B. m. indica, the great Indian rorqual, which is also found in the Indian Ocean and, although described earlier, may be the same subspecies as B. m. brevicauda.

The blue whale has a long tapering body that appears stretched in comparison with the stockier build of other whales. The head is flat and U-shaped and has a prominent ridge running from the blowhole to the top of the upper lip. The front part of the mouth is thick with baleen plates; around 300 plates (each around one metre (3.2 ft) long) hang from the upper jaw, running 0.5 m (1.6 ft) back into the mouth. Between 60 and 90 grooves (called ventral pleats) run along the throat parallel to the body length. These pleats assist with evacuating water from the mouth after lunge feeding.

The dorsal fin is small, visible only briefly during the dive sequence. Located around three-quarters of the way along the length of the body, it varies in shape from one individual to another; some only have a barely perceptible lump, but others may have prominent and falcate (sickle-shaped) dorsals. When surfacing to breathe, the blue whale raises its shoulder and blowhole out of the water to a greater extent than other large whales, such as the fin or sei whales. Observers can use this trait to differentiate between species at sea. Some blue whales in the North Atlantic and North Pacific raise their tail fluke when diving. When breathing, the whale emits a spectacular vertical single-column spout up to 12 metres (39 ft), typically 9 metres (30 ft). Its lung capacity is 5,000 litres (1320 U.S. gallons). Blue whales have twin blowholes shielded by a large splashguard.

The flippers are 3-4 metres (9.8-13 ft) long. The upper sides are grey with a thin white border; the lower sides are white. The head and tail fluke are generally uniformly grey. The whale's upper parts, and sometimes the flippers, are usually mottled. The degree of mottling varies substantially from individual to individual. Some may have a uniform slate-grey colour, but others demonstrate a considerable variation of dark blues, greys and blacks, all tightly mottled.

Blue whales can reach speeds of 50 kilometres per hour (31 mph) over short bursts, usually when interacting with other whales, but 20 kilometres per hour (12 mph) is a more typical traveling speed. When feeding, they slow down to 5 kilometres per hour (3.1 mph).

Blue whales most commonly live alone or with one other individual. It is not known how long traveling pairs stay together. In locations where there is a high concentration of food, as many as 50 blue whales have been seen scattered over a small area. However, they do not form the large, close-knit groups seen in other baleen species.

Blue whales are difficult to weigh because of their size. Most blue whales killed by whalers were not weighed whole, but cut up into manageable pieces first. This caused an underestimate of the total weight of the whale, due to the loss of blood and other fluids. Nevertheless, measurements between 150-170 metric tons (170-190 short tons) were recorded of animals up to 27 metres (89 ft) in length. The weight of an individual 30 metres (98 ft) long is believed by the American National Marine Mammal Laboratory (NMML) to be in excess of 180 metric tons (200 short tons). The largest blue whale accurately weighed by NMML scientists to date was a female that weighed 177 metric tons (195 short tons).

The blue whale is the largest animal ever known to have lived. The largest known dinosaur of the Mesozoic Era was the Argentinosaurus, which is estimated to have weighed up to 90 metric tons (99 short tons), though a controversial vertebra of Amphicoelias fragillimus may indicate an animal of up to 122 metric tons (134 short tons) and 40-60 metres (130-200 ft). Furthermore, there are weight estimates for the very poorly known Bruhathkayosaurus ranging from 140-220 metric tons (150-240 short tons), besides length estimates up to about 45 metres (148 ft). The extinct fish Leedsichthys may have approached its size. However, complete fossils are difficult to come by, making size comparisons difficult. All these animals are considered to be smaller than the blue whale.

There is some uncertainty about the biggest blue whale ever found, as most data come from blue whales killed in Antarctic waters during the first half of the twentieth century, and was collected by whalers not well-versed in standard zoological measurement techniques. The longest whales ever recorded were two females measuring 33.6 metres (110 ft) and 33.3 metres (109 ft). The longest whale measured by scientists at the NMML was 29.9 metres (98 ft).

A blue whale's tongue weighs around 2.7 metric tons (3.0 short tons) and, when fully expanded, its mouth is large enough to hold up to 90 metric tons (99 short tons) of food and water. Despite the size of its mouth, the dimensions of its throat are such that a blue whale cannot swallow an object wider than a beach ball. Its heart weighs 600 kilograms (1,300 lb) and is the largest known in any animal. A blue whale's aorta is about 23 centimetres (9.1 in) in diametre. During the first seven months of its life, a blue whale calf drinks approximately 400 litres (100 U.S. gallons) of milk every day. Blue whale calves gain weight quickly, as much as 90 kilograms (200 lb) every 24 hours. Even at birth, they weigh up to 2,700 kilograms (6,000 lb)—the same as a fully grown hippopotamus.

Blue whales feed almost exclusively on krill, though they also take small numbers of copepods. The species of this zooplankton eaten by blue whales varies from ocean to ocean. In the North Atlantic, Meganyctiphanes norvegica, Thysanoessa raschii, Thysanoessa inermis and Thysanoessa longicaudata are the usual food; in the North Pacific, Euphausia pacifica, Thysanoessa inermis, Thysanoessa longipes, Thysanoessa spinifera, Nyctiphanes symplex and Nematoscelis megalops; and in the Antarctic, Euphausia superba, Euphausia crystallorophias and Euphausia valentin.

An adult blue whale can eat up to 40 million krill in a day. The whales always feed in the areas with the highest concentration of krill, sometimes eating up to 3,600 kilograms (7,900 lb) of krill in a single day. This daily requirement of an adult blue whale is in the region of 1.5 million kilocalories.

Because krill move, blue whales typically feed at depths of more than 100 metres (330 ft) during the day and only surface-feed at night. Dive times are typically 10 minutes when feeding, though dives of up to 20 minutes are common. The longest recorded dive is 36 minutes. The whale feeds by lunging forward at groups of krill, taking the animals and a large quantity of water into its mouth. The water is then squeezed out through the baleen plates by pressure from the ventral pouch and tongue. Once the mouth is clear of water, the remaining krill, unable to pass through the plates, are swallowed. The blue whale also incidentally consumes small fish, crustaceans and squid caught up with krill.

Mating starts in late autumn and continues to the end of winter. Little is known about mating behaviour or breeding grounds. Females typically give birth once every two to three years at the start of the winter after a gestation period of 10 to 12 months. The calf weighs about 2.5 metric tons (2.8 short tons) and is around 7 metres (23 ft) in length. Blue whale calves drink 380–570 litres (100–150 U.S. gallons) of milk a day. Weaning takes place for about six months, by which time the calf has doubled in length. Sexual maturity is typically reached at eight to ten years, by which time males are at least 20 metres (66 ft) long (or more in the Southern Hemisphere). Females are larger still, reaching sexual maturity at around the age of five, by which they are about 21 metres (69 ft) long.

Scientists estimate that blue whales can live for at least 80 years; however, since individual records do not date back into the whaling era, this will not be known with certainty for many years. The longest recorded study of a single individual is 34 years, in the northeast Pacific. The whales' only natural predator is the orca. Studies report that as many as 25 per cent of mature blue whales have scars resulting from orca attacks. The mortality rate of such attacks is unknown.

Blue whale strandings are extremely uncommon, and, because of the species' social structure, mass strandings are unheard of. However, when strandings do occur, they can become the focus of public interest. In 1920, a blue whale washed up near Bragar on the Isle of Lewis in the Outer Hebrides of Scotland. It had been shot by whalers, but the harpoon had failed to explode. As with other mammals, the fundamental instinct of the whale was to try to carry on breathing at all costs, even though this meant beaching to prevent itself from drowning. Two of the whale's bones were erected just off a main road on Lewis and remain a tourist attraction.

Estimates made by researchers suggest the source level of sounds made by blue whales are between 155 and 188 decibels when measured relative to a reference pressure of one micropascal at one metre. All blue whale groups make calls at a fundamental frequency between 10 and 40 Hz; the lowest frequency sound a human can typically perceive is 20 Hz. Blue whale calls last between ten and thirty seconds. Blue whales off the coast of Sri Lanka have been repeatedly recorded making 'songs' of four notes, lasting about two minutes each, reminiscent of the well-known humpback whale songs. As this phenomenon has not been seen in any other populations, researchers believe it may be unique to the B. m. brevicauda (pygmy) subspecies.

The reason for vocalization is unknown. Researchers discuss six possible reasons:

1. Maintenance of inter-individual distance
2. Species and individual recognition
3. Contextual information transmission (for example feeding, alarm, courtship)
4. Maintenance of social organisation (for example contact calls between females and males)
5. Location of topographic features
6. Location of prey resources.

Blue whales are not easy to catch or kill. Their speed and power meant that they were rarely pursued by early whalers, who instead targeted sperm and right whales. In 1864, the Norwegian Svend Foyn equipped a steamboat with harpoons specifically designed for catching large whales. Although initially cumbersome and with a low success rate, Foyn perfected the harpoon gun, and soon several whaling stations were established on the coast of Finnmark in northern Norway. Because of disputes with the local fishermen, the last whaling station in Finnmark was closed down in 1904.

Soon, blue whales were being hunted in Iceland (1883), the Faroe Islands (1894), Newfoundland (1898), and Spitsbergen (1903). In 1904-05 the first blue whales were taken off South Georgia. By 1925, with the advent of the stern slipway in factory ships and the use of steam-driven whale catchers, the catch of blue whales, and baleen whales as a whole, in the Antarctic and sub-Antarctic began to increase dramatically. In the 1930–31 season, these ships caught 29,400 blue whales in the Antarctic alone. By the end of World War II, populations had been significantly depleted, and, in 1946, the first quotas restricting international trade in whales were introduced, but they were ineffective because of the lack of differentiation between species. Rare species could be hunted on an equal footing with those found in relative abundance.

Blue whale hunting was banned in 1966 by the International Whaling Commission, and illegal whaling by the USSR finally halted in the 1970s, by which time 330,000 blue whales had been caught in the Antarctic, 33,000 in the rest of the Southern Hemisphere, 8,200 in the North Pacific, and 7,000 in the North Atlantic. The largest original population, in the Antarctic, had been reduced to 0.15 per cent of their initial numbers.

Since the introduction of the whaling ban, studies have failed to ascertain whether the conservation reliant global blue whale population is increasing or remaining stable. In the Antarctic, best estimates show a significant increase at 7.3 per cent per year since the end of illegal Soviet whaling, but numbers remain at under one per cent of their original levels. It has also been suggested that Icelandic and Californian populations are increasing but these increases are not statistically significant. The total world population was estimated to be between 5,000 and 12,000 in 2002, although there are high levels of uncertainty in available estimates for many areas.

The IUCN Red List counts the blue whale as 'endangered' as it has since the list's inception. In the United States, the National Marine Fisheries Service lists them as endangered under the Endangered Species Act. The largest known concentration, consisting of about 2,800 individuals, is the northeast Pacific population of the northern blue whale (B. m. musculus) subspecies that ranges from Alaska to Costa Rica, but is most commonly seen from California in summer. Infrequently, this population visits the northwest Pacific between Kamchatka and the northern tip of Japan.

In the North Atlantic, two stocks of B. m. musculus are recognised. The first is found off Greenland, Newfoundland, Nova Scotia and the Gulf of Saint Lawrence. This group is estimated to total about 500. The second, more easterly group is spotted from the Azores in spring to Iceland in July and August; it is presumed the whales follow the Mid-Atlantic Ridge between the two volcanic islands. Beyond Iceland, blue whales have been spotted as far north as Spitsbergen and Jan Mayen, though such sightings are rare. Scientists do not know where these whales spend their winters. The total North Atlantic population is estimated to be between 600 and 1,500.

In the Southern Hemisphere, there appear to be two distinct subspecies, B. m. intermedia, the Antarctic blue whale, and the little-studied pygmy blue whale, B. m. brevicauda, found in Indian Ocean waters. The most recent surveys (midpoint 1998) provided an estimate of 2,280 blue whales in the Antarctic., of which fewer than 1 per cent are likely to be pygmy blue whales Estimates from a 1996 survey were that 424 pygmy blue whales were in a small area south of Madagascar alone, thus it is likely that numbers in the entire Indian Ocean are in the thousands. If this is true, the global numbers would be much higher than estimates predict.

A fourth subspecies, B. m. indica, was identified by Blyth in 1859 in the northern Indian Ocean, but difficulties in identifying distinguishing features for this subspecies led to it being used a synonym for B. m. brevicauda, the pygmy blue whale. Records for Soviet catches seem to indicate that the female adult size is closer to that of the Pygmy Blue than B. m. musculus, although the populations of B. m. indica and B. m. brevicauda appear to be discrete, and the breeding seasons differ by almost six months.

Migratory patterns of these subspecies are not well known. For example, pygmy blue whales have been recorded in the northern Indian Ocean (Oman, Maldives and Sri Lanka), where they may form a distinct resident population. In addition, the population of blue whales occurring off Chile and Peru may also be a distinct population. Some Antarctic blue whales approach the eastern South Atlantic coast in winter, and occasionally, their vocalizations are heard off Peru, Western Australia, and in the northern Indian Ocean. In Chile, the Cetacean Conservation Centre, with support from the

Chilean Navy, is undertaking extensive research and conservation work on a recently discovered feeding aggregation of the species off the coast of Chiloe Island in the Gulf of Corcovado, where 326 blue whales were spotted in the summer of 2007.

Efforts to calculate the blue whale population more accurately are supported by marine mammologists at Duke University, who maintain the Ocean Biogeographic Information System—Spatial Ecological Analysis of Megavertebrate Populations (OBIS-SEAMAP), a collation of marine mammal sighting data from around 130 sources.

Due to their enormous size, power and speed, adult blue whales have virtually no natural predators. There is, however, one documented case in National Geographic Magazine of a blue whale being attacked by orcas off the Baja California Peninsula; although the orcas were unable to kill the animal outright during their attack, the blue whale sustained massive wounds and probably died as a result of them shortly after the attack. Up to a quarter of the blue whales identified in Baja bear scars from orca attacks.

Blue whales may be wounded, sometimes fatally, after colliding with ocean vessels, as well as becoming trapped or entangled in fishing gear. The ever-increasing amount of ocean noise, including sonar, drowns out the vocalizations produced by whales, which may make it harder for them to communicate. Human threats to the potential recovery of blue whale populations also include accumulation of polychlorinated biphenyl (PCB) chemicals within the whale's body.

With global warming causing glaciers and permafrost to melt rapidly and allowing a large amount of fresh water to flow into the oceans, there are concerns that if the amount of fresh water in the oceans reaches a critical point, there will be a disruption in the thermohaline circulation. Considering the blue whale's migratory patterns are based on ocean temperature, a disruption in this circulation, which moves warm and cold water around the world, would be likely to have an effect on their migration. The whales summer in the cool, high latitudes, where they feed in krill-abundant waters; they winter in warmer, low latitudes, where they mate and give birth.

The change in ocean temperature would also affect the blue whale's food supply. The warming trend and decreased salinity levels would cause a significant shift in krill location and abundance.

The Natural History Museum in London contains a famous mounted skeleton and life-size model of a blue whale, which were both the first of their kind in the world, but have since been replicated at the University of California, Santa Cruz. Similarly, the American Museum of Natural History in New York City has a full-size model in its Milstein Family Hall of Ocean Life. A juvenile blue whale skeleton is installed at the New Bedford Whaling Museum in New Bedford, Massachusetts.

The Aquarium of the Pacific in Long Beach, California features a life-size model of a mother blue whale with her calf suspended from the ceiling of its main hall. The Beaty Biodiversity Museum at the University of British Columbia, Canada, houses a display of a blue whale skeleton (skull is cast replica) directly on the main campus boulevard. A real skeleton of a blue whale at the Canadian Museum of Nature in Ottawa, Canada was also unveiled in May 2010.

The Museum of Natural History in Gothenburg, Sweden contains the only stuffed blue whale in the world. There one can also find the skeleton of the whale mounted beside the whale.

Living blue whales may be encountered on whale-watching cruises in the Gulf of Maine and are the main attractions along the north shore of the Gulf of Saint Lawrence and in the Saint Lawrence estuary. Whale-watching, principally of blue whales, is also carried out south of Sri Lanka; boats leave from Mirissa harbour.

Seawater is water from a sea or ocean. On average, seawater in the world's oceans has a salinity of about 3.5 per cent (35 g/L, or 599 mM). This means that every kilogram (roughly one litre by volume) of seawater has approximately 35 grams (1.2 oz) of dissolved salts (predominantly sodium (Na^+) and chloride (Cl^-) ions). The average density of seawater at the ocean surface is 1.025 g/ml. Seawater is denser than both fresh water and pure water (density 1.0 g/ml @ 4°C (39°F)) because the dissolved salts add mass without contributing significantly to the volume. The freezing point of sea water decreases as salt concentration increases. At a typical salinity it freezes at about -2°C (28°F). The coldest sea water ever recorded (in a liquid state) was in 2010, in a stream under an Antarctic glacier, and measured -2.6°C (27.3°F).

Although the vast majority of seawater has a salinity of between 3.1 per cent and 3.8 per cent, seawater is not uniformly saline throughout the world. Where mixing occurs with fresh water runoff from river mouths or near melting glaciers, seawater can be substantially less saline. The most saline open sea is the Red Sea, where high rates of evaporation, low precipitation and river inflow, and confined circulation result in unusually salty water. The salinity in isolated bodies of water (for example, the Dead Sea) can be considerably greater still.

The density of surface seawater ranges from about 1,020 to 1,029 kg•m^{-3}, depending on the temperature and salinity. Deep in the ocean, under high pressure, seawater can reach a density of 1,050 kg•m^{-3} or higher. Seawater pH is limited to the range 7.5 to 8.4. The speed of sound in seawater is about 1,500 metres/second, and varies with water temperature, salinity, and pressure.

Seawater contains more dissolved ions than all types of freshwater. However, the ratios of various solutes differ dramatically. For instance; although seawater contains about 2.8 times the bicarbonate than river water based on molarity, the percentage of bicarbonate in seawater as a ratio of all dissolved ions is far lower than in river water. Bicarbonate ions also constitute 48 per cent of river water solutes, but only 0.14 per cent of all seawater ions. Differences like these are due to the varying residence times of seawater solutes;

sodium and chlorine have very long residence times, while calcium (vital for carbonate formation) tends to precipitate much more quickly. The most abundant dissolved ions in seawater are sodium, chloride, magnesium, sulfate and calcium.

Scientific theories behind the origins of sea salt started with Sir Edmond Halley in 1715, who proposed that salt and other minerals were carried into the sea by rivers after rainfall washed it out of the ground. Upon reaching the ocean, these salts concentrated as the process of evaporation removed the water. Halley noted that most lakes that don't have ocean outlets have high salt content. Halley termed this process 'continental weathering'.

Halley's theory is partly correct. In addition, sodium leached out of the ocean floor when the ocean formed. The presence of salt's other dominant ion, chloride, results from outgassing of chloride (as hydrochloric acid) with other gases from Earth's interior via volcanos and hydrothermal vents. The sodium and chloride ions subsequently became the most abundant constituents of sea salt.

Ocean salinity has been stable for billions of years, most likely as a consequence of a chemical/tectonic system which removes as much salt as is deposited; for instance, sodium and chloride sinks include evaporite deposits, pore water burial, and reactions with seafloor basalts. Since the ocean's formation, sodium no longer leaches from the ocean floor, but instead is captured in sedimentary layers covering the ocean bed. One theory is that plate tectonics forces salt under the continental land masses, where it slowly leaches again to the surface.

Accidentally consuming small quantities of clean seawater is not harmful, especially if the seawater is consumed along with a larger quantity of fresh water. However, drinking seawater to maintain hydration is counterproductive; more water must be excreted to eliminate the salt (via urine) than the amount of water that is gained from drinking the seawater itself.

This occurs because the renal system actively regulates human blood's sodium chloride within a very narrow range around 9 g/L (0.9% by weight). Seawater contains varying concentrations of dissolved sodium chloride, depending on its source, ranging from about 2 per cent in parts of the Baltic, to over 4 per cent in parts of the eastern Mediterranean and Red sea. In most open waters concentrations vary somewhat around typical values of about 3.5 per cent, all of them far higher than the body can tolerate in the blood, and most of them beyond what the kidney can deal with. A point frequently overlooked in optimistic arguments that the kidney can in fact excrete NaCl in Baltic concentrations, is that the gut cannot absorb water at such concentrations, so that logically there should be no profit in drinking seawater. At best, drinking seawater temporarily increases blood's concentration of sodium chloride. This in turn signals the kidney to excrete sodium, but seawater's sodium concentration is above the kidney's maximum concentrating ability. Eventually the blood's sodium concentration will rise to toxic levels, removing water from all cells and interfering with nerve conduction, ultimately producing fatal seizure and heart arrhythmia.

Survival manuals consistently advise against drinking seawater. For example, the book 'Medical Aspects of Harsh Environments' presents a summary of 163 life raft voyages. The risk of death was 39 per cent for those who drank seawater, compared to only 3 per cent for those who did not drink seawater. The effect of seawater intake has also been studied in laboratory settings in rats. This study confirmed the negative effects of drinking seawater when dehydrated.

The temptation to drink seawater has always been greatest for sailors who have expended their supply of fresh water, and are unable to capture enough rainwater for drinking. This frustration is described famously by a line from researcher:

"Water, water, everywhere,
And all the boards did shrink;
Water, water, everywhere,
Nor any drop to drink".

Although it is clear that a human cannot survive on seawater alone, some people claim that one can drink up to two cups a day, mixed with fresh water in a 2:3 ratio, without ill effect. The French physician Alain Bombard survived an ocean crossing in a small Zodiak rubber boat using mainly raw fish meat which contains about 40 per cent water (like most living tissues), also small amounts of seawater and other provisions harvested from the ocean. Naturally, the veracity of his findings was challenged but an alternative explanation to Bombard's survival was not given. In Kon-Tiki, Thor Heyerdahl reported drinking seawater mixed with fresh in a 40/60 per cent ratio. A few years later another adventurer named William Willis claimed to have drunk two cups of seawater and one cup of fresh per day for 70 days without ill effect when he lost part of his water supply.

Most modern ocean-going vessels create drinkable (potable) water from seawater using desalination processes such as vacuum distillation or multi-stage flash distillation in an evaporator, or more recently by reverse osmosis. However these processes are energy intensive, and most were not usually available during the Age of Sail. Larger sailing warships with large crews, such as Nelson's HMS Victory were fitted with distilling apparatus in their galleys.

Other land animals and marine animals such as fish, whales, and penguins can adapt to a high saline habitat. For example, the desert rat can survive by drinking seawater because its kidney can concentrate sodium far more efficiently than the human kidney.

17 Harbor Seal

The harbor (or harbour) seal (*Phoca vitulina*), also known as the common seal, is a true seal found along temperate and Arctic marine coastlines of the Northern Hemisphere. They are found in coastal waters of the northern Atlantic and Pacific Oceans, as well as those of the Baltic and North Seas, making them the most widely distributed of the pinnipeds (walruses, eared seals, and true seals).

Common seals are brown, tan, or gray, with distinctive V-shaped nostrils. An adult can attain a length of 1.85 metres (6.1 ft) and a mass of 132 kilograms (290 lb). Females outlive males (30-35 years versus 20-25 years). Common seals stick to familiar resting spots or haulout sites, generally rocky areas (although ice, sand and mud may also be used) where they are protected from adverse weather conditions and predation, near a foraging area. Males may fight over mates underwater and on land. Females are believed [according to whom?] to mate with the strongest males and generally bear a single pup, which they care for alone. Pups are able to swim and dive within hours of birth, and they develop quickly on their mothers' fat-rich milk. A fatty tissue layer called blubber is present under their skins and helps to maintain body temperature.

Their global population is 5-6 million, but subspecies in certain habitats are threatened. Seal hunting or sealing, once a common practice, is now illegal in most nations within the animal's range.

With each individual possessing a unique pattern of fine, dark spots (or light spots on a dark background in some variants), they vary in colour from brownish black to tan or grey; underparts are generally lighter. The body and flippers are short, with a proportionately large, rounded head. The nostrils appear distinctively V-shaped; as with other true seals, there is no ear flap, or pinna. A relatively large (for a seal) ear canal may be visible behind the eye. Including the head and flippers, they may reach an adult length of 1.85 metres (6.1 ft) and a weight of 55 to 168 kg (120 to 370 lb). Females are generally smaller than males.

With an estimated 5 million to 6 million individuals, the population is not threatened as a whole; most subspecies are secure in numbers, with the Greenland, Hokkaido- and Baltic Sea populations being exceptions. Local populations have been reduced or eliminated through outbreaks of disease (especially the phocine distemper virus) and conflict with humans, both unintentionally and intentionally, has also been linked to common seal declines. While it is legal to kill seals which are perceived to threaten fisheries in the United Kingdom, Norway and Canada, commercial hunting is illegal; the seals are also taken in subsistence hunting and accidentally as bycatch in fishing nets. Seals in the United Kingdom are protected by the 1970 Conservation of Seals Act, which prohibits killing them in most circumstances. In the United States, alternative protection applies and it is illegal to kill any seals or any marine mammals, as they fall under the Marine Mammal Protection Act. On the East Coast of the United States, their numbers seem to be increasing quite steadily as they are reclaiming parts of their range, and have been seen as far south as Florida.

Female common seals have a life span of 30-35 years, while male life spans are usually 20-25.

There are five subspecies of Phoca vitulina:

1. Western Atlantic common seals, P.v. concolor inhabit eastern North America.

2. Ungava seals, P.v. mellonae are found in eastern Canada in freshwater (included in P.v. concolor by many authors).
3. Pacific common seals, P.v. richardsi are located in western North America.
4. Insular seals, Phoca vitulina stejnegeri are in eastern Asia.
5. Eastern Atlantic common seals, P.v. vitulina from Europe and western Asia, are one of the most common seal species in the world.

Characterized as showing a strong degree of site fidelity in their choice of resting sites, they may spend several days at sea and travel up to 50 kilometres in search of feeding grounds, and will also swim some distance upstream into freshwater in large rivers. Resting sites may be both rugged, rocky coasts, such as those of the Hebrides or the shorelines of New England, or sandy beaches. They also inhabit sandy intertidal zones; some seals may also enter estuaries in pursuit of their fish prey. Some have even taken to feeding and playing in New York Harbor and Boston Harbor in recent years. The seals frequently choose to congregate in harbors, lending the animals their other common name. The feeding habits have been studied closely in many parts of their range; they are known to prey primarily upon fish, such as menhaden, anchovy, sea bass, herring, mackerel, cod, whiting and flatfish, and occasionally upon shrimp, crabs, mollusks and squid. Although primarily coastal, dives to over 500 m have been recorded. Common seals have been recorded to attack, kill and eat several kinds of seabirds.

Characterized as showing a strong degree of site fidelity in their choice of resting sites, they may spend several days at sea and travel up to 50 kilometres in search of feeding grounds, and will also swim some distance upstream into freshwater in large rivers. Resting sites may be both rugged, rocky coasts, such as those of the Hebrides or the shorelines of New England, or sandy beaches. They also inhabit sandy intertidal zones; some seals may also enter estuaries in pursuit of their fish prey. Some have even taken to feeding and playing in New York Harbor and Boston Harbor in recent years. The seals frequently choose to congregate in harbors, lending the animals their other common name. The feeding habits have been studied closely in many parts of their range; they are known to prey primarily upon fish, such as menhaden, anchovy, sea bass, herring, mackerel, cod, whiting and flatfish, and occasionally upon shrimp, crabs, mollusks and squid. Although primarily coastal, dives to over 500 m have been recorded. Common seals have been recorded to attack, kill and eat several kinds of seabirds.

While not forming groups as large as some other seals, they are gregarious animals. When not actively feeding, the seals will haul onto a terrestrial resting site. The seals tend to be coastal, not venturing more than 20 kilometres offshore. Both courtship and mating occur underwater. The mating system is not known, but thought to be polygamous. Females give birth once per year, with a gestation period of approximately nine months.

Birthing of pups occurs annually on shore. The timing of the pupping season varies with location, occurring in February for populations in lower latitudes, and as late as July in the subarctic zone. The mothers are the sole providers of care, with lactation lasting four to six weeks. Researchers have found males gather underwater, turn on their backs, put their heads together and vocalize to attract females ready for breeding. The single pups are born and well developed, capable of swimming and diving within hours. Suckling for three to four weeks, pups feed on the mother's rich, fatty milk and grow rapidly; born weighing up to 16 kilograms, the pups may double their weight by the time of weaning.

Common seals must spend a great deal of time on shore when moulting (shedding their fur), which the seals undergo shortly after breeding. This onshore time is important to the life cycle, and can be disturbed when there is substantial human presence The timing of onset of moult depends on the age and sex of the animal with yearlings moulting first and adult males last. A female will mate again immediately following the weaning of her pup. This pinniped is sometimes reluctant to haul out in the presence of humans, so shoreline development and access must be carefully studied in known locations of seal haul out.

The California population of subspecies richardsi amounted to approximately 25,000 individuals as of 1984. Pacific common seals or Californian common seals are found along the entire Pacific coast shoreline of the state. They prefer to remain relatively close to shore in subtidal and intertidal zones, and have not been seen beyond the Channel Islands as a pelagic form; moreover, they will often venture into bays and estuaries and even swim up coastal rivers.

Frequently, they will haul out in small to medium-sized groups onto rock outcrops, mudflats, sandy beaches or even fishing piers. Some of the best locations for viewing common seals up close are at Cannery Row in Monterey, Moss Landing on Monterey Bay or at Bolinas Lagoon in Marin County. They feed in shallow littoral waters on herring, flounder, hake, anchovy, codfish and sculpin.

In California, breeding occurs from March to May, and pupping between April and May, depending on local populations. There is no indication this species has territorial characteristics in water, and it definitely displays none on land. As top level feeders in the kelp forest, common seals enhance species diversity and productivity. They are preyed upon by orcas and white sharks.

Considerable scientific inquiry has been carried out by The Marine Mammal Centre and other research organisations beginning in the 1980s regarding the incidence and transmission of diseases in common seals in the wild, including analysis of phocine herpesvirus. In the San Francisco Bay, some common seals are fully or partially reddish in colour. This may be caused by an accumulation of trace elements, such as iron or selenium, in the ocean or a change in the hair follicles.

Earless Seal

The true seals or earless seals are one of the three main groups of mammals within the seal superfamily, Pinnipedia. All true seals are members of the family Phocidae. They are sometimes called crawling seals to distinguish them from the fur seals and sea lions of the family Otariidae. Seals live in the oceans of both hemispheres and are mostly confined to polar, subpolar, and temperate climates, with the exception of the more tropical monk seals.

Adult phocids vary from 1.17 metres (3.8 ft) in length and 45 kilograms (99 lb) in weight, in the ringed seal, to 4.9 metres (16 ft) and 2,400 kilograms (5,291 lb) in the southern elephant seal.

Phocids are more specialized for aquatic life than otariids. They lack external ears and have sleek, streamlined bodies. Retractable nipples, internal testicles and an internal penis sheath provide further streamlining. A smooth layer of blubber lies underneath the skin. Phocids are able to divert blood flow to this layer to help control their temperature.

Limbs

Their fore flippers are used primarily for steering, while their hind flippers are bound to the pelvis in such a way that they cannot bring them under their body to walk on them.

They are more streamlined than fur seals and sea lions and can therefore swim more effectively over long distances. However, because they cannot turn their hind flippers downward, they are very clumsy on land, having to wriggle with their front flippers and abdominal muscles.

Phocids have fewer teeth than land-based members of the Carnivora, although they retain powerful canines. Some species lack molars altogether.

Phocid respiratory and circulatory systems are adapted to allow diving to considerable depths, and they can spend a long time underwater between breaths. Air is forced from the lungs during a dive and into the upper respiratory passages, where gases cannot easily be absorbed into the bloodstream. This helps protect the seal from the bends. The middle ear is also lined with blood sinuses that inflate during diving, helping to maintain a constant pressure.

While otariids are known for speed and maneuverability, phocids are known for efficient, economical movement. This allows most phocids to forage far from land to exploit prey resources, while otariids are tied to rich upwelling zones close to breeding sites.

Phocids swim by sideways movements of their bodies, using their hind flippers to fullest effect.

Phocids spend most of their time at sea, although they return to land or pack ice to breed and give birth.

Pregnant females spend long periods foraging at sea, building up fat reserves, and then return to the breeding site to use their stored energy to nurse pups. The common seal, Phoca vitulina, also known as the harbor seal, displays a reproductive strategy similar to that of otariids in which the mother makes short foraging trips between nursing bouts.

Because a phocid mother's feeding grounds are often hundreds of kilometres from the breeding site, she must fast while lactating. This combination of fasting with lactation requires the mother to provide large amounts of energy to her pup at a time when she is not eating (and often, not drinking.) Mothers must supply their own metabolic needs while nursing. This is a miniature version of the humpback whale's strategy. They fast during their months-long migration from arctic feeding areas to tropical breeding/nursing areas and back.

Phocids produce thick, fat-rich milk that allows them to provide their pups with large amounts of energy in a short period. This allows the mother to return to the sea in time to replenish her reserves. Lactation ranges from 28 days in the northern elephant seal to just three to five days in the hooded seal. The mother ends nursing by leaving her pup at the breeding site to search for food (pups continue to nurse if given the opportunity). 'Milk stealers' that suckle from unrelated, sleeping females are not uncommon; this often results in the death of the mother's pup, since a single female can only feed one pup.

The pup's diet is so high in calories, it builds up a fat store. Before the pup is ready to forage, the mother abandons it, and the pup consumes its own fat for weeks or months while it matures. Seals, like all marine mammals, need time to develop the oxygen stores, swimming muscles, and neural pathways necessary for effective diving and foraging. Seal pups typically eat no food and drink no water during the period, although some polar species eat snow. The postweaning fast ranges from two weeks in the hooded seal to 9-12 weeks in the northern elephant seal. The physiological and behavioural adaptations that allow phocid pups to endure these remarkable fasts, which are among the longest for any mammal, remain an area of active study and research.

In the 1980s, phylogenetic analysis of the phocids has led to a few conclusions about the interrelatedness of the various genera. The four genera Hydrurga, Leptonychotes, Lobodon, and Ommatophoca form a monophyletic group, the tribe Lobodontini. Likewise, the Phocinae subfamily (Erignathus, Cystophora, Halichoerus, and Phoca) is also monophyletic. More recently, five species have been split off from Phoca, forming three additional genera. However, the family Monachinae (the lobodonts plus Monachus and Mirounga) is probably paraphyletic.

Super Family Pinnipedia

- Family Otariidae: Fur seals and sea lions
- Family Odobenidae: Walrus
- Family Phocidae
- Subfamily Monachinae
- Tribe Monachini
- Monachopsis
- Pristiphoca
- Properiptychus
- Messiphoca
- Mesotaria
- Callophoca
- Pliophoca
- Pontophoca
- Hawaiian monk seal, Monachus schauinslandi

- Mediterranean monk seal, Monachus monachus
- Caribbean monk seal, Monachus tropicalis (probably extinct around 1950)
- Tribe Miroungini
- Northern elephant seal, Mirounga angustirostris
- Southern elephant seal, Mirounga leonina
- Tribe Lobodontini
- Monotherium wymani
- Ross seal, Ommatophoca rossi
- Crabeater seal, Lobodon carcinophagus
- Leopard seal, Hydrurga leptonyx
- Weddell seal, Leptonychotes weddellii
- Acrophoca longirostris
- Piscophoca pacifica
- Homiphoca capensis
- Subfamily Phocinae
- Kawas benegasorum
- Leptophoca lenis
- Preapusa
- Cryptophoca
- Bearded seal, Erignathus barbatus
- Hooded seal, Cystophora cristata
- Tribe Phocini
- Common seal or harbor seal, Phoca vitulina
- Spotted seal, Phoca largha
- Ringed seal, Pusa hispida (formerly Phoca hispida)
- Baikal seal, Pusa sibirica (formerly Phoca sibirica)
- Caspian seal, Pusa caspica (formerly Phoca caspica)
- Harp seal, Pagophilus groenlandica (formerly Phoca groenlandicus)
- Ribbon seal, Histriophoca fasciata (formerly Phoca fasciata)
- Phocanella
- Platyphoca

- Gryphoca
- Grey seal, Halichoerus grypus
- Evolution
- Piscophoca pacifica fossil

The earliest fossil phocids date from the mid-Miocene, 15 million years ago in the north Atlantic. Until recently, many researchers believed phocids evolved separately from otariids and odobenids from otter-like animals, such as Potamotherium, which inhabited European fresh-water lakes. Recent evidence strongly suggests a monophyletic origin for all pinnipeds from a single ancestor, possibly Enaliarctos, most closely related to the bears.

Monk seals and elephant seals are believed to have first entered the Pacific through the open straits between North and South America, which closed only in the Pliocene. The various Antarctic species may have either used the same route, or traveled down the west coast of Africa.

Seal Hunting

Seal hunting, or sealing, is the personal or commercial hunting of seals. The hunt is currently practiced in five countries: Canada, where most of the world's seal hunting takes place, Namibia, the Danish region of Greenland, Norway and Russia. Canada's largest market for seals is Norway.

The Canadian Department of Fisheries and Oceans (DFO) regulates the seal hunt in Canada. It sets quotas (total allowable catch-TAC), monitors the hunt, studies the seal population, works with the Canadian Sealing Association to train sealers on new regulations, and promotes sealing through its website and spokes people.

The DFO set kill quotas of 270,000 seals in 2007, 275,000 in 2008, 280,000 in 2009, and 330,000 in 2010. The actual kills in recent years have been less than the quotas: 82,800 in 2007, 217,800 in 2008, 72,400 in 2009, and 67,000 in 2010. In 2007, Norway claimed that 29,000 harp seals were killed in its seal hunt, and Russia and Greenland claimed that 5,476 and 90,000 seals were killed in 2007, respectively.

Harp seal populations in the northwest Atlantic declined to approximately 2 million in the late 1960s as a result of Canada's annual kill rates that averaged over 291,000 from 1952 to 1970. Conservationists demanded reduced rates of killing and stronger regulations to avert the extinction of the harp seals. In response, in 1971, the Canadian government instituted a quota system. Animal rights activists were annoyed that penalties where not imposed for exceeding the quota. This displayed an ignorance of the system in use at that time. The system was competitive, with each boat catching as many seals as it could before the hunt closed, which the Department of Fisheries did when they knew that years quota had been reached. Because it was thought that the competitive element might cause sealers to cut corners, new regulations where introduced that limited the catch to 400 Seals per day, and 2000 per boat total.

A 2007 population survey conducted by the Canadian Department of Fisheries and Oceans (DFO) estimated the current population at 5.5 million (95% CI 3.8 million - 7.1 million). It is illegal in Canada to hunt newborn harp seals (whitecoats) and young hooded seals (bluebacks). When the seal pups begin to molt their downy white fur at the age of 12-14 days, they are called 'ragged-jacket' and can be commercially hunted. After molting, the seals are called 'beaters', named for the way they beat the water with their flippers. The hunt remains highly controversial, attracting significant media coverage and protests each year. Images from past hunts have become iconic symbols for conservation, animal welfare, and animal rights advocates. In 2009, Russia banned the hunting of harp seals less than one year old.

Archeological evidence indicates the Native Americans and First Nations People in Canada have been hunting seals for at least 4,000 years. Traditionally, when an Inuit boy killed his first seal or caribou, a feast was held. The meat was an important source of fat, protein, vitamin A, vitamin B_{12} and iron, and the pelts were prized for their warmth. The Inuit diet is rich in fish, whale, and seal.

Traditional Inuit seal hunting accounts for three per cent of the total hunt; it is excluded from the European Commission's call in 2006 for a ban on the import, export and sale of all harp and hooded seal products. Ringed seals were once the main staple for food, and have been used for clothing, boots, fuel for lamps, a delicacy, containers, igloo windows, and furnished harnesses for huskies. Though no longer used to this extent, ringed seals are still an important food source for the people of Nunavut. Called nayiq by the Central Alaskan Yup'ik people, the ringed seal is also hunted and eaten in Alaska.

Migratory fishermen began hunting seals in the region of Newfoundland and Labrador and the Gulf of St. Lawrence in the 1500s. Large scale commercial seal hunting outside of Europe began with the Newfoundland seal hunt, which became an annual event starting in 1723 and expanded rapidly near the turn of the 18th century. Growing from the enormous international Grand Banks fishery, the Newfoundland hunt began with small schooner-based hunts. Kill rates averaging 451,000 in the 1830s, rising to 546,000 annually during the first half of the next decade, led to a marked decline in the harp seal population, which adversely impacted profitability of the sealing industry.

In the 1870s, the industry was transformed by the arrival of large, steam-powered sealing vessels, such as the steam barquentines Bear and Terra Nova, which could smash through ice packs to the heart of large seal herds. These large and expensive ships required major capital investments from British and Newfoundland firms, and shifted the industry from merchants in small outports to companies based in St. John's, Newfoundland. By the late 19th century, the sealing industry in Newfoundland was second in importance only to cod fishing. The seal hunt provided critical winter wages for fishermen, but remained harsh and dangerous work, marked by major sealing disasters which claimed hundreds of lives, such as the loss the 1914 Newfoundland Sealing Disaster involving the SS Southern Cross, the SS Newfoundland and

SS Stephano. After World War II, the Newfoundland hunt was dominated by large Norwegian sealing vessels until the late 20th century, when the much diminished hunt shifted to smaller motor fishing vessels, based from outports around Newfoundland and Labrador. In 2007, the commercial seal hunt dividend contributed about $6 million to the Newfoundland GDP, a fraction of the industry's former importance.

Sealing spread further in the late 18th century, when seal herds in the southern hemisphere began to be hunted by whalers. In 1778, English sealers brought back from the Island of South Georgia and the Magellan Strait area as many as 40,000 seal skins and 2,800 tons of elephant seal oil. In 1791, 102 vessels, manned by 3000 sealers, were hunting seals south of the equator. The principal American sealing ports were Stonington and New Haven, Connecticut. Most of the pelts taken during these expeditions would be sold in China.

Pacific

Commercial sealing in Australasia appears to have started with Eber Bunker, master of the William and Ann who announced his intention in November 1791 to visit Dusky Sound in New Zealand, did call in that country and had skins on board when he got back to Britain. Captain Raven of the Britannia stationed a party at Dusky from 1792-93, but the discovery of Bass Strait, between mainland Australia and Van Diemen's Land, now called Tasmania, saw the sealers' focus shift there in 1798, when a gang including Daniel Cooper was landed from the Nautilus on Cape Barren Island. With Bass Strait over-exploited by 1802 attention returned to southern New Zealand where Stewart Island/Rakiura and Foveaux Strait were explored, exploited and charted from 1803 to 1804. Thereafter, attention shifted to the subantarctic Antipodes Islands, 1805-7, the Auckland Islands from 1806, the southeast coast of New Zealand's South Island, Otago Harbour and Solander Island by 1809, before focusing further to the south at the newly discovered Campbell Island and Macquarie Island from 1810. In this time sealers were active on the southern coast of mainland Australia, for example at Kangaroo Island. This whole development has been called the first sealing boom and sparked the Sealers' War in southern New Zealand. By the mid teens of the 19th century, sealing had faded. There was a brief revival from 1823, but this was very short-lived. Although highly profitable at times and affording New South Wales one of its earliest trade staples, its unregulated character saw its self-destruction. Some traders were Australia-based, notably Simeon Lord, Henry Kable, James Underwood and Robert Campbell, but American and British traders and seamen were engaged in it, too, such as the Plummers of London and the Whitneys of New York.

By 1830, most Pacific seal stocks had been seriously depleted, and Lloyd's records only showed one full-time sealing vessel on its books. Since then, a number of nations have outlawed the hunting of seals and other marine mammals. The landmark North Pacific Fur Seal Convention of 1911 was the first international treaty specifically addressing wildlife conservation. Today, commercial sealing is conducted by only five nations: Canada, Greenland, Namibia, Norway, and Russia. The United States, which had been heavily involved in the sealing industry, now maintains a complete ban on the commercial hunting of marine mammals, with the exception of indigenous peoples who are allowed to hunt a small number of seals each year.

An older and more traditional method of killing seals is with a hakapik: a heavy wooden club with a hammer head and metal hook on the end. The hakapik is used because of its efficiency; the animal can be killed quickly without damage to its pelt. The hammer head is used to crush the seals' thin skulls, while the hook is used to move the carcasses. Canadian sealing regulations describe the dimensions of the clubs and the hakapiks, and caliber of the rifles and minimum bullet velocity, that can be used. They state: "Every person who strikes a seal with a club or hakapik shall strike the seal on the forehead until its skull has been crushed", and that "No person shall commence to skin or bleed a seal until the seal is dead", which occurs when it "has a glassy-eyed, staring appearance and exhibits no blinking reflex when its eye is touched while it is in a relaxed condition". Reportedly, in one study, three out of eight times, the animal was not rendered either dead or unconscious by shooting, and the hunters would then kill the seal using a hakapik or other club of a type that is sanctioned by the governing authority.

In Canada, the season for the commercial hunt of harp seal is from November 15 to May 15. Most sealing occurs in late March in the Gulf of St. Lawrence, and during the first or second week of April off Newfoundland, in an area known as the Front. This peak spring period is generally referred to as the 'Canadian Seal Hunt'.

In 2003, the three-year harp seal quota granted by Fisheries and Oceans Canada was increased to a maximum of 975,000 animals per three years, with a maximum of 350,000 animals in any two consecutive years. In 2006, 325,000 harp seals, as well as 10,000 hooded seals and 10,400 grey seals were killed. An additional 10,000 animals were allocated for hunting by aboriginal peoples. The current northwest Atlantic harp seal population is estimated at 5.6 million animals.

Although around 70 per cent of Canadian seals killed are taken on the Front, private monitors focus on the St. Lawrence hunt, because of its more convenient location. The 2006 St. Lawrence leg of the hunt was officially closed on Apr. 3, 2006; sealers had already exceeded the quota by 1,000 animals. On March 26, 2007 the Newfoundland and Labrador government launched a seal hunt website.

Warm winters in the Gulf of St. Lawrence have led to thinner and more unstable ice there. In 2007, Canada's federal fisheries ministry reported that while the pups are born on the ice as usual, the ice floes have started to break up before the pups learn to swim, causing the pups to drown. Canada reduced the 2007 quota by 20 per cent, because overflights showed large numbers of seal pups were lost to thin and melting ice. In southern Labrador and off Newfoundland's northeast coast, however, there was extra heavy ice in 2007, and the coast guard estimated as many as 100 vessels were trapped in ice simultaneously.

The 2010 hunt was cut short because demand for seal pelts was down. Only one local pelt buyer, NuTan Furs, offered to purchase pelts; and it committed to purchase less than 15,000 pelts. Pelt prices were about C$21/pelt in 2010, which is about twice the 2009 price and about 64 per cent of the 2007 price. The reduced demand is attributable mainly to the 2009 ban on imports of seal products into the European Union.

The 2010 winter was unusually warm, with little ice forming in the Gulf of St. Lawrence in February and March, when harp seals give birth to their pups on ice floes. Around the Gulf, harp seals arrived in late winter to give birth on near-shore ice and even on beaches rather than on their usual whelping grounds: sturdy sea ice. Also, seal pups born elsewhere began floating to shore on small, shrinking pieces of ice. Many others stayed too far north, out of reach of all but the most determined hunters. Environment Canada, the weather forecasting agency, reported the ice was at the lowest level on record.

Regulations

The Fisheries Act established 'Seal Protection Regulations' in the mid-1960s. The regulations were combined with other Canadian marine mammals regulations in 1993, to form the 'Marine Mammal Regulations'. In addition to describing the use of the rifle and hakapik, the regulations state every person 'who fishes for seals for personal or commercial use shall land the pelt or the carcass of the seal'. The commercial hunting of infant harp seals (whitecoats) and infant hooded seals (bluebacks) was banned in 1987 under pressure from animal rights groups. Now, seals may only be killed once they have started molting (from 12 to 15 days of age), as this coincides with the time when they are abandoned by their mothers.

Export

Canada's biggest market for seal pelts is Norway. Carino Limited is one of Newfoundland's largest seal pelt producers. Carino is marketing its seal pelts mainly through its parent company, GC Rieber Skinn, Bergen, Norway. Canada sold pelts to eleven countries in 2004. The next largest were Germany, Greenland, and China/Hong Kong. Other importers were Finland, Denmark, France, Greece, South Korea, and Russia. Asia remains the principal market for seal meat exports. One of Canada's market access priorities for 2002 was to 'continue to press Korean authorities to obtain the necessary approvals for the sale of seal meat for human consumption in Korea'. Canadian and Korean officials agreed in 2003 on specific Korean import requirements for seal meat. For 2004, only Taiwan and South Korea purchased seal meat from Canada.

Canadian seal product exports reached C$18 million in 2006. Of this, C$5.4 million went to the EU. In 2009, the European Union banned all seal imports, shrinking the market. Where pelts once sold for more than $100, they now fetch $8 to $15 each.

Greenland

Although official figures for the Greenland seal hunt are not available, the government of Canada estimates 20,000 to 25,000 seals are killed in Greenland annually. In January 2006, the government of Greenland banned imports of Canadian seal skins, citing fears Canadian seals are brutally beaten to death. The boycott may be an effort to distance Greenland's own seal hunt from Canada's, and spare themselves negative press in the process. The ban was rescinded in May 2006, with the Greenland Home Rule Government noting the seal hunt in Canada has sensible regulations on hunting methods, drawn up in close cooperation with biologists, veterinarians, weapons experts and seal hunters. It further noted seal-hunting in Canada is subject to strict and extensive control measures, to ensure the use of effective and humane killing methods.

In Greenland, seal hunting is conducted with rifles - the seals being shot in the head from a small open boat while they sit on an ice floe. The shot needs to be very accurate and the boat must rush up to the seal to hook the carcass out of the water where it falls within a few seconds before it sinks. The economy of certain very rural Greenlandic villages, such as Aappilattoq, are highly dependent upon such seal hunting.

Namibia is the only country in the Southern Hemisphere culling seals. Although the protection and the sustainable use of natural resources is part of Namibia's constitution, it regularly conducts the second highest seal harvest in the world, mainly because of the huge amount of fish seals are estimated to consume. While a government-initiated study found seal colonies consume more fish than the entire fishing industry can catch, animal protection society Seal Alert South Africa estimated less than 0.3 per cent losses to commercial fisheries.

Harvesting is done from July to November on two places, Cape Cross and Atlas Bay, and in the past at Wolf Bay. These two colonies together account for 75 per cent of the cape fur seal population of the country.

Cape Cross is a tourism resort and the largest cape fur colony in Namibia. The Department of Tourism has stated that "Cape Cross Seal Reserve was established to protect the largest breeding colony of Cape fur seals in the world". In season, the resort is closed and sealed off during the culling in the early morning hours, journalists are not allowed to enter. Namibia's SPCA is allowed to observe the culling from 2010 onwards.

Namibia's Ministry of Fisheries announced a three-year rolling quota for the seal harvest, although different quotas per year are sometimes reported. The latest quota announced was in 2009, valid until 2011. The quotas are usually not filled by the concession holders.

In 2009, an unusual bid to end seal culling in Namibia was attempted when Seal Alert tried to raise money to purchase the only buyer of Namibian seals, Australian-based Hatem Yavuz, lock, stock, and barrel for US$14.2 million. The project did not materialise. The Government of Namibia, on the other hand, offered the International Fund for Animal Welfare (IFAW) an opportunity to buy out the two sealers in Namibia to finally end the culling. The offer was rejected.

Norway

The Norwegian sealing season runs from January to September. The hunt involves 'seal catching' by seagoing sealing boats on the Arctic ice shelf, and 'seal hunting' on the coast and islands of mainland Norway. The latter is carried out by small groups of licenced hunters shooting seals from land and using small boats to retrieve the catch.

In 2005, Norway began offering seal hunting as a tourist attraction. In 2006, 17,037 seals (including 13,390 harp and 3,647 hooded seals) were harvested. In 2007, the Norwegian Ministry of Fisheries and Coastal Affairs stated up to 13.5 million Norwegian krone (about US$2.6 million) would be given in funding to vessels in the 2007 Norwegian seal hunt.

Regulations All Norwegian sealing vessels are required to carry a qualified veterinary inspector on board. Norwegian sealers are required to pass a shooting test each year before the season starts, using the same weapon and ammunition as they would on the ice. Likewise, they have to pass a hakapik test.

Adult seals more than one year old must be shot in the head with expanding bullets, and cannot be clubbed to death. The hakapik shall be used to ensure the animal is dead. This is done by crushing the skull of the shot adult seal with the short end of the hakapik, before the long spike is thrust deep into the animal's brain. The seal shall then be bled by making an incision from its jaw to the end of its sternum. The killing and bleeding must be done on the ice, and live animals may never be brought onboard the ship. Young seals may be killed using just the hakapik, but only in the aforementioned manner, i.e., they need not be shot.

Seals in the water and seals with young may not be killed, and the use of traps, artificial lighting, aeroplanes or helicopters is forbidden.

The hakapik may only be used by certified seal-catchers (fangstmenn) operating in the pack ice of the Arctic Ocean and not by coastal seal hunters. All coastal seal hunters must be preapproved by the Norwegian Directorate of Fisheries and have to pass a large game hunting test.

In 2007, the European Food Safety Agency confirmed the animals are put to death faster and more humanely in the Norwegian sealing than in large game hunting on land.

In Norway in 2004, only Rieber worked with sealskin and seal oil. In 2001, the biggest producer of raw seal oil was Canada. (Two percent of the raw oil was processed and sold in Canadian health stores.) Rieber had the majority of all distribution of raw seal oil in the world market, but there was no demand for seal oil. From 1995 to 2005, Rieber annually received between 2 and 3 million Norwegian krone in subsidy. A 2003-2004 parliamentary report says CG Rieber Skinn is the only company in the world that delivers skin from bluebacks. Most of the skins processed by Rieber have been imported from abroad, mainly from Canada. Only a small portion is from the Norwegian hunt. Of the processed skin, five per cent is sold in Norway; the rest is exported to the Russian and Asian markets.

Fortuna Oils AS is a 100 per cent owned subsidiary of GC Rieber. They get the majority of their raw oil imported from Canada. They also have access to raw oil from the Norwegian hunt.

Russia

The Russian seal hunt has not been well monitored since the breakup of the Soviet Union. The quota in 1998 was 35,000 animals. Reportedly, many whitecoat pups are not properly killed and are transported, while injured, to processing areas. In January 2000, a bill to ban seal hunting was passed by the Russian parliament by 273 votes to 1, but was vetoed by President Vladimir Putin.

On September 21, 2007 in Arkhangelsk, the Norwegian GC Rieber Skinn AS proposed a joint Russian–Norwegian seal hunting project. The campaign was carried out from one hunt boat supplied by GS Rieber Skinn AS in 2007, lasted two weeks, and brought in 40 000 roubles per Russian hunter. GS Rieber skinn AS declared a plan to order 20 boats and donate them to the Pomor. CG Rieber Skinn AS, in 2007, established a daughter company in Arkhangelsk, called GC Rieber Skinn Pomor'e Lic.

The Norwegian company Polardrift AS, in 2007, had plans to establish a company in Russia, and operate under Russian flag, in close cooperation with GC Rieber Skinn Pomor'e.

Plans for the 2008 season included both helicopter-based hunts, mainly to take whitecoats, and boat-based hunts, mainly targeting beaters.

On March 18, 2009, Russia's Minister of Natural Resources and Ecology, Yuriy Trutnev, announced a complete ban on the hunting of harp seals younger than one year of age in the White Sea.

According to a 2002 peer-reviewed study done by five Canadian veterinarians and funded by the Canadian Veterinary Medical Association (CVMA) 2002 Daoust, *et al.* sealing report, "the large majority of seals taken during this hunt (at best, 98% in work reported here) are killed in an acceptably humane manner". These veterinarians found, "During the 2001 season in the Gulf, three (1.9%) of 158 seals brought on board of the sealing vessels and directly observed by Daoust had not been killed, and in one (0.86%) of 116 interactions between seals and sealers observed on videotapes by researchers, the seal also did not appear to have been killed before being hooked and brought on board". They thus concluded this small proportion of animals that are not killed efficiently justifies continued attention to this industry's activities, preferably by members of the veterinary profession, who are best equipped to assess the humaneness of the killing methods.

In observing four videos taken during the 2001 seal hunt in the Gulf of St. Lawrence, the authors of this report state, 'A large proportion (87%) of the sealers recorded on the four videotapes failed to palpate the skull or check the corneal reflex before proceeding to hook or bleed the seal or go to another seal'.

The Royal Commission on Seals and the Sealing Industry in Canada, also known as the Malouf Commission, concluded in a 1986 report, 'Judged by the criteria of rapidity of unconsciousness and particularly the absence of preslaughter stress, the clubbing of seal pups is, when properly performed, at least as humane as, and often more humane than, the killing methods used in commercial slaughterhouses, which are accepted by a majority of the public'. Royal Commission on Seals and the Sealing Industry in Canada 1986.

According to the Department of Fisheries and Oceans Canada (DFO), "The Marine Mammal Regulations stipulate that seals must be harvested quickly using only high-powered rifles, shotguns firing slugs, clubs or hakapiks".

However, a 2001 study, by Burdon, *et al.*,the IFAW Veterinary Report on the Canadian Commercial Seal Hunt 2001 conducted by five international veterinarians and commissioned by IFAW, an organisation that opposes the seal hunt, disputes these findings. This report concludes the Canadian commercial seal hunt results in considerable and unacceptable suffering.

The veterinarians examined 76 seal carcasses and found that in 17 per cent of the cases, there were no detectable lesions of the skull, leading them to conclude the clubbing likely did not result in loss of consciousness. In 25 per cent of the remaining cases, the carcasses had minimal to moderate skull fractures, indicative of a 'decreased level of consciousness', but probably not unconsciousness. The remaining 58 per cent of the carcasses examined showed extensive skull fractures.

This veterinary study included examination of video footage of 179 seals hunted in 1998, 1999, and 2000. In these videos, 96 seals were shot, 56 were shot and then clubbed or gaffed, 19 were clubbed or gaffed, and 8 were killed by unknown means. In 79 per cent of these cases, sealers did not check the corneal reflex to ensure that the seals were dead prior to hooking or skinning them. In only 6 per cent of these cases, seals were bled immediately, where struck. The average time from initial strike to bleeding was 66 seconds.

In 2005, IFAW published a comparison of the CVMA-funded study and its own study, entitled Canada's Commercial Seal Hunt is Not 'Acceptably Humane'. In this critique, researcher, writes, "The Burdon et al. evidence cited above addresses the question of whether seals were likely conscious or unconscious at the time they were skinned, using post-mortem examination of skulls. In marked contrast, the figure cited from Daoust et al.'s report represents the number of seals clubbed or shot that were brought on board sealing vessels while still conscious. That number ignores any and all animal suffering that occurs between the time animals are clubbed or shot until they eventually reach a sealing vessel, usually on the end of a hook or gaff". Another difference between these reports is 'Daoust *et al.*'s direct observations were made under very different conditions than those provided by Burdon *et al*. Unlike Burdon et al.'s observations, they were made directly from sealing vessels so that the sealers were unavoidably aware that observers were present. As Daoust et al. admit, the presence of an observer on a sealing vessel "may have incited sealers to hit the seals skulls more vigorously". Of course, the presence of an observer also has the potential to modify other sealing practices, including checking for a corneal reflex and bleeding animals immediately after clubbing.

In 2005, the World Wildlife Fund (WWF) commissioned the Independent Veterinarians Working Group Report. With reference to video evidence, the report states: "Perception of the seal hunt seems to be based largely on emotion, and on visual images that are often difficult even for experienced observers to interpret with certainty. While a hakapik strike on the skull of a seal appears brutal, it is humane if it achieves rapid, irreversible loss of consciousness leading to death".

Ecological Feasibility

In 2007, the Canadian Department of Fisheries and Oceans conducted a population survey. The resulting estimate of the harp seal population was 5.5 million (95% CI 3.8 million to 7.1 million). In 2005, the population estimate was similar: 5.8 million (95% CI 4.1 million to 7.6 million).

Prior to the arrival of European settlers, a much larger population of harp seals migrated to the waters off Newfoundland and Labrador. Settlers began exploiting the population, with kills peaking in the middle of the 1800s. In the first half of the 1840s, 546,000 seals were killed annually. This led to a population decline that adversely affected the industry.

In the 1950s and 1960s an average of over 291,000 seal pups were killed each year. This led to a population decline to less than 2 million seals. Conservationists became alarmed and demanded controls on kill rates. Thus in 1971, Canada instituted a quota system. In the years from 1971 to 1982, an average of 165,627 seals were killed.

In 1983, the European Union banned the import of whitecoat harp seal pup pelts (pelts from pups less than about two weeks of age, when the pups molt). As a result, the market for pelts dropped. The kill rates thus declined in subsequent years to an average of about 52,000 seals from 1983 to 1995. During this time, the harp seal population increased.

After the European Union's ban on whitecoat pelt imports, the Canadian government and sealing industry developed markets for the pelts of beaters. In 1996, the kill rates again increased to over 200,000 each year, except in the year 2000. In 2002 and 2004 to 2006, over 300,000 seal pups were killed each year.

As a result of population concerns, Norway's seal hunt is now controlled by quotas based on recommendations from International Council for the Exploration of the Sea (ICES), However, sealing in Norway has declined in recent years, and the quotas have not been reached.

In addition to hunting pressures on the population of harp seals, as ice seals that are dependent on solid sea ice for whelping, the harp seal population is affected by global climate change. The lack of sea ice in recent years has resulted in the drowning deaths of tens of thousands of newborn harp seal pups

Animal welfare advocates and organisations, such as PETA, object to the use of real fur when many synthetic 'faux fur' alternatives are available. Fur advocates claim that faux fur does not compare to real fur's superior warmth and style. They also claim it is a renewable resource and synthetic fur is a petroleum-based product and can release highly tcxic prussic acid into the environment.

Economic Impact

According to Canadian authorities, the value of the 2004 seal harvest was C$16.5 million, which significantly contributes to seal manufacturing companies, and for several thousand fishermen and First Nations peoples. For some sealers, they claim, proceeds from the hunt make up a third of their annual income. Critics, however, say this represents only a tiny fraction of the C$600-million Newfoundland fishing industry. Sealing opponents also say $16.5 million is insignificant, compared to the funding required to regulate and subsidize the hunt. For 1995 and 1996, there are confirmed reports Fisheries and Oceans Canada encouraged maximum utilization of harvested seals through a $0.20 per pound meat subsidy. The level of subsidy totalled $650,000 in 1997, $440,000 in 1998 and $250,000 in 1999. There were no meat subsidies in 2000. Some critics, such as the McCartneys, have suggested promoting that area as an ecotourism site would be far more lucrative than the annual harvest.

In March 2005, Greenpeace asked the DFO to 'dispel the myth that seals are hampering the recovery of cod stocks'. In doing so, they implied the seal hunt is, at least in part, a cull designed to increase cod stocks. Cod fishing has traditionally been a key part of the Atlantic fishery, and an important part of the economy of Newfoundland and Labrador. Fisheries and Oceans Canada responded there is no connection between the annual seal harvest and the cod fishery, and that the seal hunt is 'established on sound conservation principles'.

Many animal protection groups encourage people to petition against the harvest. Respect for Animals and Humane Society International believe the hunt will be ended only by the financial pressure of a boycott of Canadian seafood. In 2005, the Humane Society of the United States (HSUS) called for such a boycott in the United States.

Protesters frequently use images of whitecoats, despite Canada's ban on the commercial hunting of suckling pups. The HSUS explains this by saying images of the legally hunted ragged jackets are nearly indistinguishable from those of whitecoats. Also, they state, according to official DFO kill reports, 97 per cent of the estimated million harp seals killed in the last four years have been under three months old, and the majority of these are less than one month old.

On March 26, 2006, seven antisealing activists were arrested in the Gulf of St. Lawrence for violating the terms of their observer permits. By law, observers must maintain a ten-metre distance between themselves and the sealers. Five of the protesters were later acquitted. In the same month, as part of a counterprotest, Newfoundland and Labrador Premier Danny Williams encouraged people in the province to boycott Costco after the retailer decided to stop carrying seal oil capsules. Costco stated politics played no role in their decision to remove the capsules, and on April 4 that year, they were again being sold in Costco stores.

The law was approved by the Council of the European Union without debate on July 27, 2009. Denmark, Romania, and Austria abstained. The Canadian government responded to the move by stating that it will take the European Union to the World Trade Organisation if the ban does not exempt Canada. Canadian Inuits from Nunavut territory have opposed the ban and lobbied European Parliament members against it. The legislation banning seal products is likely to come into effect before the beginning of the hunting season in 2010.

Numerous celebrities have opposed the commercial seal hunt. Rex Murphy has reported celebrities have been used by antihunt activists since the mid-20th century; Yvette Mimieux and Loretta Swit were recruited to attract the attention of international gossip magazines. Other celebrities who have aligned themselves against the hunt include Richard Dean Anderson, Kim Basinger, Juliette Binoche, Sir Paul McCartney, Heather Mills, Pamela Anderson, Martin Sheen, Pierce Brosnan, Morrissey, Paris Hilton, Robert Kennedy, Jr., Rutger Hauer, Brigitte Bardot, Ed Begley, Jr., Farley Mowat, Linda Blair, and the Red Hot Chili Peppers.

In March 2006, Brigitte Bardot traveled to Ottawa to protest the hunt, though the prime minister turned down her request for a meeting. During the same month, Paul and Heather Mills McCartney toured the Gulf of St. Lawrence's sealing grounds, and spoke out against the seal hunt, including as guests on Larry King Live, where the two debated with Danny Williams, the Premier of Newfoundland and Labrador.

In 1978, marine ecologist criticized the focus on the seal hunt, arguing it is entirely emotional: "We have to be logical. We have to aim our activity first to the endangered species. Those who are moved by the plight of the harp seal could also be moved by the plight of the pig - the way they are slaughtered is horrible".

18 Dolphins

Dolphins are marine mammals that are closely related to whales and porpoises. There are almost forty species of dolphin in 17 genera. They vary in size from 1.2 m (4 ft) and 40 kg (90 lb) (Maui's dolphin), up to 9.5 m (30 ft) and 10 tonnes (9.8 LT; 11 ST) (the orca or killer whale). They are found worldwide, mostly in the shallower seas of the continental shelves, and are carnivores, mostly eating fish and squid. The family Delphinidae is the largest in the Cetacean order, and evolved relatively recently, about ten million years ago, during the Miocene. Dolphins are among the most intelligent animals, and their often friendly appearance and seemingly playful attitude have made them popular in human culture.

The name is originally from Greek (delphís), 'dolphin', which was related to the Greek (delphus), 'womb'. The animal's name can therefore be interpreted as meaning 'a 'fish' with a womb'. The name was transmitted via the Latin delphinus (the romanization of the later Greek - delphinos), which in Middle Latin became dolfinus and in Old French daulphin, which reintroduced the ph into the word. The term mereswine (that is, sea pork) has also historically been used.

The word is used in a few different ways. It can mean:

- any member of the family Delphinidae (oceanic dolphins);
- any member of the families Delphinidae and Platanistoidea (oceanic and river dolphins);

- any member of the suborder Odontoceti (toothed whales; these include the above families and some others);
- it is used casually as a synonym for bottlenose dolphin, the most common and familiar species of dolphin.

This article uses the second definition and does not describe porpoises (suborder Odontoceti, family Phocoenidae). Orcas and some closely related species belong to the Delphinidae family and therefore qualify as dolphins, even though they are called whales in common language. A group of dolphins is called a 'school' or a 'pod'. Male dolphins are called 'bulls', females 'cows' and young dolphins are called 'calves'.

Taxonomy

- Suborder Odontoceti, toothed whales
- Family Delphinidae, oceanic dolphins
- Genus Delphinus
- Long-Beaked Common Dolphin, Delphinus capensis
- Short-Beaked Common Dolphin, Delphinus delphis
- Genus Tursiops
- Common Bottlenose Dolphin, Tursiops truncatus
- Indo-Pacific Bottlenose Dolphin, Tursiops aduncus
- Genus Lissodelphis
- Northern Rightwhale Dolphin, Lissodelphis borealis
- Southern Rightwhale Dolphin, Lissodelphis peronii
- Genus Sotalia
- Tucuxi, Sotalia fluviatilis
- Costero, Sotalia guianensis
- Genus Sousa
- Indo-Pacific Hump-backed Dolphin, Sousa chinensis
- Chinese White Dolphin (the Chinese variant), Sousa chinensis chinensis
- Atlantic Humpbacked Dolphin, Sousa teuszii
- Genus Stenella
- Atlantic Spotted Dolphin, Stenella frontalis
- Clymene Dolphin, Stenella clymene

- Pantropical Spotted Dolphin, Stenella attenuata
- Spinner Dolphin, Stenella longirostris
- Striped Dolphin, Stenella coeruleoalba
- Genus Steno
- Rough-Toothed Dolphin, Steno bredanensis
- Genus Cephalorhynchus
- Chilean Dolphin, Cephalorhynchus eutropia
- Commerson's Dolphin, Cephalorhynchus commersonii
- Heaviside's Dolphin, Cephalorhynchus heavisidii
- Hector's Dolphin, Cephalorhynchus hectori
- Genus Grampus
- Risso's Dolphin, Grampus griseus
- Genus Lagenodelphis
- Fraser's Dolphin, Lagenodelphis hosei
- Genus Lagenorhynchus
- Atlantic White-Sided Dolphin, Lagenorhynchus acutus
- Dusky Dolphin, Lagenorhynchus obscurus
- Hourglass Dolphin, Lagenorhynchus cruciger
- Pacific White-Sided Dolphin, Lagenorhynchus obliquidens
- Peale's Dolphin, Lagenorhynchus australis
- White-Beaked Dolphin, Lagenorhynchus albirostris
- Genus Orcaella
- Australian Snubfin Dolphin, Orcaella heinsohni
- Irrawaddy Dolphin, Orcaella brevirostris
- Genus Peponocephala
- Melon-headed Whale, Peponocephala electra
- Genus Orcinus
- Killer Whale (Orca), Orcinus orca
- Genus Feresa
- Pygmy Killer Whale, Feresa attenuata
- Genus Pseudorca
- False Killer Whale, Pseudorca crassidens
- Genus Globicephala
- Long-finned Pilot Whale, Globicephala melas

- Short-finned Pilot Whale, Globicephala macrorhynchus
- Genus Australodelphis
- Australodelphis mirus
- Family Platanistidae
- Ganges and Indus River Dolphin, Platanista gangetica with two subspecies
- Ganges River Dolphin (or Susu), Platanista gangetica gangetica
- Indus River Dolphin (or Bhulan), Platanista gangetica minor
- Family Iniidae
- Amazon River Dolphin (or Boto), Inia geoffrensis
- Family Lipotidae
- Baiji (or Chinese River Dolphin), Lipotes vexillifer (possibly extinct, since December 2006)
- Family Pontoporiidae
- La Plata Dolphin (or Franciscana), Pontoporia blainvillei
- Six species in the family Delphinidae are commonly called 'whales', but genetically are dolphins. They are sometimes called blackfish.
- Melon-headed Whale, Peponocephala electra
- Killer Whale (Orca), Orcinus orca
- Pygmy Killer Whale, Feresa attenuata
- Wolphin Kawili'Kai at the Sea Life Park in Hawaii.
- False Killer Whale, Pseudorca crassidens
- Long-finned Pilot Whale, Globicephala melas
- Short-finned Pilot Whale, Globicephala macrorhynchus

In 1933, three strange dolphins beached off the Irish coast; they appeared to be hybrids between Risso's and bottlenose dolphins. This mating was later repeated in captivity, producing a hybrid calf. In captivity, a bottlenose and a rough-toothed dolphin produced hybrid offspring. A common-bottlenose hybrid lives at SeaWorld California. Other dolphin hybrids live in captivity around the world or have been reported in the wild, such as a bottlenose-Atlantic spotted hybrid. The best known hybrid is the wolphin, a false killer whale-bottlenose dolphin hybrid. The wolphin is a fertile hybrid. Two wolphins currently live at the Sea Life Park in Hawaii; the first was born in 1985 from a male false killer whale and a female bottlenose. Wolphins have also been observed in the wild.

Dolphins, along with whales and porpoises, are descendants of terrestrial mammals, most likely of the Artiodactyl order. The ancestors of the modern day dolphins entered the water roughly 50 million years ago, in the Eocene epoch.

Hind limb buds are apparent on an embryo of a spotted dolphin in the fifth week of development as small bumps (hind limb buds) near the base of the tail. The pin is approximately 2.5 cm (1.0 in) long.

Modern dolphin skeletons have two small, rod-shaped pelvic bones thought to be vestigial hind limbs. In October 2006, an unusual bottlenose dolphin was captured in Japan; it had small fins on each side of its genital slit, which scientists believe to be a more pronounced development of these vestigial hind limbs.

Anatomy

Dolphins have a streamlined fusiform body, adapted for fast swimming. The tail fin, called the fluke, is used for propulsion, while the pectoral fins together with the entire tail section provide directional control. The dorsal fin, in those species that have one, provides stability while swimming.

Though it varies by species, basic colouration patterns are shades of grey, usually with a lighter underside, often with lines and patches of different hue and contrast.

The head contains the melon, a round organ used for echolocation. In many species, elongated jaws form a distinct beak; species such as the bottlenose have a curved mouth which looks like a fixed smile. Some species have up to 250 teeth. Dolphins breathe through a blowhole on top of their head. The trachea is anterior to the brain. The dolphin brain is large and highly complex, and is different in structure from that of most land mammals.

Unlike most mammals, dolphins do not have hair, except for a few hairs around the tip of their rostrum which they lose shortly before or after birth. The only exception to this is the Boto river dolphin, which has persistent small hairs on the rostrum.

Dolphins' reproductive organs are located on the underside of the body. Males have two slits, one concealing the penis and one further behind for the anus. The female has one genital slit, housing the vagina and the anus. Two mammary slits are positioned on either side of the female's genital slit.

A recent study at the U.S. National Marine Mammal Foundation revealed that dolphins, like humans, develop a natural form of type 2 diabetes, which may lead to a better understanding of the disease and new treatments for both humans and dolphins.

Senses

Most dolphins have acute eyesight, both in and out of the water, and they can hear frequencies ten times or more above the upper limit of adult human hearing. Though they have a small ear opening on each side of their head, it is believed hearing underwater is also, if not exclusively, done with the lower jaw, which conducts sound to the middle ear via a fat-filled cavity in the lower jaw bone. Hearing is also used for echolocation, which all dolphins have. Dolphin teeth are believed to function as antennae to receive incoming sound and to pinpoint the exact location of an object. The dolphin's sense of touch is also well-developed, with free nerve endings densely packed in the skin, especially around the snout, pectoral fins and genital area. However, dolphins lack an olfactory nerve and lobes, and thus are believed to have no sense of smell. They do have a sense of taste and show preferences for certain kinds of fish. Since dolphins spend most of their time below the surface, tasting the water could function like smelling, in that substances in the water can signal the presence of objects that are not in the dolphin's mouth.

Though most dolphins do not have hair, they do have hair follicles that may perform some sensory function. The small hairs on the rostrum of the Boto river dolphin are believed to function as a tactile sense possibly to compensate for the Boto's poor eyesight.

Dolphins are often regarded as one of Earth's most intelligent animals, though it is hard to say just how intelligent. Comparing species' relative intelligence is complicated by differences in sensory apparatus, response modes, and nature of cognition. Furthermore, the difficulty and expense of experimental work with large aquatic animals has so far prevented some tests and limited sample size and rigor in others. Compared to many other species, however, dolphin behaviour has been studied extensively, both in captivity and in the wild. See cetacean intelligence for more details.

Social Behaviour

Dolphins are social, living in pods of up to a dozen individuals. In places with a high abundance of food, pods can merge temporarily, forming a superpod; such groupings may exceed 1,000 dolphins. Individuals communicate using a variety of clicks, whistles and other vocalizations. They make ultrasonic sounds for echolocation. Membership in pods is not rigid; interchange is common. However, dolphins can establish strong social bonds; they will stay with injured or ill individuals, even helping them to breathe by bringing them to the surface if needed. This altruism does not appear to be limited to their own species however. The dolphin Moko in New Zealand has been observed guiding a female Pygmy Sperm Whale together with her calf out of shallow water where they had stranded several times. They have also been seen protecting swimmers from sharks by swimming circles around the swimmers or charging the sharks to make them go away.

Dolphins also display culture, something long believed to be unique to humans (and possibly other primate species). In May 2005, a discovery in Australia found Indo-Pacific bottlenose dolphins (Tursiops aduncus) teaching their young to use tools. They cover their snouts with sponges to protect them while foraging. This knowledge is mostly transferred by mothers to daughters, unlike simian primates, where knowledge is generally passed on to both sexes. Using sponges as mouth protection is a learned behaviour. Another learned behaviour was discovered among river dolphins in Brazil, where some male dolphins use weeds and sticks as part of a sexual display.

Dolphins engage in acts of aggression towards each other. The older a male dolphin is, the more likely his body is to be covered with bite scars. Male dolphins engage in such acts of aggression apparently for the same reasons as humans: disputes between companions and competition for females. Acts of aggression can become so intense that targeted dolphins sometimes go into exile as a result of losing a fight.

Male bottlenose dolphins have been known to engage in infanticide. Dolphins have also been known to kill porpoises for reasons which are not fully understood, as porpoises generally do not share the same diet as dolphins, and are therefore not competitors for food supplies.

Reproduction and Sexuality

Dolphin copulation happens belly to belly; though many species engage in lengthy foreplay, the actual act is usually brief, but may be repeated several times within a short timespan. The gestation period varies with species; for the small Tucuxi dolphin, this period is around 11 to 12 months, while for the orca, the gestation period is around 17 months. They usually become sexually active at a young age, even before reaching sexual maturity. The age of sexual maturity varies by species and gender.

Dolphins are known to have sex for reasons other than reproduction, sometimes also engaging in homosexual behaviour. Various species sometimes engage in sexual behaviour including copulation with other dolphin species. Sexual encounters may be violent, with male dolphins sometimes showing aggressive behaviour towards both females and other males. Occasionally, dolphins behave sexually towards other animals, including humans.

Feeding

Various methods of feeding exist among and within species, some apparently exclusive to a single population. Fish and squid are the main food, but the false killer whale and the orca also feed on other marine mammals.

One common feeding method is herding, where a pod squeezes a school of fish into a small volume, known as a bait ball. Individual members then take turns plowing through the ball, feeding on the stunned fish. Coralling is a method where dolphins chase fish into shallow water to more easily catch them. In South Carolina, the Atlantic bottlenose dolphin takes this further with 'strand feeding', driving prey onto mud banks for easy access. In some places, orcas come to the beach to capture sea lions. Some species also whack fish with their flukes, stunning them and sometimes knocking them out of the water.

Reports of cooperative human-dolphin fishing date back to the ancient Roman author and natural philosopher Pliny the Elder. A modern human-dolphin partnership currently operates in Laguna, Santa Catarina, Brazil. Here, dolphins drive fish towards fishermen waiting along the shore and signal the men to cast their nets. The dolphins' reward is the fish that escape the nets.

Dolphins are capable of making a broad range of sounds using nasal airsacs located just below the blowhole. Roughly three categories of sounds can be identified: frequency modulated whistles, burst-pulsed sounds and clicks. Dolphins communicate with their whistles and burst-pulsed sounds, though the nature and extent of that ability is not known. At least some dolphin species can identify themselves using a signature whistle. The clicks are directional and are for echolocation, often occurring in a short series called a click train. The click rate increases when approaching an object of interest. Dolphin echolocation clicks are amongst the loudest sounds made by marine animals.

Dolphins occasionally leap above the water surface, and sometimes perform acrobatic figures (for example, the spinner dolphin). Scientists are not certain about the purpose(s) of the acrobatics. Possibilities include locating schools of fish by looking at above-water signs like feeding birds, communicating with other dolphins, dislodging parasites or simple amusement.

Play is an important part of dolphin culture. Dolphins play with seaweed and play-fight with other dolphins. At times they harass other local creatures, like seabirds and turtles. Dolphins enjoy riding waves and frequently surf coastal swells and the bow waves of boats, at times 'leaping' between the dual bow waves of a moving catamaran. Occasionally, they playfully interact with swimmers. Captive dolphins have been observed in aquariums engaging in complex play behaviour which involves the creation and manipulation of bubble rings.

Generally, dolphins sleep with only one brain hemisphere in slow-wave sleep at a time, thus maintaining enough consciousness to breathe and to watch for possible predators and other threats. Earlier sleep stages can occur simultaneously in both hemispheres. In captivity, dolphins seemingly enter a fully asleep state where both eyes are closed and there is no response to mild external stimuli. In this case respiration is automatic, a tail kick reflex keeps the blowhole above the water if necessary. Anesthetized dolphins initially show a tail kick reflex. Though a similar state has been observed with wild Sperm Whales, it is not known if dolphins in the wild reach this state. The Indus river dolphin has a different sleep method from other dolphin species. Living in water with strong currents and potentially dangerous floating debris, it must swim continuously to avoid injury. As a result, this species sleeps in very short bursts which last between 4 and 60 seconds.

Except for humans, dolphins have few natural enemies. Some species or specific populations have none, making them apex predators. For most of the smaller species of dolphins, only a few of the larger sharks, such as the bull shark, dusky shark, tiger shark and great white shark are a potential risk, especially for calves. Some of the larger dolphinic species, especially orcas (killer whales), may also prey smaller dolphins, but this seems rare. Dolphins also suffer from a wide variety of diseases and parasites.

Some dolphin species face an uncertain future, especially some river dolphin species such as the Amazon river dolphin, and the Ganges and Yangtze river dolphin, which are critically or seriously endangered. A 2006 survey found no individuals of the Yangtze river dolphin, which now appears to be functionally extinct.

Pesticides, heavy metals, plastics, and other industrial and agricultural pollutants that do not disintegrate rapidly in the environment concentrate in predators such as dolphins. Injuries or deaths due to collisions with boats, especially their propellers, are also common.

Various fishing methods, most notably purse seine fishing for tuna and the use of drift and gill nets, unintentionally kill many dolphins. Accidental by-catch in gill nets and incidental captures in antipredator nets that protect marine fish farms are common and pose a risk for mainly local dolphin populations. In some parts of the world, such as Taiji in Japan and the Faroe Islands, dolphins are traditionally considered as food, and are killed in harpoon or drive hunts. Dolphin meat is high in mercury, and may thus pose a health danger to humans when consumed.

Dolphin safe labels attempt to reassure consumers fish and other marine products have been caught in a dolphin-friendly way. The original deal with 'Dolphin safe' labels was brokered in the 1980s between marine activists and the major tuna companies, and involved decreasing incidental dolphin kills by up to 50 per cent by changing the type of nets being used to catch the tuna. It should be noted that the dolphins are only netted while fishermen are in pursuit of smaller tuna. Albacore are not netted this way, which makes albacore the only truly dolphin-safe tuna.

Loud underwater noises, such as those resulting from naval sonar use, live firing exercises, or certain offshore construction projects, such as wind farms, may be harmful to dolphins, increasing stress, damaging hearing, and causing decompression sickness by forcing them to surface too quickly to escape the noise.

Dolphins have long played a role in human culture. Dolphins are common in Greek mythology and there are many coins from ancient Greece which feature a man or boy or deity riding on the back of a dolphin. The Ancient Greeks welcomed dolphins; spotting dolphins riding in a ship's wake was considered a good omen. In Hindu mythology, the Ganges River Dolphin is associated with Ganga, the deity of the Ganges river.

In more recent times, the 1963 film Flipper and the subsequent 1964 television series popularized dolphins in Western society. The series, created by Ivan Tors, portrayed a dolphin as a kind of seagoing version of Lassie, the collie made popular in the 1950s TV series. Flipper was a Bottlenose Dolphin who understood commands and always behaved heroically. Flipper was remade as a film in 1996.

The 1973 movie The Day of the Dolphin portrayed kidnapped dolphins performing a naval military assassination using explosives. This was also explored in the similarly named The Simpsons Treehouse of Horror episode, 'Night of the Dolphin', where Lisa frees a dolphin at a aquarium exhibit and unwittingly initiates their plan to overthrow the land-dwellers and live in their place. The 1990s science fiction television series seaQuest DSV featured a bottle-nose named Darwin who could communicate using a vocoder, a fictional invention which translated clicks and whistles to English and back.

In The Hitchhiker's Guide to the Galaxy book series, dolphins are the second most intelligent species on Earth (after mice).

Killer whales have also been portrayed in film, though to a lesser extent than bottlenosed dolphins. The 1977 horror movie Orca portrayed killer whales as intelligent and capable of pair-bonding and aggressive behaviour. In the movie, a male killer whale takes revenge on fishermen after they kill his mate. The 1993 movie Free Willy made a star of the Orca playing Willy, Keiko.

The renewed popularity of dolphins in the 1960s resulted in the appearance of many dolphinaria around the world, making dolphins accessible to the public. Criticism and animal welfare laws forced many to close, although hundreds still exist around the world. In the United States, the best known are the SeaWorld marine mammal parks.

Organisations such as the Mote Marine Laboratory rescue and rehabilitate sick, wounded, stranded or orphaned dolphins, while others, such as the Whale and Dolphin Conservation Society and Hong Kong Dolphin Conservation Society, work on dolphin conservation and welfare. India has declared the Dolphin as their national aquatic animal in an attempt to protect the endangered Ganges River Dolphin. The Vikramshila Gangetic Dolphin Sanctuary has been created in the Ganges river for the protection of the animals.

Various scientists to have researched Dolphin behaviour have proposed that their unusually high intelligence compared to other animals means that dolphins should be seen as non-human persons that should have their own specific rights, and that it is morally unacceptable to keep them captive for entertainment purposes, or to kill them; either intentionally for consumption or as by-catch.

Although dolphins generally interact well with humans, some attacks have occurred, most of them with small injuries. The attacks can occur both in the wild and captivity.

Orcas, the largest species of dolphin, have been involved in fatal attacks on humans in captivity. The record-holder of documented orca fatal attacks is a male named Tilikum, that belongs to SeaWorld and has played a role in the death of three people in three different incidents. There are documented incidents in the wild too, but none of them fatal.

Fatal attacks from other species are less common, but there is a registered occurrence in the coast of Brazil in 1994, when a man died after injuries suffered during a bottlenose dolphin attack. Non-fatal incidents occur more frequently, both in wild and captivity.

While dolphin attacks are much rarer than other sea animal attacks, such as shark ones, some scientists are worried about the careless programmes of human-dolphin interaction. Researcher, who studies dolphin attacks, points that dolphins are large and wild predators, so people should be more careful when interact with them.

Dolphins are an increasingly popular choice of animal-assisted therapy for psychological problems and developmental disabilities. For example, a 2005 study found dolphins an effective treatment for mild to moderate depression. However, this study was criticized on several grounds. For example, it is not known whether dolphins are more effective than common pets. Reviews of this and other published dolphin-assisted therapy (DAT) studies have found important methodological flaws and have concluded that there is no compelling scientific evidence that DAT is a legitimate therapy or that it affords more than fleeting mood improvement.

A number of militaries have employed dolphins for various purposes from finding mines to rescuing lost or trapped humans. The military use of dolphins, however, drew scrutiny during the Vietnam War when rumors circulated that the United States Navy was training dolphins to kill Vietnamese divers. The United States Navy denies that at any point dolphins were trained for combat. Dolphins are still being trained by the United States Navy on other tasks as part of the U.S. Navy Marine Mammal Programme. The Russian military is believed to have closed its marine mammal programme in the early 1990s. In 2000 the press reported that dolphins trained to kill by the Soviet Navy had been sold to Iran.

Dolphins are also common in contemporary literature, especially science fiction novels. Dolphins play a military role in William Gibson's short story Johnny Mnemonic, in which cyborg dolphins find submarines and decode encrypted information. Dolphins play a role as sentient patrollers of the sea enhanced with a deeper empathy toward humans in Anne McCaffrey's The Dragonriders of Pern series. In the Known Space universe of author Larry Niven, dolphins play a significant role as fully recognised 'legal entities'. More humorous is Douglas Adams' The Hitchhiker's Guide to the Galaxy series of picaresque novels, in which dolphins are the second most intelligent creatures on Earth (after mice, followed by humans) and try in vain to warn humans of Earth's impending destruction. Their story is told in So Long, and Thanks for All the Fish. Much more serious is their major role in David Brin's Uplift series. A talking Dolphin named 'Howard' helps Hagbard Celine and his submarine crew fight the evil Illuminati in Robert Shea and Robert Anton Wilson's Illuminatus Trilogy.

Dolphins appear frequently in non-science fiction literature. In the book The Music of Dolphins by author Karen Hesse, dolphins raise a girl from the age of four until the coast guard eventually discovers her. Fantasy author Ken Grimwood wrote dolphins into his 1995 novel Into the Deep about a marine biologist struggling to crack the code of dolphin intelligence, including chapters written from a dolphinian viewpoint.

Dolphin meat is consumed in a small number of countries world-wide, which include Japan and Peru (where it is referred to as chancho marino, or 'sea pork'). While Japan may be the best-known and most controversial example, only a very small minority of the population has ever sampled it.

Dolphin meat is dense and such a dark shade of red as to appear black. Fat is located in a layer of blubber between the meat and the skin. When dolphin meat is eaten in Japan, it is often cut into thin strips and eaten raw as sashimi, garnished with onion and either horseradish or grated garlic, much as with sashimi of whale or horse meat (basashi). When cooked, dolphin meat is cut into bite-size cubes and then batter-fried or simmered in a miso sauce with vegetables. Cooked dolphin meat has a flavour very similar to beef liver.

19 Cetaceans

The cetaceans (whales, dolphins and porpoises) are marine mammal descendants of land mammals. Their terrestrial origins are indicated by:

- Their need to breathe air from the surface.
- The bones of their fins, which resemble the limbs of land mammals.
- The vertical movement of their spines, characteristic more of a running mammal than of the horizontal movement of fish.

The question of how land animals evolved into ocean-going leviathans was a mystery until recent discoveries in Pakistan revealed several stages in the transition of cetaceans from land to sea.

The traditional theory of cetacean evolution was that whales were related to the mesonychids, an extinct order of carnivorous ungulates (hoofed animals), which resembled wolves with hooves and were a sister group of artiodactyls (even-toed ungulates). These animals had unusual triangular teeth similar to those of whales. This is why scientists long believed that whales evolved from a form of mesonychid. But more recent molecular phylogeny data suggest that whales are more closely related to the artiodactyls, specifically the hippopotamus. The strong evidence for a clade combining cetaceans and artiodactyls is further discussed in the article Cetartiodactyla. However, the anthracothere ancestors of hippos do not appear in the fossil record until millions of years after Pakicetus, the first known whale ancestor.

The molecular data is supported by the recent discovery of Pakicetus, the earliest proto-whale . The skeletons of Pakicetus show that whales did not derive directly from mesonychids. Instead, they are artiodactyls that began to take to the water soon after artiodactyls split from mesonychids. Proto-whales retained aspects of their mesonychid ancestry (such as the triangular teeth) which modern artiodactyls have lost.

An interesting implication is that the earliest ancestors of all hoofed mammals were probably at least partly carnivorous or scavengers, and today's artiodactyls and perissodactyls became herbivores later in their evolution.

By contrast, whales retained their carnivorous diet, because prey was more available and they needed higher caloric content in order to live as marine endotherms. Mesonychids also became specialized carnivores, but this was likely a disadvantage because large prey was not yet common. This is why they were out-competed by better-adapted animals like the creodonts and later Carnivora which filled the gaps left by the dinosaurs.

Indohyus is a small deer-like creature, which lived about 48 million years ago in Kashmir. It belongs to the artiodactyls family Raoellidae, and is believed to be the closest sister group of Cetacea. About the size of a raccoon or domestic cat, this herbivorous creature shared some of the traits of whales, most notably the involucrum, which is the diagnostic characteristic of any cetacean, and is not found in any other species.

Besides, it also showed signs of adaptations to aquatic life, including a thick and heavy outer coating which is similar to the bones of modern creatures such as the hippopotamus, and reduces buoyancy so that they can stay underwater. This suggests a similar survival strategy to the African mousedeer or water chevrotain which, when threatened by a bird of prey, dives into water and hides beneath the surface for up to four minutes.

The pakicetids are hoofed mammals that are the earliest whales, with Indohyus from family Raoellidae being the closest sister group. They lived in the early Eocene, around 53 million years ago. Their fossils were first discovered in North Pakistan in 1979, located at a river not far from the shores of former Tethys Sea. After the initial discovery, more fossils were found, mainly in the late-early Eocene fluvial deposits in northern Pakistan and northwestern India.

Based on this discovery, pakicetids most likely lived in an arid environment with ephemeral streams and moderately developed floodplains millions of years ago. By using stable oxygen isotopes analysis, they were shown to drink fresh water. Their diet probably included land animals that approached water for drinking or some freshwater aquatic organisms that lived in the river.

Pakicetids were classified as cetaceans mainly based on the structure of the auditory bulla, which is formed from the ectotympanic bone only. The shape of the ear region in pakicetids is highly unusual and the skull is cetacean-like, although a blowhole is still absent at this stage. The jawbone of pakicetids also lacks the enlarged space (mandibular foramen) that is filled with fat or oil, which is used in receiving underwater sound in modern whales. They have dorsal orbits (eye sockets facing up), which are similar to crocodiles.

This eye placement helps submerged predators observe potential prey above the water. According to Thewissen et al., the teeth of pakicetids also resemble the teeth of fossil whales, being less like a dog's incisors, with a serrated triangular shape, similar to a shark's tooth, which is another link to more modern whales. It was initially thought that the ears of pakicetids were adapted for underwater hearing, but, as would be expected from the anatomy of the rest of this creature, the ears of pakicetids are specialized for hearing on land.

However, pakicetids were able to listen underwater, by using enhanced bone conduction, rather than depending on tympanic membrane like general land mammals. This method of hearing does not give directional hearing underwater.

Pakicetids have long thin legs, with relatively short hands and feet which suggest that they were poor swimmers. To compensate for that, their bones are unusually thick (osteosclerotic), which is probably an adaptation to make the animal heavier to counteract the buoyancy of the water. According to a morphological analysis by Thewissen et al., pakicetids display no aquatic skeletons adaptation; instead they display adaptations for running and jumping. Hence pakicetids were most likely an aquatic wader.

In 1994, *Ambulocetus natans*, which lived about 49 million years ago, was discovered in Pakistan. It was probably amphibious, and resembled the crocodile in its physical appearance. In the Eocene, ambulocetids inhabited the bays and estuaries of the Tethys Ocean in northern Pakistan. The fossils of ambulocetids are always found in near-shore shallow marine deposits associated with abundant marine plant fossils and littoral molluscs.

Although they are found only in marine deposits, their oxygen isotope values indicate that they consumed a range of water with different degree of salinity, with some specimens having no evidence of sea water consumption and others did not ingest fresh water at the time when their teeth are fossilized. It is clear that ambulocetids tolerated a wide range of salt concentrations. Hence, ambulocetids represent the transition phase of cetacean ancestors between fresh water and marine habitat

The mandibular foramen in ambulocetids had increased in size, which indicates that a fat pad was likely to be housed in the lower jaw. In modern whales, this fat pad in the mandibular foramen extends posteriorly to the middle ear. This allows sounds to be received in the lower jaw, and then transmitted through the fat pad to the middle ear. Similar to pakicetids, the orbits of ambulocetids are on the dorsal side of the skull, but they face more laterally than in pakicetids.

Postcranial Morphology

Ambulocetids had relatively long limbs with particular strong hind legs, and they retained a tail with no sign of fluke (the horizontal tail fin of modern cetaceans). Although they could walk on land, as well as swim, it is clear that they were not fast on either terrain. It has been speculated that Ambulocetids hunted like crocodiles, lurking in the shallows to snatch unsuspecting riparian prey and fish.

They probably swam by pelvic paddling (a way of swimming which mainly utilizes their hind limbs to generate propulsion in water) and caudal undulation (a way of swimming which uses the undulations of the vertebral column to generate force for movements), as otters, seals and whales do. This is an intermediate stage in the evolution of cetacean locomotion, as modern whales swim by caudal oscillation (a way of swimming similar to caudal undulation, but uses energy more efficiently).

Remingtonocetids lived in middle-Eocene South Asia, about 49 to 43 million years ago. Compared to family Pakicetidae and Ambulocetidae, Remingtonocetidae was a diverse family found in north and central Pakistan, and also western India. Remingtonocetids were also found in shallow marine deposits, but they are obviously more aquatic than ambulocetids.

This can be seen from the recovery of their fossils from a variety of coastal marine environments, including near-shore and lagoonal deposits. It is shown that most remingtonocetids did not ingest fresh water, and had hence lost their dependency on fresh water relatively soon after their origin.

The orbits of remingtonocetids face laterally and are small. This suggests that vision is not an important sense for them. The nasal opening, which will later evolve to become blowhole in modern cetaceans, is located near the tip of the long snout. The position of the nasal opening had remained unchanged since pakicetids. One of the notable features in remingtonocetids is that the semicircular canals, which are important for balancing in land mammals, had decreased in size. This reduction in size had closely accompanied the cetacean invasion of marine environments. According to Spoor et al., this modification of the semicircular canal system may represents a crucial 'point of no return' event in early cetacean evolution, which excluded a prolonged semi-aquatic phase.

Compared to ambulocetids, remingtonocetids had relatively short fore and hind limbs. Based on their skeletal remains, remingtonocetids were probably amphibious whales that are well adapted to swimming, and likely to swim by caudal undulation only.

The protocetids form a diverse and heterogeneous group known from Asia, Europe, Africa, and North America. They lived in the Eocene, approximately 48 to 35 million years ago. The fossil remains of protocetids were uncovered from coastal and lagoonal facies in South Asia; but unlike previous cetacean families, their fossils uncovered from Africa and North America also include open marine forms. Hence they were probably amphibious, but more aquatic compared to remingtonocetids. Protocetids were the first whales to leave the Indian subcontinent and disperse to all shallow subtropical oceans of the world.

There were many genera among the family Protocetidae, and some of these are very well known (e.g., Rodhocetus). Great variations in aquatic adaptations exist among them, with some probably able to support their weight on land, whereas others could not. Their supposed amphibious nature is supported by the discovery of a pregnant Maiacetus, in which the fossilised fetus was positioned for a head-first delivery, suggesting that Maiacetus gave birth on land.

Unlike remingtonocetids and ambulocetids, protocetids have large orbits and are oriented laterally. Increasingly lateral facing eyes might be used to observe prey that live underwater, which are similar to modern cetacean. Furthermore, the nasal openings are large and are now halfway up the snout. The great variety of teeth suggests diverse feeding modes in protocetids. In both remingtonocetids and protocetids, the size of mandibular foramen had increased. The large mandibular foramen indicates that the mandibular fat pad was present. However air-filled sinuses that are present in modern cetaceans, which function to isolate the ear acoustically to enable better underwater hearing, is still not present. The external auditory meatus (ear canal) which is absent in modern cetaceans is also present.

Hence, the method of sound transmission present in them combines aspects of pakicetids and modern odontocetes. At this intermediate stage of hearing development, the transmission of airborne sound was poor due to the modifications of ear for underwater hearing; while directional underwater hearing was also poor compared to modern cetaceans.

Some protocetids had short, large fore- and hindlimbs that are likely to be used in swimming, but the limbs give a slow and cumbersome locomotion on land. It is possible that some protocetids had flukes. However, it is clear that they are adapted even further to an aquatic life-style.

In Rodhocetus, for example, the sacrum (a bone that in land-mammals is a fusion of five vertebrae that connects the pelvis with the rest of the vertebral column) was divided into loose vertebrae. However, the pelvis was still connected to one of the sacral vertebrae. The ungulate ancestry of these early whales is still underlined by characteristics like the presence of hooves at the ends of the toes in Rodhocetus.

Basilosaurids were discovered in 1840 and initially mistaken for a reptile, hence its name. Together with dorudontids, they lived in the late Eocene around 41 to 35 million years ago, and are the oldest known obligate aquatic cetaceans. They were fully recognizable whales which lived entirely in the ocean. This is supported by their fossils usually found in deposits indicative of fully marine environments, lacking any freshwater infux. They were probably distributed throughout the tropical and subtropical seas of the world. Basilosaurids are commonly found in association with dorudontids. In fact, they are closely related to one another. The fossilised stomach contents in one basilosaurid indicates that it ate fish.

Although they look very much like modern whales, basilosaurids and dorudontids lacked the 'melon organ' that allows their descendants to use echolocation as effectively as modern whales. They had small brains; this suggests they were solitary and did not have the complex social structure of some modern cetaceans. The mandibuiar foramen of basilosaurids and dorudontids now cover the entire depth of the lower jaw as in modern cetaceans. Their orbits face laterally, and the nasal opening had moved even higher up the snout, closer to the position of blowhole in modern cetaceans. Furthermore, their ear structures are functionally modern, with the major innovation being the insertion of air-filled sinuses between ear and skull. Unlike modern cetaceans, basilosaurids retain a large external auditory meatus.

Both basilosaurids and dorudontids have skeletons that are immediately recognizable as cetaceans. A basilosaurid was as big as the larger modern whales, up to 18 m (60 ft) long; dorudontids were smaller, about 5 m (16 ft) long. The large size of basilosaurids is due to the extreme elongation of their lumbar vertebrae. They had a tail fluke, but their body proportions suggest that it swam by caudal undulation and that the fluke was not the propulsive organ. In contrast, dorudontids had a shorter but powerful vertebral column.

They too had a fluke, and unlike basilosaurids, they probably swam similarly to modern cetaceans, by using caudal oscillations. The forelimbs of basilosaurids and dorudontids were probably flipper-shaped, and the external hind limbs were tiny and are certainly not involved in locomotion. Their fingers, on the other hand, still retain the mobile joints of their ambulocetid relatives. The two tiny but well-formed hind legs of basilosaurids which were probably used as claspers when mating; they are a small reminder of the lives of their ancestors. Interestingly, the pelvic bones associated with these hind limbs was now no longer connected to the vertebral column as it was in protocetids. Essentially, any sacral vertebrae can no longer be clearly distinguished from the other vertebrae.

Ancestry of Modern Cetacea

Both basilosaurids and dorudontids are relatively closely related to modern cetacean, which belong to order Odontoceti and Mysticeti. However, according to Fordyce and Barnes, the large size and elongated vertebral body of basilosaurid preclude it from being the ancestor of the two modern orders. As for dorudontids, there are some species within the family that do not have elongated vertebral bodies, which might be the immediate ancestors of Odontoceti and Mysticeti.

Toothed whales (Odontocetes) echolocate by creating a series of clicks emitted at various frequencies. Sound pulses are emitted through their melon-shaped foreheads, reflected off objects, and retrieved through the lower jaw. Skulls of Squalodon show evidence for the first hypothesized appearance of echolocation. Squalodon lived from the early to middle Oligocene to the middle Miocene, around 33-14 million years ago.

Squalodon featured several commonalities with modern Odontocetes. The cranium was well compressed, the rostrum telescoped outward (a characteristic of the modern suborder Odontoceti), giving Squalodon an appearance similar to that of modern toothed whales. However, it is thought unlikely that squalodontids are direct ancestors of living dolphins.

All modern mysticetes are large filter-feeding or baleen whales, though the exact means by which baleen is used differs among species (gulp-feeding with balaenopterids, skim-feeding with balaenids, and bottom ploughing with eschrichtiids). The first members of some modern groups appeared during the middle Miocene. These changes may have been a result of worldwide environmental change and physical changes in the oceans.

A large scale change in ocean current and temperature could have initiated the radiation of modern mysticetes, leading to the demise of the archaic forms. Generally it is speculated the four modern mysticete families have separate origins among the cetotheres. Modern baleen whales, Balaenopteridae (rorquals and humpback whale, Megaptera novaengliae), Balaenidae (right whales), Eschrichtiidae (gray whale, Eschrictius robustus), and Neobalaenidae (pygmy right whale, Caperea marginata) all have derived characteristics presently unknown in any cetothere.

During the early Miocene (about 20 Ma), echolocation developed in its modern form. Various extinct dolphin-like families flourished. Early dolphins include Kentriodon and Hadrodelphis. These belong to Kentriodontidae, which were small to medium-sized toothed cetaceans with largely symmetrical skulls, and thought likely to include ancestors of some modern species. Kentriodontids date to the late Oligocene to late Miocene.

Kentriodontines ate small fish and other nectonic organisms; they are thought to have been active echolocators, and might have formed schools. Diversity, morphology and distribution of fossils appear parallel to some modern species.

The skeleton of a Baleen whale with the hind limb and pelvic bone structure circled in red. This bone structure stays internal during the entire life of the species.

Today, the whale hind parts are internal and reduced. Occasionally, the genes that code for longer extremities cause a modern whale to develop miniature legs (known as atavism).

Whereas early cetaceans such as the Pakicetus had the nasal openings at the end of the snout, in later species such as the Rodhocetus, the openings had begun to drift toward the top of the skull. This is known as nasal drift.

The nostrils of modern whales have become modified into blowholes that allow them to break to the surface, inhale, and submerge with convenience. The ears began to move inward as well, and, in the case of Basilosaurus, the middle ears began to receive vibrations from the lower jaw. Today's modern toothed whales use the 'melon organ', a pad of fat, for echolocation.

20 Porpoise

Porpoises are small cetaceans of the family Phocoenidae; they are related to whales and dolphins. They are distinct from dolphins, although the word 'porpoise' has been used to refer to any small dolphin, especially by sailors and fishermen. The most obvious visible difference between the two groups is that porpoises have shorter beaks and flattened, spade-shaped teeth distinct from the conical teeth of dolphins.

The name derives from French pourpois, originally from Medieval Latin porcopiscus (porcus pig + piscus fish).

Porpoises, divided into six species, live in all oceans, mostly near the shore. Freshwater populations of the finless porpoise also exist. Probably the best known species is the harbour porpoise, which can be found across the Northern Hemisphere. Like all toothed whales, porpoises are predators, using sounds (echolocation in sonar form) to locate prey and to coordinate with others. They hunt fish, squid, and crustaceans.

TAXONOMY AND EVOLUTION

Porpoises, along with whales and dolphins, are descendants of land-living ungulates (hoofed animals) that first entered the oceans around 50 million years ago (Mya). During the Miocene (23 to 5 Mya), mammals were fairly modern. The cetaceans diversified, and fossil evidence suggests porpoises diverged from dolphins and other cetaceans around 15 Mya. The oldest fossils are known from the shallow seas around the North Pacific, with animals spreading to the European coasts and Southern Hemisphere only much later, during the Pliocene.

- Suborder Odontoceti toothed whales
- Infraorder Delphinida
- Superfamily Delphinoidea
- Family Phocoenidae - porpoises
- Genus *Haborophocoena*
- H. toyoshimai
- Genus *Neophocaena*
- *N. phocaeniodes* - Finless porpoise
- Genus Numataphocoena
- *N. yamashitai*
- Genus *Phocoena*
- *P. phocoena* - harbour porpoise
- *P. sinus* - vaquita
- P. dioptrica - spectacled porpoise
- *P. spinipinnis* - Burmeister's Porpoise
- Genus Phocoenoides
- *P. dalli* - Dall's porpoise
- Genus Septemriocetus
- *S. bosselaersii*
- Genus *Piscolithax*
- *P. aenigmaticus*
- *P. longirostris*
- *P. boreios*
- *P. tedfordi*

Recently discovered hybrids between male harbour porpoises and female Dall's porpoises indicate the two species may actually be members of the same genus.

Physical Characteristics

A harbour porpoise at an aquarium, in the wild, porpoises rarely jump out of the water.

Porpoises tend to be smaller but stouter than dolphins. They have small, rounded heads and blunt jaws instead of beaks. While dolphins have a round, bulbous 'melon', porpoises do not. Their teeth are spade-shaped, whereas dolphins have conical teeth. In addition, a porpoise's dorsal fin is generally triangular, rather than curved like that of many dolphins and large whales. Some species have small bumps, known as tubercles, on the leading edge of the dorsal fin. The function of these bumps is unknown.

These animals are the smallest cetaceans, reaching body lengths up to 2.5 metres (8.2 ft); the smallest species is the vaquita, reaching up to 1.5 metres (4.9 ft). In terms of weight, the lightest is the finless porpoise at 30 to 45 kilograms (66 to 99 lb), and the heaviest is Dall's porpoise at 130 to 200 kilograms (290 to 440 lb). Because of their small size, porpoises lose body heat to the water more rapidly than other cetaceans. Their stout shape, which minimizes surface area, may be an adaptation to reduce heat loss. Thick blubber also insulates them from the cold. The small size of porpoises requires them to eat frequently, rather than depending on fat reserves.

Porpoises are relatively r-selected compared with dolphins: that is, they bear young more quickly than dolphins. Female Dall's and harbour porpoises often become pregnant with a single calf each year, and pregnancy lasts for about 11 months. Porpoises have been known to live 8-10 years, although some have lived to be 20.

Behaviour

'Rooster tail' spray around swimming Dall's porpoises.

Porpoises prey on fish, squid, and crustaceans. Although they are capable of dives up to 200 m, they generally hunt in shallow coastal waters. They are found most commonly in small groups of fewer than ten individuals, referred to as pods. Rarely, some species form brief aggregations of several hundred animals. Like all toothed whales, they are capable of echolocation for finding prey and group coordination. Porpoises are fast swimmers—Dall's porpoise is said to be one of the fastest cetaceans, with a speed of 55 km/h (34 mph). Porpoises tend to be less acrobatic and more wary than dolphins.

Accidental entanglement (bycatch) in fishing nets is the main threat to porpoises today. One of the most endangered cetacean species is the vaquita, having a limited distribution in the Gulf of California, a highly industrialized area.

In some countries, porpoises are hunted for food or bait meat.

Porpoises are rarely held in captivity in zoos or oceanaria, as they are generally not as capable of adapting to tank life nor as easily trained as dolphins.

21 Seabirds

Seabirds (also known as marine birds) are birds that have adapted to life within the marine environment. While seabirds vary greatly in lifestyle, behaviour and physiology, they often exhibit striking convergent evolution, as the same environmental problems and feeding niches have resulted in similar adaptations. The first seabirds evolved in the Cretaceous period, and modern seabird families emerged in the Paleogene.

In general, seabirds live longer, breed later and have fewer young than other birds do, but they invest a great deal of time in their young. Most species nest in colonies, which can vary in size from a few dozen birds to millions. Many species are famous for undertaking long annual migrations, crossing the equator or circumnavigating the Earth in some cases. They feed both at the ocean's surface and below it, and even feed on each other. Seabirds can be highly pelagic, coastal, or in some cases spend a part of the year away from the sea entirely.

Seabirds and humans have a long history together: they have provided food to hunters, guided fishermen to fishing stocks and led sailors to land. Many species are currently threatened by human activities, and conservation efforts are under way.

There exists no single definition of which groups, families, and species are seabirds, and most definitions are in some way arbitrary. In the words of two seabird scientists, 'The one common characteristic that all seabirds share is that they feed in saltwater; but, as seems to be true with any statement in biology, some do not'. However, by convention all of the Sphenisciformes and Procellariiformes, all of the Pelecaniformes except the darters, and some of the Charadriiformes (the skuas, gulls, terns, auks and skimmers) are classified as seabirds. The phalaropes are usually included as well, since although they are waders ('shorebirds' in North America), two of the three species are oceanic for nine months of the year, crossing the equator to feed pelagically.

Loons and grebes, which nest on lakes but winter at sea, are usually categorized as water birds, not seabirds. Although there are a number of sea ducks in the family Anatidae which are truly marine in the winter, by convention they are usually excluded from the seabird grouping. Many waders (or shorebirds) and herons are also highly marine, living on the sea's edge (coast), but are also not treated as seabirds.

Seabirds, by virtue of living in a geologically depositional environment (that is, in the sea where sediments are readily laid down), are well represented in the fossil record. They are first known to occur in the Cretaceous Period, the earliest being the Hesperornithiformes, like Hesperornis regalis, a flightless loon-like seabird that dove in a fashion similar to grebes and loons (using its feet to move underwater) but had a beak filled with sharp teeth.

While Hesperornis is not thought to have left descendants, the earliest modern seabirds also occurred in the Cretaceous, with a species called *Tytthostonyx glauconiticus*, which seems allied to the Procellariiformes and/or Pelecaniformes. In the Paleogene the seas were dominated by early Procellariidae, giant penguins and two extinct families, the Pelagornithidae and the Plotopteridae (a group of large seabirds that looked like the penguins). Modern genera began their wide radiation in the Miocene, although the genus Puffinus (which includes today's Manx Shearwater and Sooty Shearwater) might date back to the Oligocene. The highest diversity of seabirds apparently existed during the Late Miocene and the Pliocene. At the end of the latter, the oceanic food web had undergone a period of upheaval due to extinction of considerable numbers of marine species; subsequently, the spread of marine mammals seems to have prevented seabirds from reaching their erstwhile diversity.

Adaptations to Life at Sea

Seabirds have made numerous adaptations to living on and feeding in the sea. Wing morphology has been shaped by the niche an individual species or family has evolved, so that looking at a wing's shape and loading can tell a scientist about its life feeding behaviour. Longer wings and low wing loading are typical of more pelagic species, whilst diving species have shorter wings. Species such as the Wandering Albatross, which forage over huge areas of sea, have a reduced capacity for powered flight and are dependent on a type of gliding called dynamic soaring (where the wind deflected by waves provides lift) as well as slope soaring. Seabirds also almost always have webbed feet, to aid movement on the surface as well as assisting diving in some species. The Procellariiformes are unusual amongst birds in having a strong sense of smell, which is used to find widely distributed food in a vast ocean, and possibly to locate their colonies.

Salt glands are used by seabirds to deal with the salt they ingest by drinking and feeding (particularly on crustaceans), and to help them osmoregulate. The excretions from these glands (which are positioned in the head of the birds, emerging from the nasal cavity) are almost pure sodium chloride.

With the exception of the cormorants and some terns, and in common with most other birds, all seabirds have waterproof plumage. However, compared to land birds, they have far more feathers protecting their bodies. This dense plumage is better able to protect the bird from getting wet, and cold is kept out by a dense layer of down feathers. The cormorants possess a layer of unique feathers that retain a smaller layer of air (compared to other diving birds) but otherwise soak up water. This allows them to swim without fighting the buoyancy that retaining air in the feathers causes, yet retain enough air to prevent the bird losing excessive heat through contact with water.

The plumage of most seabirds is less colourful than that of land birds, restricted in the main to variations of black, white or grey. A few species sport colourful plumes (such as the tropicbirds or some penguins), but most of the colour in seabirds appears in the bills and legs. The plumage of seabirds is thought in many cases to be for camouflage, both defensive (the colour of US Navy battleships is the same as that of Antarctic Prions, and in both cases it reduces visibility at sea) and aggressive.

Seabirds evolved to exploit different food resources in the world's seas and oceans, and to a great extent, their physiology and behaviour have been shaped by their diet. These evolutionary forces have often caused species in different families and even orders to evolve similar strategies and adaptations to the same problems, leading to remarkable convergent evolution, such as that between auks and penguins. There are four basic feeding strategies, or ecological guilds, for feeding at sea: surface feeding, pursuit diving, plunge diving, and predation of higher vertebrates; within these guilds there are multiple variations on the theme.

Many seabirds feed on the ocean's surface, as the action of marine currents often concentrates food such as krill, forage fish, squid or other prey items within reach of a dipped head.

Surface feeding itself can be broken up into two different approaches, surface feeding while flying (for example as practiced by gadfly petrels, frigatebirds and storm-petrels), and surface feeding whilst swimming (examples of which are practiced by fulmars, gulls, many of the shearwaters and gadfly petrels). Surface feeders in flight include some of the most acrobatic of seabirds, which either snatch morsels from the water (as do frigate-birds and some terns), or 'walk', pattering and hovering on the water's surface, as some of the storm-petrels do. Many of these do not ever land in the water, and some, such as the frigatebirds, have difficulty getting airborne again should they do so. Another seabird family that does not land while feeding is the skimmer, which has a unique fishing method: flying along the surface with the lower mandible in the water—this shuts automatically when the bill touches something in the water. The skimmer's bill reflects its unusual lifestyle, with the lower mandible uniquely being longer than the upper one.

Surface feeders that swim often have unique bills as well, adapted for their specific prey. Prions have special bills with filters called lamellae to filter out plankton from mouthfuls of water, and many albatrosses and petrels have hooked bills to snatch fast-moving prey. Gulls have more generalised bills that reflect their more opportunistic lifestyle.

Pursuit diving exerts greater pressures (both evolutionary and physiological) on seabirds, but the reward is a greater area in which to feed than is available to surface feeders. Propulsion underwater can be provided by wings (as used by penguins, auks, diving petrels, and some other species of petrel) or feet (as used by cormorants, grebes, loons and several types of fish-eating ducks). Wing-propelled divers are generally faster than foot-propelled divers. In both cases, the use of wings or feet for diving has limited their utility in other situations: loons and grebes walk with extreme difficulty (if at all), penguins cannot fly, and auks have sacrificed flight efficiency in favour of underwater diving. For example, the razorbill (an Atlantic auk) requires 64 per cent more energy to fly than a petrel of equivalent size. Many shearwaters are intermediate between the two, having longer wings than typical wing-propelled divers but heavier wing loadings than the other surface-feeding procellariids, leaving them capable of diving to considerable depths while still being efficient long-distance travellers. The most impressive diving exhibited by shearwaters is found in the Short-tailed Shearwater, which has been recorded diving below 70 m. Some albatross species are also capable of some limited diving, with Light-mantled

Sooty Albatrosses holding the record at 12 m. Of all the wing-propelled pursuit divers, the most efficient in the air are the albatrosses, and it is no coincidence that they are the poorest divers. This is the dominant guild in polar and subpolar environments, as it is energetically inefficient in warmer waters. With their poor flying ability, many wing-propelled pursuit divers are more limited in their foraging range than other guilds, especially during the breeding season when hungry chicks need regular feeding.

Plunge Diving

Gannets, boobies, tropicbirds, some terns and Brown Pelicans all engage in plunge diving, taking fast moving prey by diving into the water from flight. Plunge diving allows birds to use the energy from the momentum of the dive to combat natural buoyancy (caused by air trapped in plumage), and thus uses less energy than the dedicated pursuit divers, allowing them to utilise more widely distributed food resources, for example, in impoverished tropical seas. In general, this is the most specialised method of hunting employed by seabirds; other non-specialists (such as gulls and skuas) may employ it but do so with less skill and from lower heights. In Brown Pelicans the skills of plunge diving take several years to fully develop—once mature, they can dive from 20 m (70 ft) above the water's surface, shifting the body before impact to avoid injury. It has been suggested that plunge divers are restricted in their hunting grounds to clear waters that afford a view of their prey from the air, and while they are the dominant guild in the tropics, the link between plunge diving and water clarity is inconclusive. Some plunge divers (as well as some surface feeders) are dependent on dolphins and tuna to push shoaling fish up towards the surface.

This catch-all category refers to other seabird strategies that involve the next trophic level up. Kleptoparasites are seabirds that make a part of their living stealing food of other seabirds. Most famously, frigatebirds and skuas engage in this behaviour, although gulls, terns and other species will steal food opportunistically. The nocturnal nesting behaviour of some seabirds has been interpreted as arising due to pressure from this aerial piracy. Kleptoparasitism is not thought to play a significant part of the diet of any species, and is instead a supplement to food obtained by hunting. A study of Great Frigatebirds stealing from Masked Boobies estimated that the frigatebirds could at most obtain 40 per cent of the food they needed, and on average obtained only 5 per cent. Many species of gull will feed on seabird and sea mammal carrion when the opportunity arises, as will giant petrels. Some species of albatross also engage in scavenging: an analysis of regurgitated squid beaks has shown that many of the squid eaten are too large to have been caught alive, and include mid-water species likely to be beyond the reach of albatrosses. Some species will also feed on other seabirds; for example, gulls, skuas and giant petrels will often take eggs, chicks and even small adult seabirds from nesting colonies.

Seabirds' life histories are dramatically different from those of land birds. In general, they are K-selected, live much longer (anywhere between twenty and sixty years), delay breeding for longer (for up to ten years), and invest more effort into fewer young. Most species will only have one clutch a year, unless they lose the first (with a few exceptions, like the Cassin's Auklet), and many species (like the tubenoses and sulids), only one egg a year.

Care of young is protracted, extending for as long as six months, among the longest for birds. For example, once Common Guillemot chicks fledge, they remain with the male parent for several months at sea. The frigatebirds have the longest period of parental care of any bird, with the chicks fledging after four to six months and with continued assistance after that for up to fourteen months. Due to the extended period of care, breeding occurs every two years rather than annually for some species. This life-history strategy has probably evolved both in response to the challenges of living at sea (collecting widely scattered prey items), the frequency of breeding failures due to unfavourable marine conditions, and the relative lack of predation compared to that of land-living birds.

Because of the greater investment in raising the young and because foraging for food may occur far from the nest site, in all seabird species except the phalaropes, both parents participate in caring for the young, and pairs are typically at least seasonally monogamous. Many species, such as gulls, auks and penguins, retain the same mate for several seasons, and many petrel species mate for life. The albatrosses and procellariids which mate for life can take many years to form a pair bond before they breed, and the albatrosses have an elaborate breeding dance that is part of pair-bond formation.

Ninety-five per cent of seabirds are colonial, and seabird colonies are amongst the largest bird colonies in the world, providing one of Earth's great wildlife spectacles. Colonies of over a million birds have been recorded, both in the tropics (such as Kiritimati in the Pacific) and in the polar latitudes (as in Antarctica). Seabird colonies occur exclusively for the purpose of breeding; non-breeding birds will only collect together outside the breeding season in areas where prey species are densely aggregated.

Seabird colonies are highly variable. Individual nesting sites can be widely spaced, as in an albatross colony, or densely packed as with a murre colony. In most seabird colonies, several different species will nest on the same colony, often exhibiting some niche separation. Seabirds can nest in trees (if any are available), on the ground (with or without nests), on cliffs, in burrows under the ground and in rocky crevices. Competition can be strong both within species and between species, with aggressive species such as Sooty Terns pushing less dominant species out of the most desirable nesting spaces. The tropical Bonin Petrel nests during the winter to avoid competition with the more aggressive Wedge-tailed Shearwater. When the seasons overlap, the Wedge-tailed Shearwaters will kill young Bonin Petrels in order to use their burrows.

Many seabirds show remarkable site fidelity, returning to the same burrow, nest or site for many years, and they will defend that site from rivals with great vigour. This increases breeding success, provides a place for returning mates to reunite, and reduces the costs of prospecting for a new site. Young adults breeding for the first time usually return to their natal colony, and often nest close to where they hatched. This tendency, known as philopatry, is so strong that a study of Laysan Albatrosses found that the average distance between hatching site and the site where a bird established its own territory was 22 m; another study, this time on Cory's Shearwaters nesting near Corsica, found that of nine out of 61 male chicks that returned to breed at their natal colony bred in the burrow they were raised in, and two actually bred with their own mother.

Colonies are usually situated on islands, cliffs or headlands which land mammals have difficulty accessing. This is thought to provide protection to seabirds, which are often very clumsy on land. Coloniality often arises in types of bird which do not defend feeding territories (such as swifts, which have a very variable prey source); this may be a reason why it arises more frequently in seabirds. There are other possible advantages: colonies may act as information centres, where seabirds returning to the sea to forage can find out where prey is by studying returning individuals of the same species. There are disadvantages to colonial life, particularly the spread of disease. Colonies also attract the attention of predators, principally other birds, and many species attend their colonies nocturnally to avoid predation.

Migration

Pelicans flock flying over Havana Bay area. These birds come to Cuba every year from North America in the north hemisphere winter season.

Like many birds, seabirds often migrate after the breeding season. Of these, the trip taken by the Arctic Tern is the farthest of any bird, crossing the equator in order to spend the Austral summer in Antarctica. Other species also undertake trans-equatorial trips, both from the north to the south, and from south to north. The population of Elegant Terns, which nest off Baja California, splits after the breeding season with some birds travelling north to the Central Coast of California and some travelling as far south as Peru and Chile to feed in the Humboldt Current. The Sooty Shearwater undertakes an annual migration cycle that rivals that of the Arctic Tern; birds that nest in New Zealand and Chile and spend the northern summer feeding in the North Pacific off Japan, Alaska and California, an annual round trip of 40,000 statute miles (64,000 km).

Other species also migrate shorter distances away from the breeding sites, their distribution at sea determined by the availability of food. If oceanic conditions are unsuitable, seabirds will emigrate to more productive areas, sometimes permanently if the bird is young. After fledging, juvenile birds often disperse further than adults, and to different areas, so are commonly sighted far from a species' normal range. Some species, such as the auks, do not have a concerted migration effort, but drift southwards as the winter approaches. Other species, such as some of the storm-petrels, diving petrels and cormorants, never disperse at all, staying near their breeding colonies year round.

Away from the Sea

While the definition of seabirds suggests that the birds in question spend their lives on the ocean, many seabird families have many species that spend some or even most of their lives inland away from the sea. Most strikingly, many species breed many tens, hundreds or even thousands of miles inland. Some of these species still return to the ocean to feed; for example, the Snow Petrel, the nests of which have been found 480 kilometres (300 mi) inland on the Antarctic mainland, are unlikely to find anything to eat around their breeding sites. The Marbled Murrelet nests inland in old growth forest, seeking huge conifers with large branches to nest on. Other species, such as the California Gull, nest and feed inland on lakes, and then move to the coasts in the winter. Some cormorant, pelican, gull and tern species have individuals that never visit the sea at all, spending their lives on lakes, rivers, swamps and, in the case of some of the gulls, cities and agricultural land. In these cases it is thought that these terrestrial or freshwater birds evolved from marine ancestors. Some seabirds, principally those that nest in tundra-like skuas and phalaropes, will migrate over land as well.

The more marine species, such as petrels, auks, and gannets, are more restricted in their habits, but are occasionally seen inland as vagrants. This most commonly happens to young inexperienced birds, but can happen in great numbers to exhausted adults after large storms, an event known as a wreck, where they provide prized sightings for birders.

Seabirds and Fisheries

Seabirds have had a long association with both fisheries and sailors, and both have drawn benefits and disadvantages from the relationship.

Fishermen have traditionally used seabirds as indicators of both fish shoals, underwater banks that might indicate fish stocks, and of potential landfall. In fact, the known association of seabirds with land was instrumental in allowing the Polynesians to locate tiny landmasses in the Pacific. Seabirds have provided food for fishermen away from home, as well as bait. Famously, tethered cormorants have been used to catch fish directly. Indirectly, fisheries have also benefited from guano from colonies of seabirds acting as fertilizer for the surrounding seas.

Negative effects on fisheries are mostly restricted to raiding by birds on aquaculture, although long-lining fisheries also have to deal with bait stealing. There have been claims of prey depletion by seabirds of fishery stocks, and while there is some evidence of this, the effects of seabirds are considered smaller than that of marine mammals and predatory fish (like tuna).

Some seabird species have benefited from fisheries, particularly from discarded fish and offal. These discards compose 30 per cent of the food of seabirds in the North Sea, for example, and compose up to 70 per cent of the total food of some seabird populations. This can have other impacts; for example, the spread of the Northern Fulmar through the United Kingdom is attributed in part to the availability of discards.] Discards generally benefit surface feeders, such as gannets and petrels, to the detriment of pursuit divers like penguins.

Fisheries also have negative effects on seabirds, and these effects, particularly on the long-lived and slow-breeding albatrosses, are a source of increasing concern to conservationists. The bycatch of seabirds entangled in nets or hooked on fishing lines has had a big impact on seabird numbers; for example, an estimated 100,000 albatrosses are hooked and drown each year on tuna lines set out by long-line fisheries. Overall, many hundreds of thousands of birds are trapped and killed each year, a source of concern for some of the rarest species (for example, only about 2,000 Short-tailed Albatrosses are known to still exist). Seabirds are also thought to suffer when overfishing occurs.

The hunting of seabirds and the collecting of seabird eggs have contributed to the declines of many species, and the extinction of several, including the Great Auk and the Spectacled Cormorant. Seabirds have been hunted for food by coastal peoples throughout history—one of the earliest instances known is in southern Chile, where archaeological excavations in middens has shown hunting of albatrosses, cormorants and shearwaters from 5000 BP. This pressure has led to some species becoming extinct in many places; in particular, at least 20 species of an original 29 no longer breed on Easter Island. In the 19th century, the hunting of seabirds for fat deposits and feathers for the millinery trade reached industrial levels. Muttonbirding (harvesting shearwater chicks) developed as important industries in both New Zealand and Tasmania, and the name of one species, the Providence Petrel, is derived from its seemingly miraculous arrival on Norfolk Island where it provided a windfall for starving European settlers. In the Falkland Islands, hundreds of thousands of penguins were harvested for their oil each year. Seabird eggs have also long been an important source of food for sailors undertaking long sea voyages, as well as being taken when settlements grow in areas near a colony. Eggers from San Francisco took almost half a million eggs a year from the Farallon Islands in the mid-19th century, a period in the islands' history from which the seabird species are still recovering.

Both hunting and egging continue today, although not at the levels that occurred in the past, and generally in a more controlled manner. For example, the Ma-ori of Stewart Island/ Rakiura continue to harvest the chicks of the Sooty Shearwater as they have done for centuries, using traditional methods (called kaitiakitanga) to manage the harvest, but now work with the University of Otago in studying the populations. In Greenland, however, uncontrolled hunting is pushing many species into steep decline.

Other human factors have led to declines and even extinctions in seabird populations, colonies and species. Of these, perhaps the most serious are introduced species. Seabirds, breeding predominantly on small isolated islands, have lost many predator defence behaviours. Feral cats are capable of taking seabirds as large as albatrosses, and many introduced rodents, such as the Pacific Rat, can take eggs hidden in burrows. Introduced goats, cattle, rabbits and other herbivores can lead to problems, particularly when species need vegetation to protect or shade their young. Disturbance of breeding colonies by humans is often a problem as well—visitors, even well-meaning tourists, can flush brooding adults off a colony leaving chicks and eggs vulnerable to predators.

The build-up of toxins and pollutants in seabirds is also a concern. Seabirds, being apex predators, suffered from the ravages of DDT until it was banned; among other effects, DDT was implicated in embryo development problems and the skewed sex ratio of Western Gulls in southern California. Oil spills are also a threat to seabird species, as both a toxin and because the feathers of the birds become saturated by the oil, causing them to lose their waterproofing. Oil pollution threatens species with restricted ranges or already depressed populations.

Conservation

The threats faced by seabirds have not gone unnoticed by scientists or the conservation movement. As early as 1903, U.S. President Theodore Roosevelt was convinced of the need to declare Pelican Island in Florida a National Wildlife Refuge to protect the bird colonies (including the nesting Brown Pelicans), and in 1909 he protected the Farallon Islands. Today many important seabird colonies are given some measure of protection, from Heron Island in Australia to Triangle Island in British Columbia.

Island restoration techniques, pioneered by New Zealand, enable the removal of exotic invaders from increasingly large islands. Feral cats have been removed from Ascension Island, Arctic Foxes from many islands in the Aleutian Islands, and rats from Campbell Island. The removal of these introduced species has led to increases in numbers of species under pressure and even the return of extirpated ones. After the removal of cats from Ascension Island, seabirds began to nest there again for the first time in over a hundred years.

Seabird mortality caused by long-line fisheries can be greatly reduced by techniques such as setting long-line bait at night, dying the bait blue, setting the bait underwater, increasing the amount of weight on lines and by using bird scarers, and their deployment is increasingly required by many national fishing fleets. The international ban on the use of drift nets has also helped reduce the mortality of seabirds and other marine wildlife.

One of the Millennium Projects in the UK was the Scottish Seabird Centre, near the important bird sanctuaries on Bass Rock, Fidra and the surrounding islands. The area is home to huge colonies of gannets, puffins, skuas and other seabirds. The centre allows visitors to watch live video from the islands as well as learn about the threats the birds face and how we can protect them, and has helped to significantly raise the profile of seabird conservation in the UK. Seabird tourism can provide income for coastal communities as well as raise the profile of seabird conservation. For example, the Northern Royal Albatross colony at Taiaroa Head in New Zealand attracts 40,000 visitors a year.

The plight of albatross and large seabirds, as well as other marine creatures, being taken as bycatch by long-line fisheries, has been addressed by a large number of non-governmental organisations (including BirdLife International, the American Bird Conservancy, and the Royal Society for the Protection of Birds). This led to the Agreement on the Conservation of Albatrosses and Petrels, a legally binding treaty designed to protect these threatened species, which has been ratified by eleven countries as of 2008 (namely Argentina, Australia, Chile, Ecuador, France, New Zealand, Norway, Peru, South Africa, Spain, and the United Kingdom).

Many seabirds are little studied and poorly known, due to living far out to sea and breeding in isolated colonies. However, some seabirds, particularly, the albatrosses and gulls, have broken into popular consciousness. The albatrosses have been described as 'the most legendary of birds', and have a variety of myths and legends associated with them, and today it is widely considered unlucky to harm them, although the notion that sailors believed that is a myth which derives from Samuel Taylor Coleridge's famous poem, 'The Rime of the Ancient Mariner', in which a sailor is punished for killing an albatross by having to wear its corpse around his neck.

Gulls are one of the most commonly seen seabirds, given their use of human-made habitats (such as cities and dumps) and their often fearless nature. They therefore also have made it into the popular consciousness – they have been used metaphorically, as in Jonathan Livingston Seagull by Richard Bach, or to denote a closeness to the sea, such as their use in The Lord of the Rings – both in the insignia of Gondor and therefore Númenor (used in the design of the films), and to call Legolas to (and across) the sea. Other species have also made an impact; pelicans have long been associated with mercy and altruism because of an early Western Christian myth that they split open their breast to feed their starving chicks.

Seabird Families

The following are the groups of birds normally classed as seabirds:

- Sphenisciformes (Antarctic and southern waters; 16 species)
- Spheniscidae penguins
- Procellariiformes (Tubenoses: pan-oceanic and pelagic; 93 species)
- Diomedeidae albatrosses
- Procellariidae fulmars, prions, shearwaters, gadfly and other petrels
- Pelacanoididae diving-petrels
- Hydrobatidae storm-petrels
- Pelecaniformes (Worldwide; 57 species)
- Pelecanidae pelicans
- Sulidae gannets and boobies
- Phalacrocoracidae cormorants
- Fregatidae frigatebirds
- Phaethontidae tropicbirds
- Charadriiformes (Worldwide; 305 species, but only the families listed are classed as seabirds).
- Stercorariidae skuas
- Laridae gulls
- Sternidae terns
- Rhynchopidae skimmers
- Alcidae auks

References

Bryant, D., Burke, L., McManus, J., *et al*. (1998) 'Reefs at Risk: A Map-based Indicator of Threats to the World's Coral Reefs". World Resources Institute, Washington, D.C.

Collis, K., Adamany, S. – Columbia River Inter-Tribal Fish Commission, Roby, D.D., Craig, D.P., Lyons, D.E., – Oregon Cooperative Fish and Wildlife Research Unit, (2000), "Avian Predation on Juvenile Salmonids in the Lower Columbia River", 1998 Annual Report to Bonneville Power Administration, Portland.

Croxall, J.P. & Prince, P.A. (1994). "Dead or Alive, Night or Day: How do Albatrosses Catch Squid?" *Antarctic Science* 6: pp. 155-162.

Foley, Jonathan A.; Karl E. Taylor, Steven J. Ghan (1991). 'Planktonic Dimethylsulfide and Cloud Albedo: An Estimate of the Feedback Response'. *Climatic Change* 18 (1): 1.

Gaston, A. J., and S. B. C. Dechesne. (1996). Rhinoceros Auklet (Cerorhinca monocerata). In The Birds of North America, No. 212 (A. Poole and F. Gill, eds.). The Academy of Natural Sciences, Philadelphia, PA, and The American Ornithologists' Union, Washington, D.C.

Goreau, T.J. (1992) "Bleaching and Reef Commumity Change in Jamaica: 1951-1991". *Amer. Zool.* 32: 683-695.

Hamblin, Jacob Darwin (2005) *Oceanographers and the Cold War: Disciples of Marine Science*. University of Washington Press. ISBN 978-02-9598-482-7.

Harris, M. & Wanless, S., (1996) "Differential responses of Guillemot Uria aalge and Shag Phalacrocorax Aristotelis to a Late Winter Wreck" Bird Study 43(2): 220-230.

J. Calambokidis and G. Steiger (1998). Blue Whales. Voyageur Press.

Lang, Michael A., Ian G. Macintyre, and Klaus Rützler, eds. *Proceedings of the Smithsonian Marine Science Symposium.* Smithsonian Contributions to the Marine Sciences, No. 38. Washington, D.C.: Smithsonian Institution Scholarly Press, 2009.

Manuwal, D.A. and A.C. Thoresen. 1993. Cassin's Auklet (Ptychoramphus aleuticus). In *The Birds of North America,* No. 50 (A. Poole and F. Gill, Eds.). Philadelphia: The Academy of Natural Sciences; Washington, D.C.: The American Ornithologists' Union.

Metz, V.G. & Schreiber, E.A. (2002) "Great Frigatebird (Fregata minor)" In *The Birds of North America,* No. 681, (Poole, A. & Gill, F., eds) The Birds of North America Inc: Philadelphia.

Nelson, S. K. 1997. Marbled Murrelet (Brachyramphus marmoratus). In *The Birds of North America,* No. 276 (A. Poole and F. Gill, eds.). The Academy of Natural Sciences, Philadelphia, PA, and The American Ornithologists' Union, Washington, D.C.

NOAA (1998) *Record-breaking Coral Bleaching Occurred in Tropics this Year.* National Oceanic and Atmospheric Administration, Press Release (October 23, 1998). ICRS (1998).

Oro, D., Ruiz, X., Pedrocchi, V. & Gonzalez-Solis, J. (1997) "Diet and Adult Time Budgets of Audouin's Gull Larus Audouinii in response to Changes in Commercial Fisheries" Ibis 139: 631-637.

Punta, G, Herrera, G. (1995) "Predation by Southern Giant Petrels Macronectes Giganteus on Adult Imperial Cormorants Phalacrocorax Atriceps" *Marine Ornithology* 23 166-167.

Randall R. Reeves, Brent S. Stewart, Phillip J. Clapham and James A. Powell (2002). National Audubon Society Guide to Marine Mammals of the World. Alfred A. Knopf, Inc.

Robertson, C.J.R. (1993). "Survival and Longevity of the Northern Royal Albatross Diomedea Epomophora Sanfordi at Taiaroa Head" 1937-93. *Emu* 93: 269-276.

Sea Snakes at Food and Agriculture Organisation of the United Nations. Accessed 7 August 2007.

Sebens, K.P. (1994) 'Biodiversity of Coral Reefs: What are We Losing and Why?" *Amer Zool*, 34: 115-133.

Sousa, Wayne P (1986) [1985]. "7, Disturbance and Patch Dynamics on Rocky Intertidal Shores". *The Ecology of Natural Disturbance and Patch Dynamics*. eds. Steward T.A. Pickett & P.S. White. Academic Press. ISBN 0125545215.

Statement on Global Coral Bleaching in 1997-1998. International Coral Reef Society, October 15, 1998.

Steele, J., K.Turekian and S. Thorpe. (2001). *Encyclopedia of Ocean Sciences.* San Diego: Academic Press. (6 Vols.)

Stidworthy J. 1974. Snakes of the World. Grosset & Dunlap Inc. p. 160. ISBN 0-448-11856-4.

Sverdrup, Keith A., Duxbury, Alyn C., Duxbury, Alison B. (2006). *Fundamentals of Oceanography*, McGraw-Hill.

Vickery, J & Brooke, M. (1994) 'The Kleptoparasitic Interactions Between Great Frigatebirds and Masked Boobies on Henderson Island, South Pacific" Condor 96: 331-340.

Wilkinson, C.R., and Buddemeier, R.W. (1994) 'Global Climate Change and Coral Reefs: Implications for People and Reefs'. Report of the UNEP-IOC-ASPEI-IUCN Global Task Team on the Implications of Climate Change on Coral Reefs. IUCN, Gland, Switzerland.

Winkler, D.W. 1996. California Gull (Larus californicus). In *The Birds of North America*, No. 259 (A. Poole and F. Gill, eds.). The Academy of Natural Sciences, Philadelphia, PA, and The American Ornithologists' Union, Washington, D.C.

Thompson, P.M., (2004) "Identifying Drivers of Change; did Fisheries Play a Role in the Spread of North Atlantic fulmars?" in Management of Marine Ecosystems: Monitoring Change in Upper Trophic Levels. Cambridge: Cambridge University Press.

Index